Cascading Style Sheets

DESIGNING FOR THE WEB

Third Edition

Cascading Style Sheets

DESIGNING FOR THE WEB

Third Edition

Håkon Wium Lie
Bert Bos

✦✦Addison-Wesley

Upper Saddle River, NJ • Boston • Indianapolis • San Francisco
New York • Toronto • Montreal • London • Munich • Paris • Madrid
Capetown • Sydney • Tokyo • Singapore • Mexico City

Library of Congress Catalog Number: 2004116047

ISBN 0-321-19312-1

Text printed in the United States on recycled paper at R.R. Donnelley and Sons Company in Crawfordsville, Indiana.

First printing, April 2005

o o o o o

Foreword 2005

Watson and Crick. Fred and Ginger. Bert and Håkon. The first of these immortal duos cracked the secret of life. The second pair dazzled Depression-era audiences with gravity defying dance routines that remain the very icon of charm and grace. As for the third pair – the authors of the book you now hold in your hands – the achievement that ensures their immortality benefits everyone who uses the Web or creates content for it.

For it was Bert and Håkon's gift, not only to recognize the Web's importance long before many of us had so much as heard the word "modem," but also to recognize the danger posed by the medium's lack of a standard visual formatting language which could be abstracted from the semantics of a page's structure and content. In the early (and not-so-early) days, an unholy hodge-podge of proprietary, nonstandard tags was used to cobble page layouts together. All such Web pages were fat and slow, and the way they were built made their content unavailable to far too many would-be readers, users, or customers.

The authors of this book solved all those problems at a single stroke: namely, the invention of Cascading Style Sheets (CSS), a standard layout language for the Web. The key to their invention – the biggest thing Bert and Håkon did for us – is that CSS separates presentation from underlying structure and semantics. CSS takes the visual instructions out of HTML, where they never belonged anyway, and sticks them into one or more lean, cache-able, documents that are powerful enough to present your site one way in a traditional graphic browser, another way in a phone browser, a third way in kiosk mode, and a fourth for your printer.

If you designed or built Web pages during the 1990s, you might not have learned much about CSS. After all, in those days, the CSS standard was still in its infancy. Besides, certain browser makers (no names please) were almost pathologically reluctant to support CSS completely or even accurately. In fact, some didn't even bother to accurately or completely support HTML.

But times have changed. So has CSS: in its latest incarnation as CSS 2.1, it packs surprising power and flexibility, allowing us as designers to create almost any layout we can imagine. As to today's Web browsers, while they are not perfect (and some are more imperfect than others), their CSS support has traveled light years since the 1990s. This improved support allows anyone who understands CSS to create lean, fast-loading, content-rich Web pages that score as big with search engines as they do with readers. Best of all, the content of your pages is available to more people because it is accessible to more types of browsers and devices.

It's pretty clear: if you design or program Web pages, or create Web content, or own or manage a website, you need to know how CSS works. And who better to show you than the dynamic duo that invented CSS in the first place?

In this updated edition to their original best-selling classic, the co-creators of CSS clearly, logically, and painlessly explain the hows and whys and ins and outs of the visual formatting language that is their gift to us. The examples are simple enough for novices yet detailed enough for experts. If you missed the previous edition, you are in for a treat. If, like the rest of us, you own a dog-eared copy of the previous edition, you will appreciate how this new edition makes sense of CSS 2.1, clearing up points that have sometimes confused even the experts.

The Web would be a poorer place without Messieurs Bos and Lie. Your shelf will be richer for the addition of this book. Rely on it. Study it. Savor it.

Jeffrey Zeldman
New York
November 2004

o o o o o

Foreword 1999

This Foreword was written by Robert Cailliau for the first edition of this book, which appeared in 1997. The following text is the slightly revised version published in the second edition from 1999.

When the Web was in its infancy, seven years ago or so, I felt greatly relieved at the final removal of all the totally unsolvable problems of fixed format presentation. In the young Web, there were no more pagination faults, no more footnotes, no silly word breaks, no fidgeting the text to gain that extra line that you sorely needed to fit everything on one page. In the window of a Web page on the NeXTStep system, the text was always clean. Better than that: I decided what font it came out in, how big I wanted the letters, what styles I chose for definition lists and where tabs went.

Then we descended into the Dark Ages for several years, because the Web exploded into a community that had no idea that such freedom was possible, but worried about putting on the remote screen exactly what they thought their information should look like. I've read recommendations against using structured markup because you have no control over what comes out the other side. Sad.

You have by now understood that I'm firmly in the camp of those who think that quality of content comes first, and presentation comes later. But of course, I'm not entirely right here: presentation is important. Mathematical formulas are always presented in a two-dimensional layout.

Fortunately, SGML's philosophy allows us to separate structure from presentation, and the Web DTD, HTML, is no exception. Even in the

NeXTStep version of 1990, Tim Berners-Lee provided for style sheets, though at a rudimentary level (we had other things to do then!).

Today, style sheets are becoming a reality again, this time much more elaborate. This is an important milestone for the Web, and we should stop for a minute to reflect on the potential benefits and pitfalls of this technology.

I followed the CSS effort from its inception – mostly over cups of coffee with Håkon at CERN – and I've always had one concern: is it possible to create a powerful enough style sheet "language" without ending up with a programming language?

The CSS described in this book shows that you can create some quite stunning presentations without programming. While the programmer in me may be a little disappointed, the minimalist in me is comforted. In fact, I'll never need this much freedom and special effects, but then I'm not a graphic artist. Anything that needs more complication effectively becomes an image, and should be treated as such. I feel therefore that the middle part of the spectrum between pure ASCII text and full images is effectively covered by the power of CSS, without introducing the complexity of programming.

You have here a book on presentation. But it is presentation of information that should also remain structured, so that your content can be effectively used by others, while retaining the specific visual aspects you want to give it. Use CSS with care. It is the long-awaited salt on the Web food: a little is necessary, too much is not good cooking.

The efforts of the authors have finally brought us what we sorely needed: the author's ability to shape the content without affecting the structure. This is good news for the Web!

Robert Cailliau
CERN, Geneva
January 1999

o o o o o

Table of contents

Cascading Style Sheets

Chapter 5

Fonts... **89**

Chapter 8

Space around boxes.. 170

Chapter 9

Relative and absolute positioning......................................205

Chapter 12

Printing and other media.. **266**

Chapter 13

Cascading and inheritance... **281**

Chapter 14

External style sheets... **293**

o o o o o

Preface

Since its introduction in 1996, Cascading Style Sheets (CSS) has revolutionized Web design. Now, in 2004, most Web pages use CSS, and many designers base their layouts entirely on CSS. To do so successfully requires a good understanding of how CSS works. The purpose of this book is to describe how designers can take full advantage of CSS 2.1, which is the newly released update of the specification.

CSS's journey from an idea to a specification – and then on to a specification designers can rely on – has been long and arderous. The creator of the CSS Zen Garden (described in Chapter 11, "From HTML extensions to CSS") describes it this way:

> Littering a dark and dreary road lay the past relics of browser-specific tags, incompatible DOMs, and broken CSS support. Today, we must clear the mind of past practices. Web enlightenment has been achieved thanks to the tireless efforts of folk like the W3C, WaSP, and the major browser creators.

Indeed, we believe that the web is a more enlightened place now that CSS has matured to a stage where it can be used for advanced layouts in a range of browsers. This book tells you all you need to know to start using CSS.

ACKNOWLEDGMENTS

Creating a lasting specification for the Web is not a job for one person. That's why the two authors joined forces. Then, we found out two wasn't enough, and a W3C Working Group (which includes W3C technical staff and W3C member representatives) was formed. The CSS 2.1 specification is the product of that working group. We are indebted to Tantek Çelik and Ian Hickson, who are co-editors of the CSS 2.1 specification, and to the other members of the group. In particular, we want to thank David Baron, Jim Bigelow, Kimberly Blessing, Frederick Boland, Ada Chan, Don Day, Michael Day, Elika Etemad, Daniel Glazman, David Hyatt, Björn Höhrmann, and Kevin Lawver.

CSS 2.1 is only the most recent version of the CSS specification. The foundation for CSS was laid by CSS1 and CSS2, and many people helped write, maintain, and promote those documents. In roughly chronological order:

- David Raggett and Steven Pemberton were influential in establishing the concept of style sheets for the Web.
- Eric Meyer created the test suite for the CSS1 specification and has promoted CSS tirelessly ever since.
- Todd Fahrner created the *W3C Core Styles* (described in Chapter 14), the "acid" test, and the *Ahem* font.
- Ian Jacobs and Chris Lilley were co-editors of the CSS2 specification.
- Brian Wilson provided extensive documentation of CSS and its implementations.
- Jeffrey Zeldman has publicized widely on why standards, including CSS, are good for you.
- Dave Shea created the wonderful CSS Zen Garden.
- Michael Day and Xuehong Liu for making it possible to print CSS. Thanks to the Prince formatter, we were able to produce the book ourselves using the same methods we preach in this book.

Lastly, our thanks to Tim Berners-Lee, without whom none of this would have been possible.

Håkon Wium Lie & Bert Bos
Oslo/Antibes
February 2005

TRADEMARK NOTICE

Chapter 1

The Web and HTML

Cascading Style Sheets (CSS) represent a major breakthrough in how Web-page designers work by expanding their ability to control the appearance of Web pages, which are the documents that people publish on the Web.

For the first few years after the World Wide Web (the Web) was created in 1990, people who wanted to put pages on the Web had little control over what those pages looked like. In the beginning, authors could only specify structural aspects of their pages (for example, that some piece of text would be a heading or some other piece would be straight text). Also, there were ways to make text bold or italic, among a few other effects, but that's where their control ended.

In the scientific environments where the Web was born, people are more concerned with the content of their documents than the presentation. In a research report, the choice of typefaces (or fonts, as we call them in this book) is of little importance compared to the scientific results that are reported. However, when authors outside the scientific environments discovered the Web, the limitations of Web document formats became a source of continuing frustration. Authors often came from a paper-based publication environment where they had full control of the presentation. They wanted to be able to make text red or black, make it look more spaced out or more squeezed, to center it or put it against the right margin, or anywhere else they wanted. Many Web designers have a desktop-publishing background, in which they can do all these things and more to improve the appearance of printed material. They want the same capabilities when they design Web pages. However, such capabilities have been slow to develop – slow by Internet speed standards, that is. So, designers devised techniques to sidestep these limitations, but these techniques sometimes have unfortunate side effects. We discuss those techniques and their side effects later in this chapter.

CSS also works with XML, which is another document format for the Web. See Chapter 16, "XML Documents," for how to use CSS and XML together.

This book discusses a new method to design Web pages. CSS works with HTML (the HyperText Markup Language), which is the primary document format on the Web. HTML describes the document's *structure*; that is, the roles the various parts of a document play. For example, a piece of text may be designated as a heading or a paragraph. HTML doesn't pay much attention to the document's *appearance,* and in fact, it has only very limited capability to influence appearance. CSS, however, describes how these elements are to be presented to the document's reader. Now, using CSS, you can better specify the appearance of your HTML pages and make your pages available to more Web users worldwide. CSS greatly enhances the potential of HTML and the Web.

A *style sheet* is a set of stylistic guidelines that tell a browser how an HTML document is to be presented to users. With CSS, you can specify such styles as the size, color, and spacing of text, as well as the placement of text and images on the page. CSS can also do much more.

A key feature of CSS is that style sheets can *cascade.* That is, several different style sheets can be attached to a document and all of them can influence the document's presentation. In this way, an author can create a style sheet to specify how the page should look, while a reader can attach a personal style sheet to adjust the appearance of the page for human or technological limitations, such as poor eyesight or a personal preference for a certain font.

CSS is a simple language that can be read by humans, in contrast to some computer languages. Perhaps even more important, however, is that CSS is easy to write. All you need to know is a little HTML and some basic desktop-publishing terminology: CSS borrows from that terminology when expressing style. So, those of you who have experience in desktop publishing should grasp CSS quickly. But, if you're new to HTML, desktop publishing, or Web-page design, don't despair. You are likely to find CSS surprisingly easy to grasp. This book includes a brief review of basic HTML and tips on page design.

To understand how revolutionary CSS is, you first need to understand Web-page design as it has been and the problems that CSS can help solve. In this chapter, we begin with a brief tour of the Web and the problems Web designers and others have faced prior to the introduction of CSS. Then, we quickly review the basics of HTML. For those of you who are already publishing on the Web, this all may be old news. For those of you who are new to the idea of designing Web pages, this helps put things in perspective. In Chapter 2, "CSS," we step you through the basics of how to use CSS. In subsequent chapters, we delve more deeply into CSS, covering how you can specify the text, background, color, spacing, and more in the design of Web pages.

THE WEB

The Web is a vast collection of documents on the *Internet* that are linked together via hyperlinks. The Internet consists of millions of computers worldwide that communicate electronically. A *hyperlink* is a predefined link between two documents. The hyperlinks allow a user to access documents on various Web servers without concern for where they are located. A *Web server* is a computer on the Internet that serves out Web pages on request. From a document on a Web server in California, the user is just one mouse click away from a document that is stored, perhaps, on a Web server in France. Hyperlinks are integral to the Web. Without them, there would be no Web.

Users gain access to the Web through a browser. A *browser* is a computer program that lets users browse – or "surf" – the Web by fetching documents from Web servers and displaying them to the user. To move from one document to another, the user clicks a <u>highlighted</u> (often underlined) word or image that represents a hyperlink. The browser then retrieves the document that is at the other end of the hyperlink and displays it on the screen. For example, a user could be in a document about baroque music and click the highlighted words <u>Johann Sebastian Bach</u> that are linked to "Bach's home page." (On the Web, all celebrities – and everyone else who wants one – have a home page.) After the browser fetches Bach's home page (instantly, in the best case), it appears on the user's screen.

Development of the Web

The Web was invented around 1990 by Tim Berners-Lee with Robert Cailliau as a close ally. Both of them were then working at CERN, which is the European Laboratory for Particle Physics. Tim is a graduate of Oxford University and a long-time computer and software expert, and is now the director of the World Wide Web Consortium (W3C), an organization that coordinates the development of the Web. He also is a principal research scientist at Massachusetts Institute of Technology's Laboratory for Computer Science and Artificial Intelligence (MIT CSAIL). Robert is a 30-year veteran at CERN, where he still works. Robert organized the first Web conference in Geneva in 1993. Both Tim and Robert were awarded the ACM Software System Award in 1995 because of their work on the Web. (Robert wrote the Foreword to this book.)

Tim created the language HTML, which is used by people to exchange information on the Web. We discuss what HTML is in the next section and give a brief review of its basics later in the chapter. Tim also began work on style sheets soon afterward, but when the Web really started taking off in 1993, the work on them was not complete.

The world outside scientific laboratories discovered the Web around 1994. Since then, the Web's growth has been tremendous. Had style sheets been available on the Web from its beginning, Web-page designers would have been spared much frustration. However, releasing CSS1 two years later did offer some advantages. First, in the interim, we learned much about what visual effects Web designers want to achieve on their pages. Second, we learned that users also want their say in how documents are presented on their computer screens; for example, the visually impaired may want to make fonts bigger so that they can be read more easily. As a result, we were able to provide functionality to meet as many of these needs as possible, and even more was added when CSS2 was issued in 1998. Hence, the CSS of 1999 is a better solution than a style-sheet solution years earlier would have been.

MARKUP LANGUAGES

HTML is a markup language. A *markup language* is a method of indicating within a document the roles that the document's pieces are to play. Its focus is on the structure of a document rather than its appearance. For example, you can indicate that one piece of text is a paragraph, another is a top-level heading, and another is a lower-level heading. You indicate these by placing codes, called *tags,* into the document. HTML has around 30 commonly used tags, which are reviewed later in this chapter. You could, for example, use a tag that says, in effect, "Make this piece of text a heading."

In contrast, desktop-publishing (DTP) programs emphasize the presentation of a document rather than its structure. Authors can select font families, text colors, and margin widths and thereby accurately control what the final product – which normally ends up on paper – looks like.

The distinction between structural and presentational systems isn't always as clear cut as what we've described. HTML, while having its roots in structured documents, has some tags that describe presentation rather than structure. For example, you can specify that a text should be presented in bold or italic. Also, some DTP programs let you describe the structure – in addition to the presentation – of a document. When you create a new document in applications such as Microsoft Word or Adobe FrameMaker, a standard set of styles is available. A *style* is a group of stylistic characteristics that you can apply to a piece of text. For example, you may have a style called *title1,* that has the characteristics that sets the text to 18 point Helvetica bold italic. (If you're not familiar with what "18 point Helvetica bold italic" means, don't worry; we explain it in Chapter 5, "Fonts.") By applying the style *title1* to selected parts of your document, you effectively mark it up. At the same time, you also specify how those pieces of text should be presented. Figure 1.1 shows what 18 point Helvetica bold italic looks like.

Conceptually, this is similar to HTML and CSS. In HTML, *title 1* would be a tag, and the stylistic characteristics (namely, 18 point Helvetica bold italic) would be written in a CSS style sheet. If you already know a DTP program that supports this notion of styles, the transition to HTML and CSS will be easy.

18 point Helvetica bold italic

Figure 1.1 18 point Helvetica bold italic.

DODGING THE LIMITATIONS OF HTML

HTML is a simple, easy-to-learn markup language designed for hypertext documents on the Web. In fact, a computer-literate person can learn to write basic HTML in less than a day. This simplicity is one reason for the huge success of the Web.

From the beginnings of HTML, Web-page designers have tried to sidestep its stylistic limitations. Their intentions have been the best – to improve the presentation of documents – but often, the techniques have had unfortunate side effects. Typically, the techniques work for some of the people some of the time, but never for all the people all the time. They include the following:

- Using proprietary HTML extensions
- Converting text into images
- Placing text in tables
- Writing a program instead of using HTML

We discuss these techniques and their side effects in the next sections.

Proprietary HTML extensions

One way to sidestep HTML's limitations has been for browser vendors to create their own tags that give designers who use their browser a little more control over the appearance of a Web page. At some point, it seemed that every new version of a browser introduced a few new elements that designers could play with. For example, Netscape introduced the **CENTER** element in 1994 to allow text to be centered on the screen, and more recently, the **SPACER** element for, among other things, indenting the first line of a paragraph. Microsoft introduced the **MARQUEE** element in 1995 to make text slide across the screen. (Chapter 17, "Tables," shows more extensions with their CSS replacements.)

But, these HTML extensions have their problems. First, they are not universal. Although the W3C officially added **CENTER** to HTML 3.2 to avoid problems with browsers behaving differently at a time when CSS was not ready, the others remain specific to a particular browser.

Another problem is that the extensions are meaningless on non-visual browsers, such as speech browsers (that read pages aloud) or Braille browsers. Some of the extensions, such as the **FONT** element, won't even work on certain visual browsers, such as the text-only browser Lynx or browsers on hand-held devices. The standard HTML elements, on the other hand, are all designed to be device-independent. An element such as **EM** ("emphasis"), which is usually shown as italic text on graphical browsers, can be rendered underlined or in reverse video by Lynx or with a more emphatic voice by a speech browser.

Luckily, CSS offers more powerful alternatives to these HTML extensions, as we will show in this book. Moreover, the CSS equivalents are standardized by W3C, which means all major browser makers agree on them. CSS also offers control over non-visual presentations, which none of the extensions do.

The availability of CSS has even made possible the removal from HTML of the oldest extensions. Now that there is a better place to put layout information, elements such as **CENTER** and **FONT** are no longer needed in HTML. In HTML 4 (and XHTML 1, its cousin in XML), which is the current version at the time of writing, they have been relegated to a special "transitional module" and are no longer part of the main standard. In the next version of HTML, they may disappear completely.

Converting text into images

A second way by which designers have sought to get around the limitations of HTML has been to make text into images. With an image, the designer can fully control colors, spacing, and fonts, among other features. Then, the designer simply inserts the appropriate link in the document where the image is to appear on the page, thereby linking the image's file to the page. When the browser displays the page, the text — in the form of an image — appears on the page.

This method, too, has downsides: It compromises accessibility to a page, and it requires readers to wait longer for documents to display.

Accessibility is the ability of people or programs to use the information on a page. Accessibility of a page is compromised in two ways when you use images to hold text. First, certain types of software called *robots* (also known as *crawlers* or *spiders*) roam the Web (so to speak) seeking what's out there and then creating and updating indexes that users can use to find Web pages. Indexing services, such as AltaVista, AllTheWeb, and Google, use robots to build their indexes.

Robots work by loading a Web page, and then automatically loading all the pages that are linked from that page, and then loading all the pages that are linked to those pages, and so on, usually for the purpose of creating a database of all the words on all the pages. When a user searches for a particular word or set of words, all the pages containing that selection are made available. Robots, however, cannot read images. So they just skip them. Hence, they simply miss text that is part of an image.

Accessibility of your page is compromised in a second way. Not all users have a browser that provides a graphical user interface (GUI) such as what's provided by Navigator and Explorer. Some browsers can display only text, not images. Also, some people may have configured their browser to not display images. So, the user loses the content of those images. Some people *do* have a graphical brower with images, but need

7

to set the fonts to a large size to be able to read them. They will find that the text in the images is too small or doesn't have enough contrast.

Currently, the only way around these accessibility problems, apart from CSS, is to enclose a textual description of the image that robots and text-only browsers can use. In the latter, for example, the user would receive this textual description of the image rather than the image – not a great substitute for the real thing, but it's better than nothing.

The second downside to using images to hold text is that images take longer to load and draw on the screen than text. The user may become impatient and back out of a page before it's loaded completely. Also, the preponderance of images as a substitute for attractive type can account for much of the reputed slowness of the Web to respond when drawing pages onscreen.

Placing text in a table

A third technique designers have used to bypass HTML's limitations is to put text into a table. Doing this enables the designer to control the layout of the text. For example, to add a margin of a certain width on the left side of a page, you would put the entire document inside a table and then add an empty column along the left side to create the "margin."

The downside (you knew there would be one): Not all browsers support tables, so pages that use tables do not display well on those browsers. Depending on how you use tables, the results on such browsers can be somewhere between "weird" and "disastrous."

The use of tables also complicates the writing of HTML. You have to add many more tags even for a simple table. The more complex the table or table structure is – you can create tables within tables to any depth you want – the more complex your code becomes.

Tables also have severe accessibility problems. Tables used for layout pose problems to programs that try to read pages without displaying them visually. For example, a browser that gives access to the Web over the phone (by reading the pages out loud) would indicate to the listener that it enters a table and then make some specific sound at the start of every cell, which is rather disturbing if the text isn't actually made up of tabular data. The voice browser has to do it that way, however, because it has to assume that a table contains data for which it is important to know the precise arrangement in rows and columns, such as price lists or sales figures. Browsers with a limited display area, such as browsers in mobile phones, Braille browsers, or browsers set to display text with a large font, have the same problem. They often display only one table cell at a time. Users won't like it when they have to navigate through the cells of a table that isn't one.

Used with care, tables can sometimes be the right solution. CSS can nearly always replace tables, so the designer has a choice: Is the arrangement in rows and columns a matter of style (and thus for CSS), or is it an intrinsic part of the structure of the text, that even non-visual browsers need to know about?

Writing a program instead of using HTML

A fourth technique designers use to bypass HTML's limitations is to create a program that displays pages. Although it's more complex than any other alternative, this technique has the advantage of giving designers control over every pixel on the screen – something not even CSS style sheets can do. However, this technique shares some of the drawbacks of the previous three that we just discussed. A program cannot be searched by robots, and it cannot be used by text-only browsers. Furthermore, because it is an actual programming language (which HTML is not), it is more difficult to learn. It may contain a computer virus. It is questionable whether, 15 years from now, there will be computers that can run the program. (Examples of programming languages for creating Web documents are Java and JavaScript.)

Why should all this matter?

HTML has become a universal data format for publishing information. Thanks to its simplicity, anyone with a computer and Internet connection can publish in HTML without expensive DTP applications. Likewise, on the user side, HTML documents can be shown on various devices without the user having to buy proprietary software. Also, perhaps the strongest point in HTML's favor: It allows for electronic documents that have a much higher chance of withstanding the years than proprietary data formats. The methods of dodging the limitations of HTML undermine these benefits: The "extended HTML" that you all too often find on the Web is a complicated proprietary data format that cannot be freely exchanged. By allowing authors to express their desire for influence over document presentation, CSS will help HTML remain the simple little language that it's meant to be.

This is why we developed CSS.

There are aesthetic and commercial reasons for why the Web needs a powerful style-sheet language. Today, placing a page on the Web is no longer just a matter of posting some text and hoping someone stumbles across it. Web pages have become an important means whereby people around the world can get together to share ideas, hobbies, interests, and more. It also is becoming an increasingly important medium for advertising products and services. A page needs to attract and stimulate as well as inform. It needs to stand out among the enormous and rapidly growing repertoire of pages that make up the Web. Aesthetics have become more important. The old HTML tools simply aren't enough for the Web-page designer who wants to make good-looking pages.

Let's get started. In the next section, we review the basics of writing HTML. In Chapter 2, we introduce CSS and show you how it works with HTML. From there, we lead you on an exploration of CSS and explain how to use it to create distinctive and manageable Web pages.

HTML BASICS

CSS was designed to work with HTML. To take advantage of CSS, you need to know some HTML. As stated in the Preface, we assume most readers have had some exposure to HTML. However, to ensure we all talk about the same thing, we now review the basics of HTML.

Elements

HTML is simple to write. It is essentially a series of elements that define the structure of your document. An *element* normally has three parts:

- Start tag
- Content
- End tag

Figure 1.2 illustrates the three parts of an element.

Figure 1.2 Anatomy of an element.

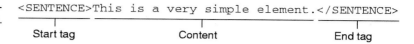

All tags in HTML start with a "<" and end with a ">." Between these comes the name of the element. In Figure 1.2, the name of the element is **SENTENCE**. The content of the element is a string of characters (but we will soon see that the content of an element can be another element). After that comes the end tag. End tags look like the start tag, except they have a "/" (slash) before the element name.

Building a simple HTML document

In this book, all element names are printed using small-cap letters (for example, **BODY**). HTML elements are case-insensitive. That is, any combination of uppercase and lowercase letters can be used. Hence, "TITLE," "Title," and "title" are all the same. XML, however, is case-sensitive.

HTML has approximately 30 commonly used elements. **SENTENCE** isn't one of them, in fact, **SENTENCE** isn't an HTML element at all. We used it as an example to show the basic structure of all elements. Let's look at a real HTML element:

    <HTML></HTML>

One of the elements in HTML is called **HTML**. The **HTML** start tag (<HTML>) marks the beginning of an HTML document, and the **HTML** end tag (</HTML>) marks the end. Everything between these two tags is the content of the **HTML** element. In the example, nothing is between the start and the end tag. In the next example, we add some content:

    <HTML><TITLE>**Bach's home page**</TITLE></HTML>

What we added from the last example is marked in bold letters (this is a convention we will use throughout this chapter). Unlike the **SENTENCE** example, the content of the **HTML** element is not just a string of characters — it's actually another element. The **TITLE** element contains the title of an HTML document. The title of the document we build in this chapter is "Bach's home page." Figure 1.3 maps out the two elements we have so far.

Figure 1.3 Diagram of an element.

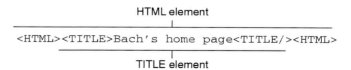

When a browser displays an HTML document in a window onscreen, the content of the title element generally goes into the title bar of the window. The title bar is at the top of the window. Below that is often the browser's control panel. Further below that is the most interesting part of the browser window: the canvas. The canvas is the part of the window where documents are actually displayed. See Figure 1.4.

As you can see, we have yet to put anything in the document that will be displayed on the canvas. To have something actually show up on the canvas, you must place it in the **BODY** element. The **BODY** element is inside the **HTML** element:

To make it easier to see where elements start and end, we show the HTML examples over several lines and indent elements that are inside others. We do this because it makes the code easier to read. The browser ignores the extra space and the line breaks that separate one line from another.

```
<HTML>
  <TITLE>Bach's home page</TITLE>
  <BODY>
  </BODY>
</HTML>
```

The content of the **HTML** element now consists of not one, but two other elements. By themselves, the **BODY** tags do not add anything to the canvas; we need to give the **BODY** element some content. Let's start by adding a first-level heading to the sample document. The standard HTML tag for a first-level heading is **H1**. Here's the HTML code:

```
<HTML>
  <TITLE>Bach's home page</TITLE>
  <BODY>
    <H1>Bach's home page</H1>
  </BODY>
</HTML>
```

The title of the document is the same as the first-level heading. This will often be the case in HTML documents, but it doesn't have to be.

HTML also has other headings you can use: **H2**, **H3**, **H4**, **H5**, and **H6**. The higher the number, the less important the heading is. If **H1** corresponds to a chapter, **H2** is a section, **H3** a subsection, etc. Typically, also, the higher the number, the smaller the font size. Here's the document with a couple of extra headings added:

```
<HTML>
  <TITLE>Bach's home page</TITLE>
  <BODY>
    <H1>Bach's home page</H1>
```

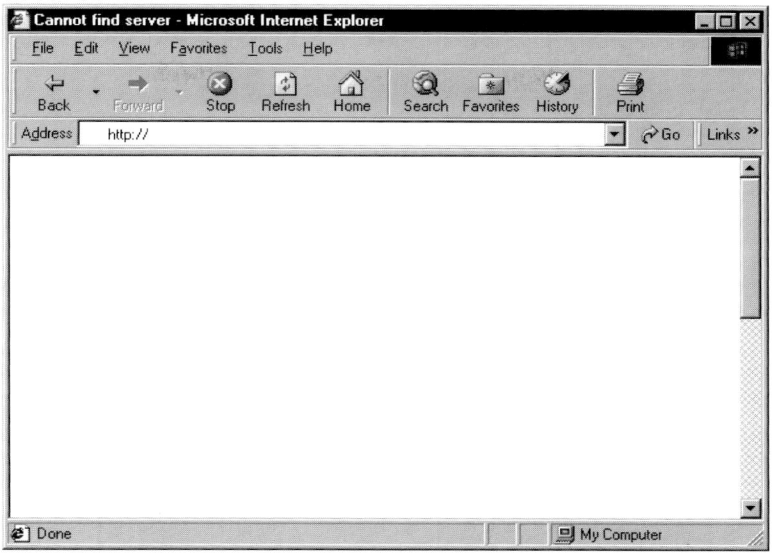

Figure 1.4 The parts of a browser's window. The top line is the title bar, the large grey area is the canvas. CSS only deals with the content of the canvas.

```
    <H2>Bach's compositions</H2>
    <H3>The keyboard music</H3>
  </BODY>
</HTML>
```

Figure 1.5 shows the heading levels as they might appear onscreen.

Figure 1.5 Three heading levels.

However, we don't need those two extra headings right now, so we delete them and add a paragraph of text instead. We do this using the paragraph element, **P**:

```
<HTML>
  <TITLE>Bach's home page</TITLE>
  <BODY>
    <H1>Bach's home page</H1>
```

```
          <P>Johann Sebastian Bach was a prolific
             composer.
     </BODY>
     </HTML>
```

Figure 1.6 shows the new paragraph.

Figure 1.6 Adding a paragraph of text.

Bach's home page

Johann Sebastian Bach was a prolific composer.

Note that we left out the ending paragraph tag, </P>. Normally, an element begins with a start tag and ends with an end tag. However, for some HTML elements, the end tag may be omitted. The end tag notifies the browser when the element ends, but in some cases, the browser can figure this out for itself, so the tag is not needed. For example, the **P** element cannot exist outside of the **BODY** element. So, when the browser encounters the **BODY** end tag (</BODY>), it knows that the **P** element has also ended. Still, including the **P** end tag is perfectly legal. HTML specifies that leaving out the </P> has no effect on the way the document is displayed.

You can also see that the browser ignored the spaces and line breaks in the source document. There is only one space between each pair of words and the line breaks are gone.

Next, suppose we want to emphasize a word relative to the surrounding text. Several HTML elements can express this; among them, we find **STRONG** and **EM** (**EM** stands for emphasis). These elements do not say anything about how they are to be displayed, but there are some conventions: **STRONG** elements are normally displayed in **bold**, and **EM** elements are displayed in *italic*.

The following code shows the use of the **STRONG** element:

```
<HTML>
  <TITLE>Bach's home page</TITLE>
  <BODY>
    <H1>Bach's home page</H1>
    <P>Johann Sebastian Bach was a
      <STRONG>prolific</STRONG>
      composer.
  </BODY>
  </HTML>
```

Figure 1.7 shows how this code is displayed.

Figure 1.7 An example of using the **STRONG** element.

Bach's home page

Johann Sebastian Bach was a **prolific** composer.

Notice how the word "prolific" stands out relative to the surrounding text. Also note that although the **H1** and **P** elements start on a new line, the **STRONG** element continues on the same line where the **P** element started. **H1** and **P** are examples of *block-level* elements, while the **STRONG** element is an *inline* element. We discuss block-level and inline elements in the next section.

Block-level and inline elements

In the previous section, the **STRONG** element was placed in the middle of an element, **P**, while the **P** and **H1** elements both began and ended a line. You can't insert a **P** element in the middle of another **P** or **H1** element or vice versa. But, you can insert an element like **STRONG** in the middle of most other elements. This is because the **P** and **H1** elements are *block-level elements,* while the **STRONG** element is an *inline element.*

Elements can be divided into three groups:

- Block-level
- Inline
- Invisible

A *block-level element* is an element that begins and ends a line or, put another way, that has a line break before and after its content. Examples of block-level elements that you've seen so far in this chapter are **H1** and **P**. Others are given in Table 1.1.

An *inline element* is an element that does not begin and end a line, although it may be placed at either end. Examples of inline elements are **STRONG**, which you saw in the earlier example, and **EM**. Others are given in Table 1.1.

An *invisible element* is an element whose content isn't displayed on the canvas. We have seen only one invisible element so far: **TITLE**. It's not really an invisible element because it appears in the title bar of the window, but it is not displayed on the canvas. HTML only has a few invisible elements, and you will find them in Table 1.1.

Element overview

Confused about the different elements? Don't worry. Table 1.1 gives you an overview of the most common HTML elements. We've introduced you to several of these already and will discuss others shortly. We talk about others when appropriate throughout the rest of this book and use them in many examples. Also, we suggest that you refer to the table as needed as you work your way through this book. The last column of the table ("Empty? Replaced?") is explained later in this chapter.

Among the elements that are not included in Table 1.1 are the elements that create forms and tables. Also, the non-standard elements have been left out.

Element name	Abbreviation for	Block, inline, or invisible	Typical visual effect	End tag can be omitted?	Empty? Replaced?
A	anchor	inline	highlighted	no	
BLOCK-QUOTE		block-level	indented	no	
BODY		block-level	inside canvas	yes	
BR	break	block-level	breaks the line	yes*	empty
DD	definition description	block-level		yes	
DL	definition list	block-level		no	
DIV	division	block-level		no	
DT	definition term	block-level		yes	
EM	emphasis	inline	italic	no	
H1, H2... H6	heading levels	block-level	large fonts	no	
HR	horizontal rule	block-level	horizontal rule	yes*	empty
HTML		block-level		yes	
I	italic	inline	italic	no	
IMG	image	inline	as an image	yes*	empty and replaced

Element name	Abbreviation for	Block, inline, or invisible	Typical visual effect	End tag can be omitted?	Empty? Replaced?
LI	list item	block-level	with a list item marker in front	yes	
LINK		invisible		yes*	empty
OBJECT		block-level		no	replaced
OL	ordered list	block-level		no	
P	paragraph	block-level		yes	
PRE	preformatted	block-level	in monospace font	no	
SPAN		inline		no	
STRONG		inline	bold	no	
STYLE		invisible		no	
TITLE		invisible	shown in title bar, not on canvas	no	
TT	teletype	inline	in monospace font	no	
UL	unordered list	block-level		no	

* indicates that the element is empty and that the end tag doesn't exist.

Table 1.1 The most common HTML elements.

In the next several sections, we add to your repertoire of HTML tags by discussing elements that you can use to create lists, add a horizontal rule, force a line break, and link to text and images.

Comments

Most of your documents will consist of elements. However, you can also insert HTML *comments* into the document. A comment is anything you want to say about what is going on with your document that you don't want to be displayed. The user won't see the comment on the canvas because browsers ignore comments; that is, they do not display a comment's contents. Comments can be a helpful way of communicating something about your document to other designers who will see your code.

To ensure that the comment really is not viewable by the user, you enclose it between special strings that the browser will recognize as enclosing a comment. You begin the comment with the string `<!--` and end it with the string `-->`. (That's two hyphens in both cases.) Here's a sample comment:

```
<!-- CSS is the greatest thing
     to hit the Web since hyperlinks -->
```

Lists

Lists are common in HTML documents. HTML has three elements that create lists:

- **OL**, which creates an *ordered* list. In an ordered list, each list item has a label that indicates the order, e.g., a digit (1, 2, 3, 4 or I, II, III, IV) or letter (a, b, c, d). In desktop-publishing terminology, ordered lists are often called numbered lists.
- **UL**, which creates an *unordered* list. In an unordered list, each list item has a mark that does not indicate order, e.g., a bullet symbol. In desktop-publishing terminology, unordered lists are often called bulleted lists.
- **DL**, which creates a *definition* list. A definition list is a list of terms with their corresponding definitions. For example, a dictionary is a (long!) definition list.

Bach's home page must surely include a list of some of his compositions. Let's add an ordered list:

```
<HTML>
  <TITLE>Bach's home page</TITLE>
  <BODY>
    <H1>Bach's home page</H1>
    <P>Johann Sebastian Bach was a
      <STRONG>prolific</STRONG>
      composer. Here are his best works:
    <OL>
      <LI>the Goldberg Variations
      <LI>the Brandenburg Concertos
```

```
      <LI>the Christmas Oratorio
   </OL>
  </BODY>
</HTML>
```

Notice that an **LI** doesn't need an end tag, but an **OL** does. Figure 1.8 shows the result.

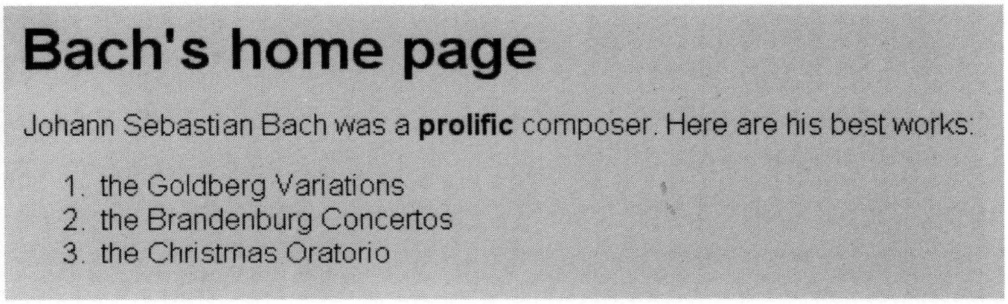

Figure 1.8 An ordered list.

Bach's home page

Johann Sebastian Bach was a **prolific** composer. Here are his best works:

1. the Goldberg Variations
2. the Brandenburg Concertos
3. the Christmas Oratorio

This ordered list is unfair to all the other great compositions by Bach. (What about the Mass in B-minor?) Let's change the ordered list into an unordered list. To do this, we simply change the **OL** to **UL**:

```
<HTML>
  <TITLE>Bach's home page</TITLE>
  <BODY>
    <H1>Bach's home page</H1>
    <P>Johann Sebastian Bach was a
      <STRONG>prolific</STRONG>composer.
      Among his works are:
    <UL>
      <LI>the Goldberg Variations
      <LI>the Brandenburg Concertos
      <LI>the Christmas Oratorio
    </UL>
  </BODY>
</HTML>
```

Figure 1.9 shows the result.

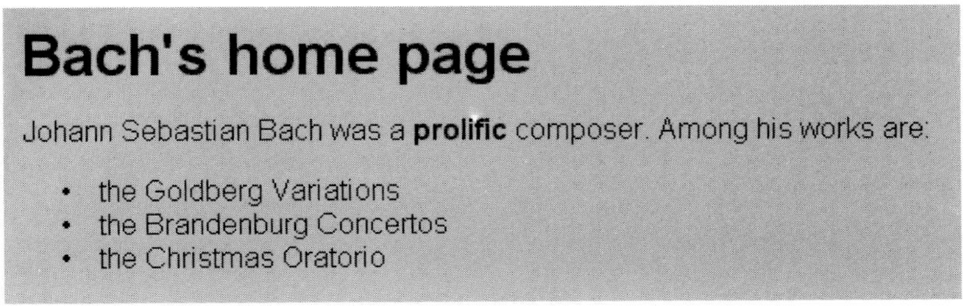

Figure 1.9 An unordered list.

Bach's home page

Johann Sebastian Bach was a **prolific** composer. Among his works are:

• the Goldberg Variations
• the Brandenburg Concertos
• the Christmas Oratorio

Notice that we do not have to change the **LI** elements to change the list from unordered to ordered: Both **UL** and **OL** use **LI** as the list item element. But, because the **LI** elements are now inside the **UL** element, they will look different.

A **DL**, or definition list, is used for lists that have terms and their corresponding definitions. Each term is contained in a **DT** element, and each definition in a **DD** element. An example of a **DL** is a dictionary or glossary. In the next example, we change our **OL** to a **DL**. Notice how the **LI**s change to **DT**s and that like the **LI**s, they do not require end tags. Figure 1.10 shows the result.

```
<HTML>
  <TITLE>Bach's home page</TITLE>
  <BODY>
    <H1>Bach's home page</H1>
    <P>Johann Sebastian Bach was a
      <STRONG>prolific</STRONG> composer.
      Among his works are:
    <DL>
      <DT>the Goldberg Variations
      <DD>composed in 1741, catalog number BWV988
      <DT>the Brandenburg Concertos
      <DD>composed in 1713, catalog numbers
          BWV1046-1051
      <DT>the Christmas Oratorio
      <DD>composed in 1734, catalog number BWV248
    </DL>
  </BODY>
</HTML>
```

Figure 1.10 A definition list.

Bach's home page

Johann Sebastian Bach was a **prolific** composer. Among his works are:

the Goldberg Variations
    composed in 1741, catalog number BWV988
the Brandenburg Concertos
    composed in 1713, catalog numbers BWV1046-1051
the Christmas Oratorio
    composed in 1734, catalog number BWV248

Empty elements HR and BR

All the HTML elements that we have discussed so far have had content. HTML also has some elements that do not have content; they are called *empty elements*. One example is the **HR** element, which inserts a horizontal rule in the document. It doesn't need any content. Also, the **BR** element's sole purpose is to force a line break. Because empty elements do not have any content, they don't need any end tags.

We can add a horizontal rule to a document by using the **HR** (horizontal rule) element. **HR** is an empty element, so you should omit its end tag. Here's the code for adding an **HR** element:

```
<HTML>
  <TITLE>Bach's home page</TITLE>
  <BODY>
    <H1>Bach's home page</H1>
    <P>Johann Sebastian Bach was a
      <STRONG>prolific</STRONG>
      composer. Among his works are:
    <UL>
      <LI>the Goldberg Variations
      <LI>the Brandenburg Concertos
      <LI>the Christmas Oratorio
    </UL>
    <HR>
  </BODY>
</HTML>
```

Figure 1.11 shows the result.

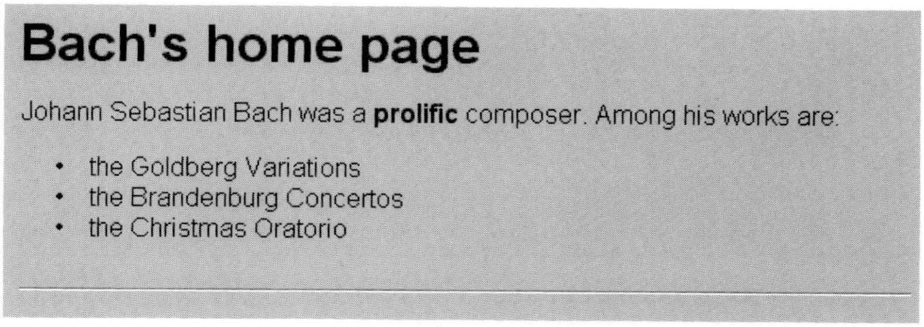

Figure 1.11 Adding a horizontal rule.

Bach's home page

Johann Sebastian Bach was a **prolific** composer. Among his works are:

* the Goldberg Variations
* the Brandenburg Concertos
* the Christmas Oratorio

We can force a line break in the middle of an element by using the **BR** (break) element. The browser normally ignores line breaks in the HTML document and automatically breaks a line when needed when it displays the document. However, if you want to force a line break at a certain spot in the document, **BR** enables you to do this. Because **BR** is an empty element, you can omit its end tag.

Here is our example with a **BR** element added:

```
<HTML>
  <TITLE>Bach's home page</TITLE>
  <BODY>
    <H1>Bach's <BR>home page</H1>
    <P>Johann Sebastian Bach was a
      <STRONG>prolific</STRONG>
      composer. Among his works are:
    <UL>
      <LI>the Goldberg Variations
      <LI>the Brandenburg Concertos
      <LI>the Christmas Oratorio
    </UL>
  </BODY>
</HTML>
```

Figure 1.12 shows the result.

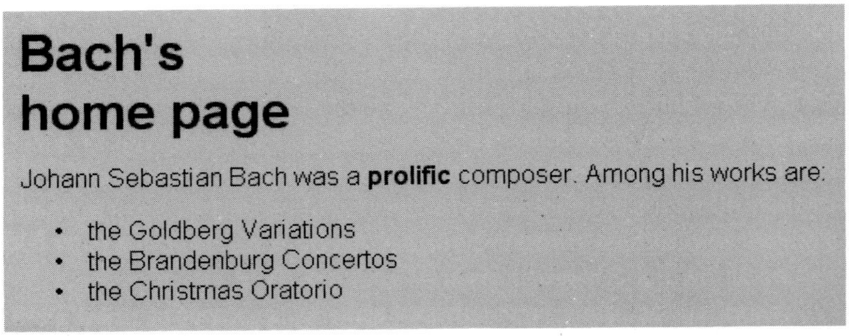

Figure 1.12 Adding a line break.

Bach's home page

Johann Sebastian Bach was a **prolific** composer. Among his works are:

- the Goldberg Variations
- the Brandenburg Concertos
- the Christmas Oratorio

It is usually better to let the browser determine the line breaks, because as an author, you cannot know how wide the user's window is or how large the fonts are. So, we'll take out the **BR** element as we move on.

Maintaining preformatted text

In the previous example, we mentioned that a browser generally ignores line breaks, except for those that you enter using the **BR** element. The browser also ignores tabs and extra white space. Tabspaces are converted to single white-space characters, while extra white-space characters — any more than one — are collapsed into one white-space character. Generally, this is what we want. This feature enables us to space out our code so that it is more readable and reflects the structure of the document, secure in the knowledge that the browser ignores all the extra white spaces.

Sometimes, however, you may want to insert white space and have the browser display your text exactly as you formatted it. The **PRE** (preformatted) element allows you do this. Simply enclose within <PRE> tags the information whose formatting you want to preserve. The **PRE** element is often used for simple tables where columns need to align vertically:

```
<HTML>
   <TITLE>Bach's home page</TITLE>
   <BODY>
      <H1>Bach's <BR>home page</H1>
      <P>Johann Sebastian Bach was a
         <STRONG>prolific</STRONG>
         composer. Among his works are:
         <PRE>
COMPOSITION                  YEAR   CATALOG#
Goldberg Variation           1741   BWV988
Brandenburg Concertos 1713          BWV1046-1051
Christmas Oratorio           1734   BWV248
</PRE>
   </BODY>
</HTML>
```

Notice that the content of the **PRE** element cannot be aligned with the other elements because the extra white space would appear on the canvas. Figure 1.13 shows the result.

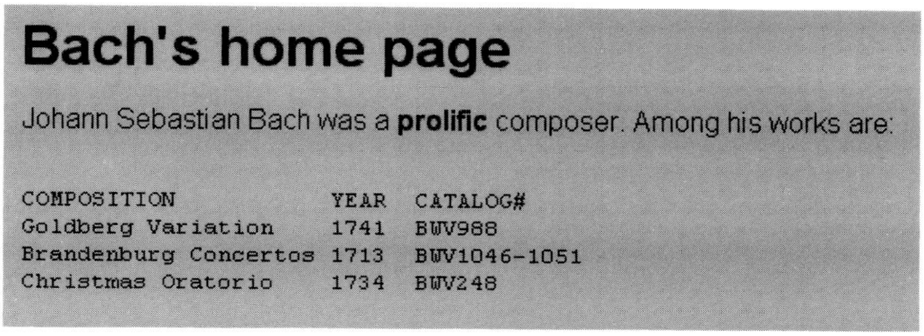

Figure 1.13 Preserving preformatted text.

Bach's home page

Johann Sebastian Bach was a **prolific** composer. Among his works are:

```
COMPOSITION                  YEAR   CATALOG#
Goldberg Variation           1741   BWV988
Brandenburg Concertos 1713          BWV1046-1051
Christmas Oratorio           1734   BWV248
```

This is actually not a very good example because by using **PRE**, we hide the fact that the content is a table. This is a case where using a table is in fact the right thing to do because it enhances accessibility (see the section "Placing text in a table" earlier in this chapter).

Adding hyperlinks

We can make our document more interesting by adding hyperlinks to it. When hyperlinks are in place, users can click on them to access related documents from somewhere else on the Web. Hyperlinks are integral to HTML and the Web. Without hyperlinks, there would be no Web.

To make a hyperlink, you use the **A** (anchor) element. When the user clicks on the **A** element, the browser fetches the document at the other end of the hyperlink. The browser needs to be told where it can find the other document, and this information goes into an attribute on the **A** element. An *attribute* is a characteristic quality of the element, other than the type or content of an element. The **A** element uses an attribute called **HREF** (hypertext reference) to add a hyperlink:

```
<HTML>
  <TITLE>Bach's home page</TITLE>
  <BODY>
    <H1>Bach's home page</H1>
    <P>Johann Sebastian Bach was a
      <STRONG>prolific</STRONG>
      composer. Among his works are:
    <UL>
      <LI>the <A HREF="goldberg.html">Goldberg</A>
        Variations
      <LI>the Brandenburg Concertos
      <LI>the Christmas Oratorio
    </UL>
    <HR>
  </BODY>
</HTML>
```

Let's take a closer look at the newly added **A** element. Figure 1.14 shows the different parts of the **A** element.

Figure 1.14 The parts of an **A** element.

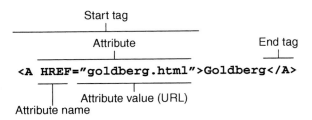

The **A** start tag is a bit more complicated than the other start tags we have seen so far; in addition to the element name, it includes an attribute. Different element types have different attributes; among the most common ones is the **HREF** attribute on the **A** element. Attributes can only go into the start tag of the element, after the element name. Most attributes need a value: The **HREF** attributes always takes a URL as a value. A URL (Universal Resource Locator) is a Web address that the browser uses to locate the hyperlinked document. When URLs are used as values on the **HREF** attribute, they should always be quoted ("…").

URLs come in two flavors:

- A *relative URL* gives the location of the document relative to the document where it is referenced (that is, the document where the **A** element is). You can only use relative URLs when you link to a document on the same Web server as the document you are linking from.
- An *absolute URL* gives the location of the document independent of any other document. You must use absolute URLs when you link to a document on a different server. Absolute URLs can be typed into any machine on the Internet and the browser will find it. That's why you see absolute URLs on T-shirts, in TV commercials, etc.

In the previous example, the **HREF** attribute had a relative URL (gold-berg.html) as value. If the user clicks on the word "Goldberg," the browser fetches the document called goldberg.html from the same location as where our sample document is found.

We can also put an absolute URL into our document:

```
<HTML>
  <TITLE>Bach's home page</TITLE>
  <BODY>
    <H1>Bach's home page</H1>
    <P>Johann Sebastian Bach was a
      <STRONG>prolific</STRONG> composer.
      Among his works are:
    <UL>
      <LI>the <A HREF="goldberg.html">Goldberg</A>
          Variations
      <LI>the Brandenburg Concertos
      <LI>the <A HREF="http://example.org/christmas.html">
      Christmas</A> Oratorio
    </UL>
    <HR>
  </BODY>
</HTML>
```

As you can see, absolute URLs are slightly more complicated than relative ones. In fact, when Tim Berners-Lee invented the URL scheme, they were only meant to be seen by machines. Figure 1.15 shows the various parts of this URL.

Figure 1.15 Structure of a URL.

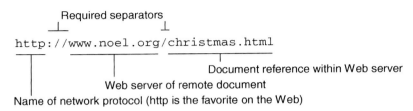

The details of URLs are not the main topic for this book and as long as you are aware of the two types of URL, you may safely proceed.

Adding images

Images proliferate on the Web. It wasn't until the Mosaic browser added support for images in 1993 that a critical mass of people realized the potential of the Web. You can add images to your documents with the **IMG** element – **IMG** is short for image.

IMG is a peculiar element. First, it's empty. That's not so strange, we've seen those before. (Quick reminder: an empty element is an element without content, e.g., **HR**, **BR**.) Second, it's a replaced element. A *replaced* element is a placeholder for some other content that is being pointed to from the element. In the case of **IMG**, it points to an image that is fetched by the browser when the **IMG** element is encountered. Unlike the **A** element, which gives the user the option of jumping to a link or not, the browser automatically fetches the image **IMG** points to. Also, unlike the **A** element, **IMG** uses an attribute called **SRC** to point to the image.

Let's add an image to the sample document. Not many portraits of Bach are known, but those that exist are on the Web:

```
<HTML>
  <TITLE>Bach's home page</TITLE>
  <BODY>
    <H1><IMG SRC="jsbach.png" ALT="Portrait of
    J.S. Bach">Bach's home page</H1>
    <P>Johann Sebastian Bach was a
      <STRONG>prolific</STRONG>
```

```
composer. Among his works are:
<UL>
  <LI>the <A HREF="goldberg.html">Goldberg</A>
      Variations
  <LI>the Brandenburg Concertos
  <LI>the <A HREF="http://example.org/christmas.html">
  Christmas</A> Oratorio
</UL>
<HR>
</BODY>
</HTML>
```

Let's take a closer look at the attributes on the **IMG** element (see Figure 1.16).

Figure 1.16 **IMG** element.

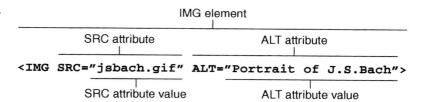

The **SRC** attribute on **IMG** is similar to the **HREF** attribute on **A**: They both take a URL as a value. The **ALT** attribute is new. The purpose of **ALT** is to provide an alternative (from which it gets its name) textual description of the image. Sometimes, a browser cannot fetch the image (perhaps the Web server is broken?) or it may be configured to ignore images, for example, in the case of a text-only browser. In these cases, the browser will look for the alternative textual description and display that instead of the image. The **ALT** text is also essential for people who cannot see. Therefore, you should always try to include a textual alternative for the image so users can still get a sense of what is going on.

Figure 1.17 shows how Microsoft Internet Explorer shows the page while the image is being fetched.

When the image is ready, the page looks like Figure 1.18.

DOCUMENT TREES

In this chapter, we have demonstrated how elements in HTML are placed inside one another. We did this by indenting the code, as shown in all the previous code examples. The **HTML** element itself is the outermost element that encompasses all the other elements. Inside the

Figure 1.17 Waiting for an element to be fetched.

Bach's home page

Johann Sebastian Bach was a **prolific** composer. Among his works are:

- the Goldberg Variations
- the Brandenburg Concertos
- the Christmas Oratorio

Figure 1.17 Waiting for an element to be fetched.

Bach's home page

Johann Sebastian Bach was a **prolific** composer. Among his works are:

- the Goldberg Variations
- the Brandenburg Concertos
- the Christmas Oratorio

Figure 1.18 The image has been loaded.

HTML element are the **TITLE** and **BODY** elements, with the latter encompassing all the other elements, such as **H1** and **P**. Within some of those elements are other elements. For example, within the **UL** element are the **LI** elements. If you were to diagram this idea of elements within elements, the result might be as shown in Figure 1.19.

```
<HTML>
  <TITLE>Bach's home page</TITLE>
  <BODY>
    <H1>Bach's home page</H1>
    <P>Johann Sebastian Bach was a
      <STRONG>prolific</STRONG>
      composer. Among his works are:
    <UL>
      <LI>the Goldberg Variations
      <LI>the Brandenburg Concertos
```

```
            <LI>the Christmas Oratorio
        </UL>
      </BODY>
    </HTML>
```

Figure 1.19 Diagram of elements within elements in a tree
structure.

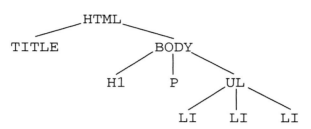

Notice how Figure 1.19 resembles a person's genealogical chart, with
parents and children spread out in a top-to-bottom fashion, where parents can also be children. This is called a *tree structure*. In the tree structure of an HTML document, the **HTML** element is the earliest ancestor
– the top parent. All other elements are children, grandchildren, and
great-grandchildren – in short, descendants – of the **HTML** element. An
element can have from zero to many children, but it always has only
one parent, with the exception of the **HTML** element, which is an
orphan. In Figure 1.19, note that **TITLE** and **BODY** are children of
HTML. **TITLE** has no children, but **BODY** has three: **H1**, **P**, and **UL**. In
turn, **UL** has three children: the **LI**s. Also note that in this example,
BODY is both a child and a parent, as is **UL**.

We encounter tree structures in many situations outside HTML and
genealogy. Trees – real trees such as spruce and pine – are (not surprisingly) tree structures. Organizational charts for companies are often set
out in a tree structure. Books and technical documents, too, are usually
set out in a tree structure, where sections and subsections are branches
of the whole. (The fact that books are made from trees doesn't seem to
have anything to do with it…) The last example is probably the reason
why HTML documents always have a tree structure.

Nested elements

In HTML, there are some restrictions on which elements can be children of which elements. Usually, an element cannot contain children of
its own type. That is, a **P**, for example, cannot be a child element of
another **P**. You would not typically want to put a paragraph inside

another paragraph, anyway. Similarly, an **HI** cannot be a child element of another **HI**.

Some elements, however, may contain children of their own type. One example is **BLOCKQUOTE**, the element that is used to put quoted material within a document. This element can have nested within it quoted material that is the content of another **BLOCKQUOTE** element, that is, you can put a quote within a quote. This ability of an element to have children of its own type is called *nesting*.

The following is an example using no less than three nested **BLOCK-QUOTE** elements (shown in bold, italic, and bold italic, respectively):

```
<HTML>
 <TITLE>Fredrick the Great meets Bach</TITLE>
 <BODY>
  <H1>Fredrick the Great meets Bach</H1>
  <P>In his book "Gödel, Escher, Bach," Douglas
   Hofstadter writes:
   <BLOCKQUOTE>
   Johann Nikolaus Forkel, one of
   Bach's earliest biographers, tells the story
   as follows:
   <BLOCKQUOTE>
     One evening, just as he was getting
     his flute ready, and his musicians
     were assembled, an officer brought
     him a list of the strangers who had
     arrived. With his flute in his hand
     he ran over the list, but
     immediately turned to the assembled
     musicians, and said, with a kind of
     agitation:
     <BLOCKQUOTE>
      Gentlemen,
      old Bach is come.
     </BLOCKQUOTE>
    </BLOCKQUOTE>
   </BLOCKQUOTE>
 </BODY>
</HTML>
```

This can be displayed as shown in Figure 1.20.

Notice how with the nested elements, the second element is indented even more than the first is. This is a visual indication that it is a child of the first **BLOCKQUOTE**.

BLOCKQUOTE marks content as a quote. When you use it for all quotes in your document, you or others, such as robots, can easily

Figure 1.20 Nested **BLOCK-QUOTE** elements.

Fredrick the Great meets Bach

In his book "Gödel, Escher, Bach" Douglas Hofstadter writes:

> Johann Nikolaus Forkel, one of Bach's earliest biographers, tells the story as follows:
>
>> One evening, just as he was getting his flute ready, and his musicians were assembled, an officer brought him a list of the strangers who had arrived. With his flute in his hand he ran over the list, but immediately turned to the assembled musicians, and said, with a kind of agitation:
>>
>>> Gentlemen, old Bach is come.

extract all the quotes. It is much used also as a means of indenting material other than quotes. It is common to see stacks of **BLOCKQUOTE** elements, not because there are so many levels of quotes, but because designers think indentation looks good. Here's an example of that (see Figure 1.21):

```
<HTML>
  <BODY>
    <BLOCKQUOTE>
      <BLOCKQUOTE>
        <BLOCKQUOTE>
          <BLOCKQUOTE>
            Indentation is great!
          </BLOCKQUOTE>
        </BLOCKQUOTE>
      </BLOCKQUOTE>
    </BLOCKQUOTE>
  </BODY>
</HTML>
```

Figure 1.21 Using **BLOCK-QUOTE** for indentation.

Indentation is great!

Unfortunately, when robots or others search for quotes, they find not only quotes, but also everything else tagged as quotes.

With the arrival of CSS, this misuse of **BLOCKQUOTE** should no longer be necessary. CSS provides easy-to-use methods for indenting text and images, as we will show you in subsequent chapters.

Well, there you have it. The elements we described in this chapter, plus a few others we discuss later, form the basics of HTML. With these, you can write and publish many literary gems. Of course, they may not look all that great. But, we fix that with CSS.

Chapter 2

CSS

HTML is the most popular document format on the Web, and it is used in most of the examples in this book. However, you can use CSS to style other document languages, including XHTML (which is a dialect of HTML) and XML (which uses different tags than HTML does).

As we explained in Chapter 1, "The Web and HTML," HTML elements enable Web-page designers to mark up a document's structure. The HTML specification lists guidelines on how browsers should display these elements. For example, you can be reasonably sure that the contents of a **STRONG** element will be displayed as boldfaced. Also, you can pretty much trust that most browsers will display the content of an **H1** element using a big font size – at least bigger than the **P** element and bigger than the **H2** element. But beyond trust and hope, you don't have any control over your text's appearance.

CSS changes that. CSS puts the designer in the driver's seat. We devote much of the rest of this book to explaining what you can do with CSS. In this chapter, we begin by introducing you to the basics of how to write style sheets and how CSS and HTML work together to describe both the structure and style of your document.

RULES AND STYLE SHEETS

To start using CSS, you don't even have to write style sheets. Chapter 14, "External Style Sheets," tells you how to point to existing style sheets on the Web.

You can create style sheets in two ways. You can either use a normal text editor and write the style sheets "by hand" or you can use a dedicated tool – for example, a Web authoring tool. The dedicated tools enable you to create style sheets without learning the syntax of the CSS language. However, in many cases, the designer wants to tweak the style sheet by hand afterwards, so we recommend that you learn to write and edit CSS by hand. Let's get started! Here is a simple example:

```
h1 { color: green }
```

This code is a simple CSS rule that contains one rule. A *rule* is a statement about one stylistic aspect of one or more elements. A *style sheet* is a set of one or more rules that apply to an HTML document. This rule sets the color of all first-level headings (**H1**). Figure 2.1 shows what the visual result of this rule might be.

Figure 2.1 The headline in our sample document.

Bach's home page

Unfortunately, this chapter is printed in black and white; you have to trust us that the color really is green.

Anatomy of a rule

A rule consists of two parts (see Figure 2.2):

- Selector: The part before the left curly brace
- Declaration: The part within the curly braces

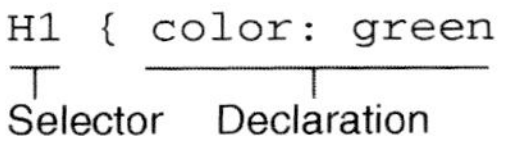

Figure 2.2 Two main parts of a rule.

```
H1 { color: green }
 ┬   ────────────
Selector   Declaration
```

The *selector* links the HTML document and the style sheet. It specifies what elements are affected by the declaration. The *declaration* is the part of the rule that sets forth what the effect will be. In this example, the selector is **H1** and the declaration is `color: green`. Hence, the declaration affects all **H1** elements and, as a result, they will be green.

The example selector is based on the *type* of the element: It selects all elements of the **H1** type. This kind of selector is called *type selector*. Any HTML element type can be used as a type selector. Type selectors are the simplest kind of selectors. We discuss other kinds of selectors in Chapter 4, "CSS selectors."

Anatomy of a declaration

A declaration has two parts separated by a colon (see Figure 2.3):

- Property. The part before the colon
- Value: The part after the colon

Figure 2.3 Two main parts of a declaration.

```
H1 { color: green }
     Property Value
```

The *property* is a quality or characteristic that something possesses. In the previous example, it is **color**. CSS 2.1 (see the box on the next page) defines approximately 120 properties, and we can assign values to all of them.

The *value* is a precise specification of the property. In the example, it is "green," but it could just as easily be blue, red, yellow, or another color.

Figure 2.4 shows all the ingredients of a rule. The curly braces ({ }) and colon (:) make it possible for the browser to distinguish between the selector, property, and value.

Figure 2.4 Diagram of a rule.

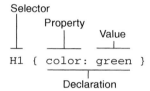

```
Selector
    Property
        Value
H1 { color: green }
        Declaration
```

Grouping selectors and rules

In designing CSS, brevity was a goal. We figured that if we could reduce the size of the style sheets, we could enable designers to write and edit style sheets "by hand." Also, short style sheets load faster than longer ones. CSS therefore includes several mechanisms to shorten style sheets by way of grouping selectors and declarations.

For example, consider these three rules:

```
H1 { font-style: italic }
H2 { font-style: italic }
H3 { font-style: italic }
```

All three rules have exactly the same declaration – they set the font style to *italic*. (This is done using the **font-style** property, which we discuss in Chapter 5, "Fonts.") Because all three declarations are identical, we can group the selectors into a *comma-separated list* and only list the declaration once, like this:

```
h1, h2, h3 { font-style: italic }
```

CSS SPECIFICATIONS

Cascading Style Sheets is formally described in three W3C specifications: CSS1, CSS2, and CSS 2.1. (As discussed in the previous chapter, W3C is the organization that coordinates the technical development of the Web.) The first specification, CSS1, was issued in December 1996 and describes a simple style sheet language mostly for screen-based presentations. CSS1 has around 50 properties (for example, **color** and **font-size**). CSS2 was finalized in May 1998 and builds on CSS1. CSS2 includes all CSS1 properties and adds around 70 of its own, such as properties to describe aural presentations and page breaks.

CSS 2.1 is the most recent specification published by W3C. It adds some new features, but CSS 2.1 is mostly a scaled-down version of CSS2. CSS2 was an ambitious attempt to describe functionality, which Web authors had requested. However, not all the functionality is reliably supported by all browsers. CSS 2.1 is a specification that describes the parts that *are* supported by two or more browsers. Because CSS 2.1 is similar to CSS2, the specification was given a minor version number (that is, 2.1) rather than a major number (such as CSS3). In this book, we do not try to distinguish between the different specifications and use the term "CSS" unless the distinction is important. If you would like to read the CSS specifications themselves, you can find them at this Web site:

```
http://www.w3.org/TR
```

This rule produces the same result as the first three.

A selector may have more than one declaration. For example, we could write a style sheet with these two rules:

```
h1 { color: green }
h1 { text-align: center }
```

In this case, we set all **H1**s to green and to be centered on the canvas. (This is done using the **text-align** property, which is discussed in Chapter 5.)

But, we can achieve the same effect faster by grouping the declarations that relate to the same selector into a *semicolon-separated list*, like this:

```
h1 {
  color: green;
  text-align: center;
}
```

All declarations must be contained within the pair of curly braces. A semicolon separates the declarations and may — but doesn't have to — also appear at the end of the last declaration. Also, to make your code easier to read, we suggest that you place each declaration on its own line, as we did here. (Browsers won't care; they'll just ignore all the extra white space and line breaks.)

Now you have the basics of how to create CSS rules and style sheets. However, you're not done yet. For the style sheet to have any effect, you have to "glue" your style sheet to your HTML document.

"GLUING" STYLE SHEETS TO THE DOCUMENT

For any style sheet to affect the HTML document, it must be "glued" to the document. That is, the style sheet and the document must be combined so that they can work together to present the document. This can be done in any of four ways:

- Apply the basic, document-wide style sheet for the document by using the **STYLE** element.
- Apply a style sheet to an individual element using the **STYLE** attribute.
- Link an external style sheet to the document using the **LINK** element.
- Import a style sheet using the CSS @import notation.

In the next section, we discuss the first method: using the **STYLE** element. We discuss using the **STYLE** attribute in Chapter 4 and using the **LINK** element and the @import notation in Chapter 14.

Gluing by using the STYLE element

You can glue together the style sheet and the HTML document by putting the style sheet inside a **STYLE** element at the top of your document. The **STYLE** element was introduced in HTML specifically to allow style sheets to be inserted inside HTML documents. Here's a style sheet (shown in bold) glued to a sample document by using the **STYLE** element. The result is shown in Figure 2.5.

```
<HTML>
  <TITLE>Bach's home page</TITLE>
  <STYLE>
    H1, H2 { font-style: italic }
  </STYLE>
```

```
<BODY>
  <H1>Bach's home page</H1>
  <P>Johann Sebastian Bach was a prolific
     composer. Among his works are:
  <UL>
    <LI>the Goldberg Variations
    <LI>the Brandenburg Concertos
    <LI>the Christmas Oratorio
  </UL>
  <H2>Historical perspective</H2>
  <P>Bach composed in what has been referred
     to as the Baroque period.
</BODY>
</HTML>
```

Figure 2.5 The result of gluing the style sheet to the document is that **H1** and **H2** elements are shown in italics. The style sheet is inserted into the **STYLE** element.

Bach's home page

Johann Sebastian Bach was a prolific composer. Among his works are:

- the Goldberg Variations
- the Brandenburg Concertos
- the Christmas Oratorio

Historical perspective

Bach composed in what has been referred to as the Baroque period.

Notice that the **STYLE** element is placed after the **TITLE** element and before the **BODY** element. The title of a document does not appear on the canvas, so CSS styles do not affect it.

The content of a **STYLE** element is a style sheet. However, whereas the content of such elements as **H1**, **P**, and **UL** appears on the canvas, the content of a **STYLE** element does not show up on the canvas. Rather, it is the *effect* of the content of the **STYLE** element – the style sheet – that appears on the canvas. So, you don't see H1, H2 { font -style: italic } displayed onscreen; instead, you see two slanted elements. No rules have been added that affect any of the other elements, so those elements appear in the browser's default style.

BROWSERS AND CSS

For CSS to work as described in this book, you must use a CSS-enhanced browser, that is, a browser that supports CSS. A CSS-enhanced browser recognizes the **STYLE** element as a container for a style sheet and presents the document accordingly. Most browsers in use today support CSS, including Microsoft's Internet Explorer (IE), Firefox (FF), Opera (O), Safari (S), and Konqueror (K). CSS is also supported by most Web authoring tools, and the Prince (P) formatter prints CSS beautifully. The symbols in parenthesis identify the browser in the capabililty charts you will see later in this book.

It wasn't always this way. CSS was first published in 1996, so browsers created before then have a valid excuse for not supporting style sheets. Also, the first generation of browsers that supported CSS (Internet Explorer 3 and Netscape Navigator 4) were filled with bugs. (A few people still use these browsers.) Also, some browsers on special devices do not support style sheets. For example, on a mobile phone where the connection speed is limited, a Web browser may ignore style sheets to speed up the Web.

For these reasons, it is important that HTML pages can be displayed even if the style sheet is not taken into account. CSS was designed with this in mind, and all content remains visible even if the style sheet is ignored. This is because of the fundamental principles of style sheets: the separation of content and presentation. By only describing the *presentation* of documents, all the *content* of the documents are available even if the style sheets are ignored.

If you expect that your pages will be viewed in older browsers, you may want to use a special trick to hide the style sheet. Because older browsers do not know about style sheets, they display the *content* of the **STYLE** element. Thus, the user ends up with the style sheet printed on the top of the canvas. At the time of writing, less than one percent of Web users experience this problem. To avoid this, you can put your style sheet inside an *HTML comment*, which we discussed in Chapter 1. Because comments don't display onscreen, by placing your style sheet inside an HTML comment, you prevent the oldest browsers from displaying the **STYLE** element's content. CSS-enhanced browsers are aware of this trick and treat the content of the **STYLE** element as a style sheet.

Recall that HTML comments start with <!-- and end with -->. Here's an excerpt from the previous code that shows how you write a style sheet in an HTML comment. The comment encloses only the **STYLE** element content:

```
<HTML>
  <TITLE>Bach's home page</TITLE>
  <STYLE>
    <!--
      H1 { font-style: italic }
    -->
  </STYLE>
  <BODY>
    ..
  </BODY>
</HTML>
```

CSS also has its own set of comments that you can use within the style sheet. A CSS comment begins with "/*" and ends with "*/." (Those familiar with the C programming language will recognize these.) CSS rules inside a CSS comment will not have any effect on the presentation of the document.

The browser also needs to be told that you are working with CSS style sheets. CSS is currently the only style sheet language in use with HTML documents, and we don't expect this to change. But, just as there is more than one image format (GIF, JPEG, and PNG come to mind), there could be more than one style sheet language. So, it's a good habit to tell browsers that they are dealing with CSS. (In fact, HTML requires you to.) This is done with the **TYPE** attribute of the **STYLE** element. The value of **TYPE** indicates what type of style sheet is being used. For CSS, that value is text/css. The following excerpt from our previous sample document shows you how to write this (in combination with the use of the HTML comment):

```
<html>
  <title>Bach's home page</title>
  <style type="text/css">
    <!--
      h1 { font-style: italic }
    -->
  </style>
  <body>
    ..
  </body>
</html>
```

When the browser loads a document, it checks to see if it understands the style sheet language. If it does, it tries to read the sheet; otherwise, it ignores it. The **TYPE** attribute on the **STYLE** element is a way to let the browser know which style sheet language is being used (see Chapter 1 for a discussion on HTML attributes). The **TYPE** attribute must be included.

To make the examples easier to read, we chose not to wrap style sheets in HTML comments, but we do use the **TYPE** attribute throughout this book.

TREE STRUCTURES AND INHERITANCE

From Chapter 1, recall the discussion about HTML representing a document with a tree-like structure and how elements in HTML have children and parents. There are many reasons for having tree-structured documents. For style sheets, there is one excellent reason: inheritance. HTML elements inherit traits from their parents, just like children do. Instead of inheriting genes and money, HTML elements inherit stylistic properties.

Let's start by looking at the sample document:

```
<html>
  <title>Bach's home page</title>
  <body>
    <h1>Bach's home page</h1>
    <p>Johann Sebastian Bach was a
      <strong>prolific</strong> composer. Among his
        works are:
    <ul>
      <li>the Goldberg Variations
      <li>the Brandenburg Concertos
      <li>the Christmas Oratorio
    </ul>
  </body>
</html>
```

Figure 2.6 shows the tree structure of this document.

Figure 2.6 The tree structure of a simple document.

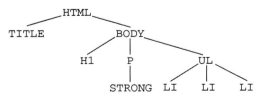

Through inheritance, CSS property values that are set on one element are transferred down the tree to its descendants. For example, until now, our examples have set the font style to italic for **H1** and **H2** elements. Now, say you want to set all the text in the document to be italic. You can do this by listing all the element types in the selector:

```
<style type="text/css">
  h1, h2, p, li { font-style: italic }
</style>
```

However, most HTML documents are more complex than our sample document, and your style sheet would soon become lengthy. There is a better and shorter way to do this. Instead of setting the style on each element type, set it on their common ancestor, the **BODY** element:

```
<style type="text/css">
  body { font-style: italic }
</STYLE>
```

Because other elements inherit properties from the **BODY** element, they all inherit the the font style (see Figure 2.7).

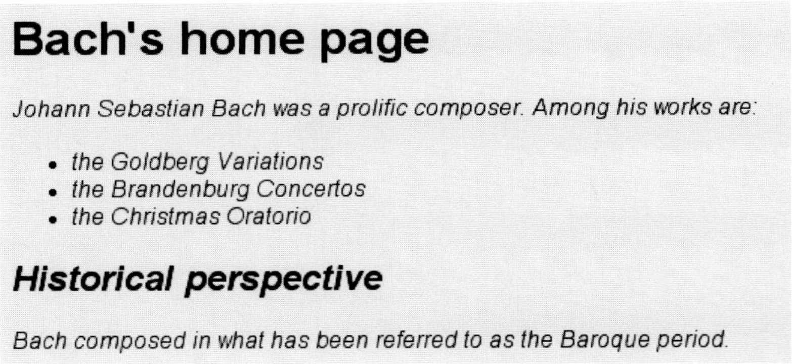

Figure 2.7 The result of inheritance.

Bach's home page

Johann Sebastian Bach was a prolific composer. Among his works are:

- *the Goldberg Variations*
- *the Brandenburg Concertos*
- *the Christmas Oratorio*

Historical perspective

Bach composed in what has been referred to as the Baroque period.

As previously mentioned, inheritance is a transport vehicle that distributes stylistic properties to an element's descendants. Because the **BODY** element is a common ancestor for all visible elements, **BODY** is a convenient selector when you want to set stylistic rules for an entire document.

OVERRIDING INHERITANCE

In the previous example, all elements were given the same font style through inheritance. Sometimes, however, children don't look like their parents. Not surprisingly, CSS also accounts for this. Say you want **H1** elements to be in italic and the rest of the text to be normal. This is easily expressed in CSS:

```
<style TYPE="text/css">
  body { font-style: italic }
  h1 { font-style-normal }
</style>
```

Because **H1** is a child element of **BODY** (and therefore inherits from **BODY**), the two rules in the previous style sheet conflict with each other. The first one sets the font style of the **BODY** element — and thereby also the font style of **H1** through inheritance — while the second one sets the font style specifically on the **H1** element. Which rule will win? Let's find out by reviewing Figure 2.8.

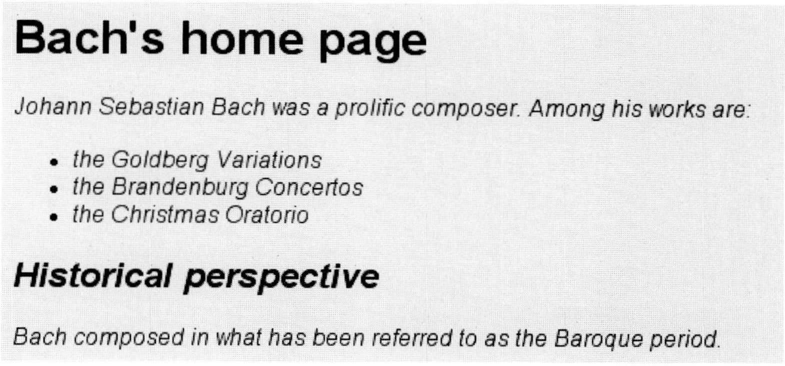

Figure 2.8 The headline is normal while the other text is slanted.

Bach's home page

Johann Sebastian Bach was a prolific composer. Among his works are:

- *the Goldberg Variations*
- *the Brandenburg Concertos*
- *the Christmas Oratorio*

Historical perspective

Bach composed in what has been referred to as the Baroque period.

The reason why the second rule wins is that it is more *specific* than the first. The first rule is extremely general — it affects all elements on the canvas. The second rule affects only **H1** elements in the document and is, therefore, more specific.

If CSS had been a programming language, the order in which the rules were specified would determine which one of them would win. CSS is not a programming language, and in the previous example, the order is irrelevant. The result is exactly the same if we use this style sheet:

```
<style type="text/css">
  h1 { font-style: normal }
  body { font-style: italic }
</style>
```

CSS has been designed to resolve conflicts between style sheet rules such as this one. Specificity is one aspect of that. You can find the details in Chapter 13, "Cascading and inheritance."

PROPERTIES THAT DON'T INHERIT

As a general rule, properties in CSS inherit from parent to child elements as described in the previous examples. Some properties, however, don't inherit and there is always a good reason why. We use the **background** property (which is described in Chapter 10, "Colors") as an example of a property that doesn't inherit.

Say you want to set a background image for a page. This is a common effect on the Web. In CSS, you can write the following:

```
<html>
  <title>Bach's home page</title>
  <style TYPE="text/css">
    body {
      background: url(texture.gif) white;
      color: black;
    }
  </style>
  <body>
    <h1>Bach's <em>home</em> page</h1>
    <p>Johann Sebastian Bach was a prolific
      composer.
  </body>
</html>
```

The **background** property has a URL (`texture.gif`) that points to a background image as value. When the image loads, the canvas looks like Figure 2.9.

Figure 2.9 Sample document with a background image.

Bach's *home* page

Johann Sebastian Bach was a prolific composer.

Figure 2.9 contains some noteworthy items:

- The background image covers the surface like a wallpaper. Also, the backgrounds of the **H1** and **P** elements have been covered. This is not because of inheritance, but because of the fact that unless otherwise set, all backgrounds are transparent. So, because we haven't set the backgrounds of the **HI** or **P** elements to something else, the parent element, **BODY**, shines through.

- In addition to the URL of the image, a color (white) has also been specified as the background. In case the image can't be found, you see the color instead.

- The color of the **BODY** element has been set to black. To ensure contrast between the text and the background, it is a good habit to always set a color when the **background** property is set.

So, exactly why doesn't the **background** property inherit? Visually, the effect of transparency is similar to inheritance: It looks like all elements have the same backgrounds. There are two reasons: First, transparent backgrounds are faster to display (there is nothing to display!) than other backgrounds. Second, because background images are aligned relative to the element to which they belong, you would otherwise not always end up with a smooth background surface.

COMMON TASKS WITH CSS

Setting colors and backgrounds (as previously described) are among the most common tasks performed by CSS. Other common tasks include setting fonts and white space around elements. This section guides you through the most commonly used properties in CSS.

Common tasks: fonts

Let's start with fonts. If you have used desktop-publishing applications in the past, you should be able to read this little style sheet:

```
h1 { font: 36pt serif }
```

This rule sets the font for **HI** elements. The first part of the value, 36pt, sets the font size to 36 points. A *point* is an old typographic unit of measure that survived into the digital age. In the next chapter, we tell you why you should use the "em" unit instead of "pt," but for now, we stick to points. The second part of the value, serif, tells the browser to use a font with serifs, which are hooks at the ends of the strokes; Chapter 5 tells you all about them. The more decorated serif fonts suit

Bach's home page well because the modern sans-serif fonts (fonts without serifs) weren't used in his time. Figure 2.10 shows the result.

Bach's home page

Johann Sebastian Bach was a prolific composer. Among his works are:

- the Goldberg Variations
- the Brandenburg Concertos
- the Christmas Oratorio

The **font** property is a shorthand property that simultaneously sets several other properties. By using it, you can shorten your style sheets and set values on all the properties it replaces. If you choose to use the expanded version, you would have to set all these to replace the previous example:

```
H1 {
    font-size: 36pt;
    font-family: serif;
    font-style: normal;
    font-weight: normal;
    font-variant: normal;
    line-height: normal;
}
```

Sometimes, you only want to set some of these. For example, you may want to emphasize the list items by setting the font weight to bold and the font style to italic. You can emphasize all list items by setting the declarations on the their ancestor element:

```
ul {
    font-style: italic;
    font-weight: bold;
}
```

Figure 2.11 shows the result of this code.

Figure 2.11 The sample document with bold slanted list items.

Bach's home page

Johann Sebastian Bach was a prolific composer. Among his works are:

- *the Goldberg Variations*
- *the Brandenburg Concertos*
- *the Christmas Oratorio*

The last properties, **font-variant** and **line-height**, haven't been widely supported in browsers up to now; therefore, they are not as commonly used yet.

Common tasks: margins

Setting space around elements is a basic tool in typography. The headline above this paragraph has space above it and (slightly less) space below it. This paragraph, as printed in this book, has space on the left and (slightly less) on the right. CSS can be used to express how much space should exist around different kinds of elements.

By default, your browser knows quite a bit about how to display the different kinds of elements in HTML. For example, it knows that lists and **BLOCKQUOTE** elements should be indented to set them apart from the rest of the text. As a designer, you can build on these settings while, at the same time, provide your own refinements. Let's use the **BLOCKQUOTE** element as an example. Here's a simple test document:

```
<HTML>
  <TITLE>Fredrick the Great meets Bach</TITLE>
  <BODY>
    <P>One evening, just as Fredrick the Great was
       getting his flute ready, and his musicians
       were assembled, an officer brought him a
       list of the strangers who had arrived. With
       his flute in his hand he ran over the list,
       but immediately turned to the assembled
       musicians, and said, with a kind of
       agitation:
    <BLOCKQUOTE>"Gentlemen, old Bach is come."
    </BLOCKQUOTE>
    <P>The flute was now laid aside, and old Bach, who
```

```
                    had alighted at his son's lodgings, was immediately
                    summoned to the Palace.
                </BODY>
            </HTML>
```

Figure 2.12 shows how a typical HTML browser would display the document.

One evening, just as Fredrick the Great was getting his flute ready, and his musicians were assembled, an officer brought him a list of the strangers who had arrived. With his flute in his hand he ran over the list, but immediately turned to the assembled musicians, and said, with a kind of agitation:

"Gentlemen, old Bach is come."

The flute was now laid aside, and old Bach, who had alighted at his son's lodgings, was immediately summoned to the Palace.

As you can see, the browser added space on all sides of the quoted text. In CSS, this space is called *margins* and all elements have margins on all four sides. The properties are called **margin-top**, **margin-right**, **margin-bottom**, and **margin-left**. You can change how the **BLOCKQUOTE** element is displayed by writing a style sheet:

```
BLOCKQUOTE {
   margin-top: 1em;
   margin-right: 0em;
   margin-bottom: 1em;
   margin-left: 0em;
   font-style: italic;
}
```

The "em" unit is detailed in the next chapter, but we can already now reveal its secret: It scales relative to the font size. So, the previous example results in the vertical margins being as high as the font size (1em) of the **BLOCKQUOTE** and horizontal margins having zero width. To make sure the quoted text can still be distinguished, it has been given an italic slant. Figure 2.13 shows the result.

Just like **font** is a shorthand property to simultaneously set several font-related properties, **margin** is a shorthand property that sets all margin properties. The previous example can therefore be written as follows:

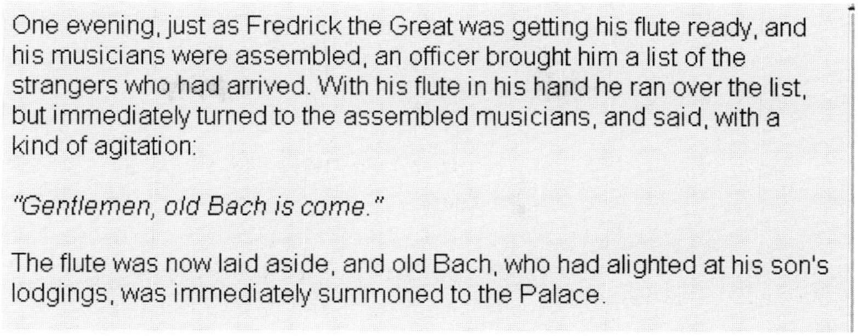

Figure 2.13 The sample document with a styled **BLOCKQUOTE** element.

One evening, just as Fredrick the Great was getting his flute ready, and his musicians were assembled, an officer brought him a list of the strangers who had arrived. With his flute in his hand he ran over the list, but immediately turned to the assembled musicians, and said, with a kind of agitation:

"Gentlemen, old Bach is come."

The flute was now laid aside, and old Bach, who had alighted at his son's lodgings, was immediately summoned to the Palace.

```
BLOCKQUOTE {
    margin: 1em 0em 1em 0em;
    font-style: italic;
}
```

The first part of the value, 1em, is assigned to **margin-top**. From there, it's clockwise: 0em is assigned to **margin-right**, 1em is assigned to **margin-bottom**, and 0em is assigned to **margin-left**.

With the left margin set to zero, the quoted text needs more styling to set it apart from the rest of the text. Setting **font-style** to italic helps and giving the element a darker background further amplifies the quote:

```
BLOCKQUOTE {
    margin: 1em 0em 1em 0em;
    font-style: italic;
    background: #DDD;
}
```

Figure 2.14 shows the result.

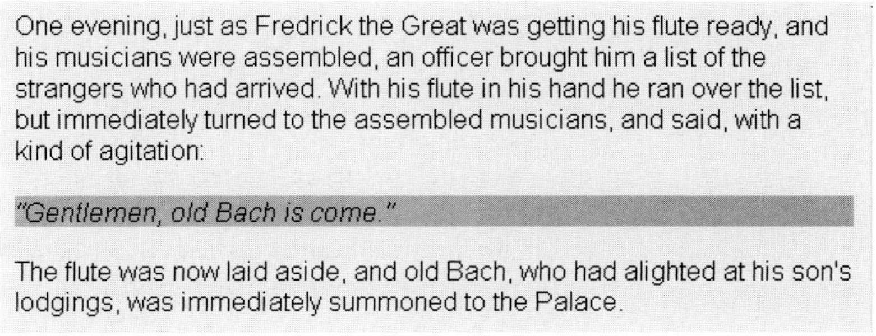

Figure 2.14 The **BLOCKQUOTE** element is styled with a background and margin.

One evening, just as Fredrick the Great was getting his flute ready, and his musicians were assembled, an officer brought him a list of the strangers who had arrived. With his flute in his hand he ran over the list, but immediately turned to the assembled musicians, and said, with a kind of agitation:

"Gentlemen, old Bach is come."

The flute was now laid aside, and old Bach, who had alighted at his son's lodgings, was immediately summoned to the Palace.

As expected, the background color behind the quote has changed. Unlike previous examples, the color was specified in red/green/blue (RGB) components. (RGB colors are described in detail in Chapter 10.)

One stylistic problem in this example is that the background color barely covers the quoted text. The space around the quote – the margin area – does not use the element's background color. CSS has another kind of space, called *padding*, which uses the background color of the element. In other respects, the padding properties are like the margin properties: They add space around an element. Let's add some padding to the quote:

```
BLOCKQUOTE {
    margin: 1em 0em 1em 0em;
    font-style: italic;
    background: #DDD;
    padding: 0.5em;
}
```

The result of setting the padding is added space between the text and the rectangle that surrounds it (see Figure 2.15).

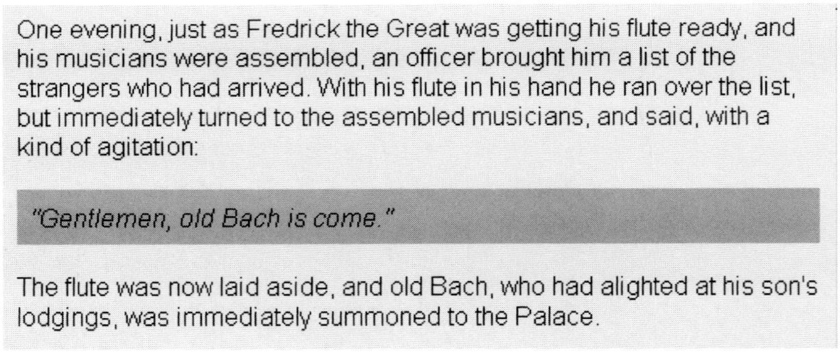

Figure 2.15 The result of adding a padding to the **BLOCK-QUOTE** element. Notice the extra space around the quoted text.

One evening, just as Fredrick the Great was getting his flute ready, and his musicians were assembled, an officer brought him a list of the strangers who had arrived. With his flute in his hand he ran over the list, but immediately turned to the assembled musicians, and said, with a kind of agitation:

"Gentlemen, old Bach is come."

The flute was now laid aside, and old Bach, who had alighted at his son's lodgings, was immediately summoned to the Palace.

Notice that the **padding** property was given only one value (0.5em). Just like the **margin** property, **padding** could have taken four values, which would have been assigned to the top, right, bottom, and left padding, respectively. However, when the same value is to be set on all sides, listing it once suffices. This is true both for **padding** and **margin** (and some other border properties, which are described in Chapter 8, "Space around boxes").

Common tasks: links

To make it easier for users to browse hypertext documents, the links should have a style that distinguishes them from normal text. HTML browsers often have underlined hyperlink text. Also, various color schemes have been used to indicate if the user has previously visited the link or not. Because hyperlinks are such a fundamental part of the Web, CSS has special support for styling them. Here's a simple example:

```
A:link { text-decoration: underline }
```

This example specifies that unvisited links should be underlined (see Figure 2.16).

Figure 2.16 Links in the document are underlined.

Bach's home page

Johann Sebastian Bach was a prolific composer. Among his works are:

- the Goldberg Variations
- the Brandenburg Concertos
- the Christmas Oratorio

The links are underlined, as we have specified, but they are also blue, which we have not specified. When authors do not specify all the possible styles, browsers use default styles to fill the gaps. The interaction between author styles, browser default styles, and user styles (the user's own preferences) is another example of CSS's conflict resolution rules. It is called the *cascade* (the "C" of CSS). We discuss the cascade in the next section.

The selector (a:link) deserves special mentioning. You probably recognize "a" as being an HTML element, but the last part is new. :link is one of several so-called pseudo-classes in CSS. Pseudo-classes give style to elements based on information outside of the document itself. For example, the author of a document cannot know whether a certain link will be visited or not. Pseudo-classes are described in detail in Chapter 4, and we give only a few more examples here:

```
A:visited { text-decoration: none }
```

This rule gives style to visited links, just like a:link gives style to unvisited links. Here is a slightly more complex example:

```
A:link, A:visited { text-decoration: none }
A:hover { background: black }
```

The last rule introduces a new pseudo-class (:hover). Assuming the user is moving a pointing device (such as a mouse), the specified style will be applied to the element when the user moves the pointer over (*hovers* over) the link. A common effect is to change the background color. Figure 2.17 shows what it looks like.

Figure 2.17 The effect of the :hover pseudo-class.

Bach's home page

Johann Sebastian Bach was a prolific composer. Among his works are:

- the Goldberg Variations
- the Brandenburg Concertos
- the Christmas Oratorio

The :hover pseudo-class has an interesting history. It was introduced in CSS2 after the hover effect became popular among JavaScript programmers. The JavaScript solution requires complicated code compared to the CSS pseudo-class, and this is an example of CSS picking up effects that have become popular among Web designers.

A WORD ABOUT CASCADING

A fundamental feature of CSS is that more than one style sheet can influence a document's presentation. This feature is known as *cascading* because the different style sheets are thought of as coming in a series. Cascading is a fundamental feature of CSS, because we realized that any single document could likely end up with style sheets from multiple sources: the browser, the designer, and possibly, the user.

In the last set of examples, you saw that the text color of the links turned blue without the style sheet specifying it. Also, the browser knew how to format **BLOCKQUOTE** and **H1** elements without being told so explicitly. Everything that the browser knows about formatting is stored in the browser's *default style sheet* and is merged with author and user style sheets when the document is displayed.

For years, we have known that designers want to develop their own style sheets. However, we discovered that users also want the option of influencing the presentation of their documents. With CSS, they can do this by supplying a personal style sheet that merges with the browser's and the designer's style sheets. Any conflicts between the various style sheets are resolved by the browser. Usually, the designer's style sheet has the strongest claim on the document, followed by the user's, and then the browser's default. However, the user can say that a rule is extremely important, and it then overrides any author or browser styles.

We detail cascading in Chapter 13. Before that, there is much to learn about fonts, space, and colors.

Chapter 3

The amazing em unit and other best practices

This chapter is about writing style sheets with style. By showing you case studies and how they are constructed, we give you a sense of how CSS can encode the visual presentation you want to achieve. More importantly, if you follow the guidelines in this chapter, your documents will behave well on a wide range of Web devices. For example, they will scale gracefully from one screen size to another.

The foremost tool for writing scalable style sheets is the *em* unit, and it therefore goes on top of the list of guidelines that we compile throughout this chapter: *Use ems to make scalable style sheets*. Named after the letter "M," the em unit has a long-standing tradition in typography where it has been used to measure horizontal widths. For example, the long dash (—) often found in American texts is known as an "em dash" because historically, it has had the same width as the letter "M." Its narrower cousin (–), often found in European texts, is similarly referred to as "en dash."

The meaning of "em" has changed over the years. Not all fonts have the letter "M" in them (for example, Chinese), but all fonts have a height. The term has therefore come to mean the height of the font – not the width of the letter "M."

In CSS, the em unit is a general unit for measuring lengths (for example, page margins and padding around elements). You can use it both horizontally and vertically, and this shocks traditional typographers who have always used the em exclusively for horizontal measurements. By extending the em unit to also work vertically, it has become a very powerful unit – so powerful that you seldom have to use other units of length.

Use ems to make scalable style sheets!

Chapter 3: The amazing em unit and other best practices

Let's look at a simple example where we use the em unit to set font sizes:

```
<HTML>
  <STYLE>
    H1 { font-size: 2em }
  </STYLE>
  <BODY>
    <H1>Movies</H1>
  </BODY>
</HTML>
```

When used to specify font sizes, the em unit refers to the font size of the parent element. So, in the previous example, the font size of the **H1** element is set to be twice the font size of the **BODY** element. To find what the font size of the **H1** element will be, we need to know the font size of **BODY**. Because this isn't specified in the the style sheet, the browser must find it from somewhere else – a good place to look is in the user's preferences. So, if the user sets the normal font size to 10 points, the size of the **H1** element is 20 points. This makes document headlines stand out relative to the surrounding text. Therefore: *Always use ems to set font sizes!*

Always use ems to set font sizes!

Designers who come from a desktop-publishing background may be inclined to skip the indirection that em introduces and specify directly that the font size should be 20 points. This is possible in CSS (see the description of the **font-size** property in Chapter 5, "Fonts") but using em is a better solution. Say, for example, that a sight-impaired user sets his normal font size to 20pt (20 points). If the font size of **H1** is 2em, as we recommend, **H1** elements will scale accordingly and be displayed in 40 points. If, however, the style sheet sets the font size to be 20pt, there will be no scaling of fonts and the size of headlines will have the same size as the surrounding text.

The usefulness of the em unit isn't limited to font sizes. Figure 3.1 shows a page design where all lengths – including the padding and margins around elements – are specified in ems.

Let's first consider the *padding*. In CSS, padding is space around an element that is added to set the element apart from the rest of the content. The color of the padding is always the same as the background color of the element it surrounds. In Figure 3.1, the menu on the right has been given a padding with this rule:

```
DIV.menu { padding: 1.5em }
```

Figure 3.1 All lengths on this page are specified using ems.

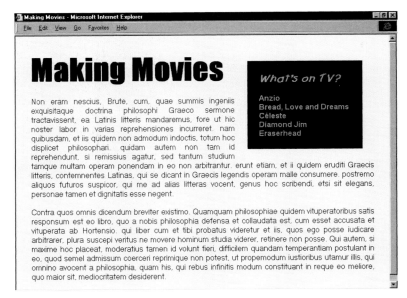

By specifying the padding width in ems, the width of the padding is relative to the font size of the **DIV** element. As a designer, you don't really care what the exact width of the padding is on the user's screen; what you care about is the proportions of the page you are composing. If the font size of an element increases, the padding around the element should also increase. This is shown in Figure 3.2 where the font size of the menu has increased while the proportions remain constant.

Outside the menu's padding is the margin area. The *margin area* ensures that there is enough space around an element so that the page doesn't appear cramped. This rule sets the margin around the menu:

```
DIV.menu { margin: 1.5em }
```

Figure 3.2 identifies the margin area. Again, the use of ems ensures scalable designs.

Another use of ems can be found in this book where the indent of the first line of most paragraphs is set to 1.8 em. The same value is used for the left margin of code examples, such as this:

```
P { text-indent: 1.8em }
PRE { margin-left: 1.8em }
```

So, if ems are so great, why does CSS have other units as well? There are cases when it makes sense to use other units. For example, here is a

Figure 3.2 Because margins and padding are specified in ems, they scale relative to the font size.

case where percentages may work just as well, if not better: setting the margins of the **BODY** element. Remember that everything that is displayed in an HTML page is inside **BODY**, so setting the margins of that element sets the overall shape of the page. You could give the page nice wide margins on both sides with these two rules:

```
BODY {
    margin-left: 15%;
    margin-right: 10%
}
```

This makes the text 75% of the total width, and the left margin a bit wider than the right one. Try it! Your page immediately looks more professional. Percentage values set on the **BODY** element are typically calculated with respect to the browser window. So, in the previous example, the text will cover 75% of the browser window.

Both ems and percentages are *relative units,* which means that they are computed with respect to something. We can distill a general rule from this: *Use relative units for lengths.* But, how about the *absolute units* in CSS – inches, centimeters, points, and picas – why are they in there at all if you never recommend to use them?

Use relative units for lengths!

Cases may arise when you'll need to use absolute units. Say, for example, that you are creating your wedding invitations using XML and CSS. You have carefully crafted tags such as <BESTMAN> and <RSVP/>, and you plan to distribute the invitations through the Web. However, some parts of your families are not yet connected and require printed

Only use absolute length units when the physical characteristics of the output medium are known!

invitations — on handmade paper, of course, and with proper margins. And 12 point fonts, exactly. This is the time to pull out the ~~obsolete~~ absolute length units: *Only use absolute length units when the physical characteristics of the output medium are known.* In practice, this happens only when you hand-tailor a style sheet for a specific printer paper size. In all other cases, you are better off using relative length units.

A common presentation on the Web is to move elements to the sides of the page. Typically, this is achieved by using a table for layout purposes. Although you can use CSS to describe table layout (see Appendix A, "HTML 4.0 quick reference"), there is a simpler way to "put stuff on the side." In HTML, images can float; i.e., they move over to the side while allowing text to "wrap around" them. In CSS, all elements — not just images — can float. The menu in Figures 3.1 and 3.2 is an example of a floating element that has been set to float to the right side of the page. To achieve this effect, you must complete two steps. First, the element must be declared to be floating using the **float** property. Second, the element must be given an appropriate width (in ems, of course). This is done through the **width** property. Here are the two rules needed:

```
DIV.menu {
   float: right;
   width: 15em;
}
```

Use floating elements instead of tables!

By using floating text elements instead of tables, your markup can remain simple while achieving many of the visual effects that are often accomplished with tables in HTML. Thus, we have another guideline: *Use floating elements instead of tables.* Simpler markup isn't the only reason why floating elements are good replacements for tables. Flexible layout schemes are another. By changing a few lines in the style sheet which generated the page shown in Figure 3.1, we can, for example, move the menu to the left side (see Figure 3.3). Also, many text-only browsers have problems displaying tables because content within the table doesn't come in its logical order.

Put content in its logical order!

This brings us to the next guideline: *Put content in its logical order.* Although CSS allows you to move text around on the screen by means of floats and other ways of positioning, do not rely on that. By putting content in its logical order, you ensure that your document makes sense in browsers that don't support CSS. That includes browsers that work in text mode, such as Lynx, older browsers that date from before

Figure 3.3 By changing a few lines in the style sheets, you can achieve a different design.

CSS, browsers whose users have turned off style sheets, or browsers that don't work visually at all, such as voice browsers and Braille browsers. Voice browsers may actually support CSS because CSS can also describe the style of spoken pages, but aural CSS (not described in this book) doesn't allow text to be spoken out of order.

Even a browser that supports CSS may sometimes fail to load the style sheet because of a network error. Therefore, you should always *make sure your documents are legible without style sheets.* Documents must be legible to humans, but also to Web robots and other software that try to index, summarize, or translate your documents. Also, think of the future: Five years from now, the style sheet may be lost; in 50 years, there may not be a browser that knows CSS; and in 500 years...

> Make sure your documents are legible without style sheets!

A good way to make sure your documents are really legible is to *test your documents on several browsers.* Alas, not all browsers that claim to support CSS do so according to W3C's specification. How much effort you should put into testing your style sheets depends on the target audience of your documents. If you publish on a closed intranet where everyone uses the same browser, your testing job will be easy. If, on the other hand, your documents are openly available on the Web, testing can be a time-consuming task. One way to avoid doing all the testing yourself is to use one of the W3C Core Styles, which are freely available on the Web (see Chapter 14, "External style sheets").

> Test your documents on several browsers!

Realize that your document will end up on systems that have different fonts. CSS specifies five so-called *generic fonts* that are guaranteed to exist in all browsers: `serif`, `sans-serif`, `monospace`, `cursive`, and `fantasy`. When specifying a font family in CSS, you have the option of supplying a list to increase the chance of finding a specified font at the user's system. The last font family in the list should always be a generic font. So *always specify a fallback generic font.* This book, for example, has been set in Gill Sans. But, not everybody has a copy of that font, so we actually specified the font as

Always specify a fallback generic font!

```
BODY { font-family: Gill Sans, sans-serif }
```

This code says that the font for the document's body is Gill Sans when available, or any other sans serif font when not. Depending on your browser and your machine's configuration, you may get Helvetica, Arial, or something similar. You can learn more about setting fonts in Chapter 5.

Know when to stop!

A word of warning at the end: *Know when to stop.* Be critical when designing your style sheet. Just because you can use 10 different fonts and 30 different colors on the same page doesn't mean you have to – or should. Simple style sheets often convey your message better than overloaded ones. That single word of red in a page of black gets more attention than any of the words on a page with a dozen different fonts and colors. If you think a piece of your text deserves more attention, give it larger margins, maybe even on all four sides. A little extra space can do wonders.

Chapter 4

CSS selectors

In the preceding chapters, we used a number of selectors, most of which select elements by their type (for example, **H1** or **P**). This chapter describes all the possible ways in which elements can be selected, from simple ones, such as the type selectors, to advanced, such as selectors that look for elements with a combination of characteristics.

We start with the simple selectors, and most common ones, and show how they can be combined into powerful – but still simple – selectors. The second half of this chapter discusses advanced selectors.

SELECTOR SCHEMES

To give you enough freedom to select which elements a style is applied to, CSS2.1 supports four selector schemes. Each is based on some aspect of an element:

- An element's type
- An element's attributes
- The context in which the element is used
- External information about the element

Also, CSS2.1 includes a way of attaching style rules to an element without using a traditional selector; the **STYLE** attribute effectively bypasses the entire selector mechanism.

The four schemes can be combined in a single selector to put style properties on elements that exhibit a combination of characteristics.

For example, the selector H1 EM uses element types (**HI** and **EM**) and context (**EM** must be inside **HI**).

TYPE SELECTORS

The simplest kind of selector in CSS is the name of an element type. Using this kind of selector, which is called a *type selector,* you apply the declaration to every instance of the element type. For example, the selector of the following simple rule is H1, so the rule affects all **HI** elements in a document:

```
H1 { color: red }
```

We used type selectors in Chapter 2, "CSS."

If you find yourself writing several style rules that are the same except for the selector, for example:

```
H1 { color: red }
H2 { color: red }
H3 { color: red }
```

you can write this more briefly by *grouping* the selectors in a comma-separated list:

```
H1, H2, H3 { color: red }
```

It is a matter of taste whether you want to use this grouping mechanism or not.

When selecting **HTML** elements, type selectors are case-insensitive. Therefore, the following four rules are equivalent:

```
BLOCKQUOTE { margin-left: 2em }
BlockQuote { margin-left: 2em }
blockquote { margin-left: 2em }
BLockQUoTE { margin-left: 2em }
```

(For now, don't worry about the margin declarations; margins are explained in Chapter 8, "Space around boxes.")

SIMPLE ATTRIBUTE SELECTORS

One of the most powerful ways on which to base selection is on an attribute. Recall from Chapter 1, "The Web and HTML," that an attribute is a characteristic quality, other than the type or content of an element. In that chapter, we discussed the attributes **HREF**, **SRC**, and **ALT**. In this section, we discuss two other attributes: **CLASS** and **ID**.

Both these attributes can be used with any HTML element, and we will see how they can create powerful selectors. They are not the only attributes that can occur in a selector, but they are very common, and CSS makes using **CLASS** and **ID** especially easy. How to refer to other attributes is explained in the section, "Advanced attribute selectors."

The CLASS attribute

The **CLASS** attribute enables you to apply declarations to a group of elements that have the same value on the **CLASS** attribute. All elements inside **BODY** can have a **CLASS** attribute. Essentially, you *classify* elements with the **CLASS** attribute, create rules in your style sheet that refer to the value of the **CLASS** attribute, and then the browser automatically applies those rules to the group of elements.

For example, say that you are an actor rehearsing for the role of Polonius in Shakespeare's *Hamlet*. In your copy of the manuscript, you want all the lines by Polonius to stand out. The first step to achieve this is to classify Polonius' lines; that is, set the **CLASS** attribute on all elements that contain lines by Polonius. Figure 4.1 shows how you set the **CLASS** value.

Figure 4.1 Setting a **CLASS** attribute on an HTML element.

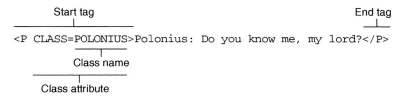

In Figure 4.1, the class name chosen is POLONIUS. Authors pick class names.

Class names must be single words, although you can use digits and dashes. The following are all acceptable class names:

- `POLONIUS`
- `name-10`
- `first-remark`

But the following are not:

- The `man` (contains a space)
- `item+12` (contains a plus sign)
- `last!!` (contains exclamation marks)

In contrast to element names, class names are case-sensitive, which means you must spell class names in the style sheet with exactly the same uppercase and lowercase letters as in the HTML source file.

The next step is to write style rules with selectors that refer to the class name. A selector that includes a class name is called a *class selector*. Figure 4.2 shows a rule with a selector that selects all of Polonius' elements.

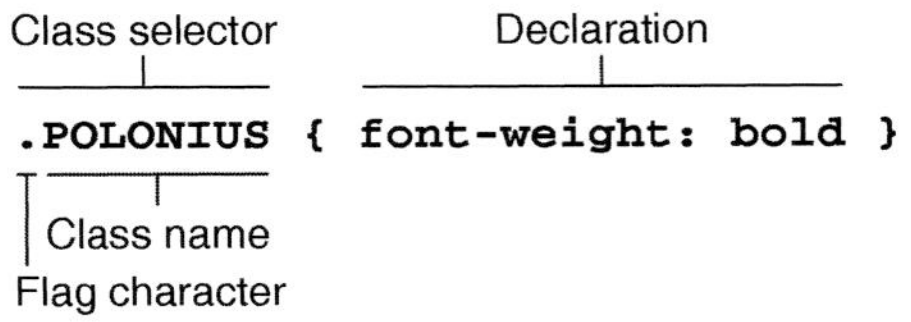

Figure 4.2 Anatomy of a rule with a class selector.

Class selector   Declaration

`.POLONIUS { font-weight: bold }`

Class name

Flag character

The class selector starts with a *flag character* (the period), which signals what type of selector follows. For class selectors, the period was chosen because it is associated with the term "class" in many programming languages. Translated into English, the flag character reads "elements with class name." The whole selector says, "elements with class name POLONIUS." Authors are free to choose class names. Assuming that you have consistently classified elements containing lines by Polonius, they will be printed in a bold font.

Let's look at a complete example that introduces a second class:

```
<HTML>
  <TITLE>Hamlet, excerpt from act II</TITLE>
  <STYLE TYPE="text/css">
    .POLONIUS { font-weight: bold }
    .HAMLET { font-weight: normal }
  </STYLE>
  <BODY>
    <P CLASS=POLONIUS>
      Polonius: Do you know me, my lord?
    <P CLASS=HAMLET>
```

```
    Hamlet: Excellent well,
    you are a fishmonger.
<P CLASS=POLONIUS>
    Polonius: Not I, my lord.
<P CLASS=HAMLET>
    Hamlet: Then I would you
    were so honest a man.
</BODY>
</HTML>
```

In this example, two classes have been defined, HAMLET and POLONIUS. The style sheet in the **STYLE** element sets the font weight (the "thickness" of the fonts; see Chapter 5) to be different. The result is shown in Figure 4.3.

Figure 4.3 The formatted fragment with Polonius' lines in bold.

Polonius: Do you know me, my lord?
Hamlet: Excellent well, you are a fishmonger.
Polonius: Not I, my lord.
Hamlet: Then I would you were so honest a man.

As you can see, Polonius' lines stand out. This is an invaluable tool when you rehearse a role.

One could argue that the same result could be achieved without style sheets. By enclosing Polonius' lines in **STRONG** or **B** elements, they would also come out bold. This is true, but consider the consequences when the actor who is scheduled to play Hamlet catches a cold and you have to replace him. Now, you suddenly need Hamlet's lines to stand out and Polonius' lines to use the normal font weight. If you had been using **STRONG** elements to emphasize Polonius' lines, you'd have to remove them and add them to Hamlet's lines instead. But, if you use CSS, you simply change two lines in the style sheet:

```
.POLONIUS { font-weight: normal }
.HAMLET { font-weight: bold }
```

This reverses the effect and Hamlet's lines stand out now, as shown in Figure 4.4.

Cascading Style Sheets

Figure 4.4 The same fragment from Shakespeare, but with the font weights reversed.

> Polonius: Do you know me, my lord?
> **Hamlet: Excellent well, you are a fishmonger.**
> Polonius: Not I, my lord.
> **Hamlet: Then I would you were so honest a man.**

The **CLASS** attribute is a powerful feature of CSS. We recommend that you use the **CLASS** attribute to add more information about elements — information that can enhance the presentation of your documents. We do not recommend that you use the **CLASS** attribute to completely change the presentation of an element. For example, you can easily change an **LI** element to look like an **HI** element by classifying it. If you want an element to look like **HI**, we recommend that you mark it up as **HI**. Do not let style sheets replace the structure of your documents; instead, let the style sheets enhance the structure.

The ID attribute

The **ID** attribute works like the **CLASS** attribute with one important difference: The value of an **ID** attribute must be unique throughout the document. That is, every element inside **BODY** can have an **ID** attribute, but the values must all be different. This makes the **ID** attribute useful for setting style rules on individual elements. A selector that includes an **ID** attribute is called an *ID selector*. The general form of an ID selector resembles that of the class selector in the previous section (see Figure 4.5).

Figure 4.5 Anatomy of a rule with an ID selector.

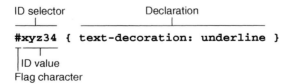

Notice that the flag character for ID selectors is a hash mark (#). The flag character alerts the browser that an **ID** value is coming up next. In English, the selector says "the element with an **ID** value equal to xyz34." The entire rule reads, "The element with an **ID** value equal to xyz43 is to be underlined." The author is free to pick the value of the **ID** attribute, and the chosen value is case-insensitive.

The HTML syntax of the element on which you want to use the **ID** attribute resembles that of other elements with attributes; for example:

```
<P ID=xyz34>Underlined text</P>
```

Combined with this style sheet rule, the content of the element will be underlined. Because the value of the **ID** attribute must be unique, you could not also include in the same document another usage of it, such as the following:

```
<H1 ID=xyz34>A headline</H1>
<P ID=xyz34>Underlined text</P>   <!-- WRONG! -->
```

Instead, you would have to give the two elements different **ID** values:

```
<H1 ID=xyz34>A headline</H1>
<P ID=xyz35>Underlined text</P>
```

Here is a complete example using an ID selector:

```
<HTML>
  <TITLE>ID showoff</TITLE>
  <STYLE TYPE="text/css">
    #xyz34 { text-decoration: underline }
  </STYLE>
  <BODY>
    <P ID=xyz34>Underlined text</P>
  </BODY>
</HTML>
```

By using the ID selectors, you can set style properties on a per-element basis. Like **CLASS**, **ID** is a powerful feature. It carries the same cautions we set out in the previous section.

THE STYLE ATTRIBUTE

The **STYLE** attribute is different from the other attributes described in this chapter. Whereas **CLASS** and **ID** attribute values can be used in selectors, the **STYLE** attribute is actually a replacement for the entire selector mechanism. Instead of having a value that can be referred to in a selector (which is what **ID** and **CLASS** have), the value of the **STYLE** attribute is actually one or more CSS declarations.

Normally, using CSS, a designer will put all style rules into a style sheet that goes into the **STYLE** element at the top of the document (or is linked externally as described in Chapter 14, "External style sheets"). However, using the **STYLE** attribute, you can bypass the style sheet and put declarations directly into the start tags of your document.

Figure 4.6 shows one example of this.

Figure 4.6 An HTML element with style rules embedded in the start tag.

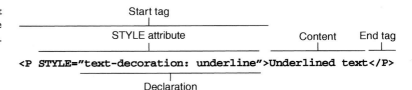

Figure 4.6 attaches a declaration to a single element and results in underlining the content of the element. Recall from the example in the previous section that the **ID** attribute accomplishes the same thing: setting style on a single element. But whereas the **ID** attribute involves an indirection, the **STYLE** attribute bypasses the style sheet and puts the declaration directly into the start tag of the element it applies to. Properties set using the **STYLE** attribute are treated exactly in the same manner as if the property had been set in a style sheet using an ID selector.

You could conceivably use the **STYLE** attribute to apply styles to just about anything and everything. For example, you could use the **STYLE** attribute this way (shown in bold):

```
<HTML>
  <TITLE>Hamlet, excerpt from act II</TITLE>
  <BODY STYLE="color: black; background: white">
    <P STYLE="font-weight: bold">
      Polonius: Do you know me, my lord?
    <P STYLE="font-weight: normal">
      Hamlet: Excellent well,
      you are a fishmonger.
    <P STYLE="font-weight: bold">
      Polonius: Not I, my lord.
    <P STYLE="font-weight: normal">
      Hamlet: Then I would you
      were so honest a man.
  </BODY>
</HTML>
```

This use of the **STYLE** attribute is legal, but there are two reasons why you should not, in general, use the **STYLE** attribute. First, it's the long way to set styles. Because the declarations in the **STYLE** attribute apply only to the element where they are specified, there is no way to reuse your declarations, so your documents become longer. Also, if you later want to change the presentation of your document, you have to make changes in more places. Second, by interleaving style and content, you miss out on an important advantage of style sheets: the separation of content and presentation. By putting all of your style settings into a style sheet, you can make your style sheets apply to more than one document (see Chapter 14 for how the **LINK** element can be used for this).

The rather messy use of the **STYLE** attribute can be rewritten into the following:

```
<HTML>
  <TITLE>Hamlet, excerpt from act II</TITLE>
  <STYLE TYPE="text/css"gt;
    BODY { color: black; background: white }
    .POLONIUS { font-weight: bold }
    .HAMLET { font-weight: normal }
  </STYLE>
  <BODY>
    <P CLASS=POLONIUS>
      Polonius: Do you know me, my lord?
    <P CLASS=HAMLET>
      Hamlet: Excellent well,
      you are a fishmonger.
    <P CLASS=POLONIUS>
      Polonius: Not I, my lord.
    <P CLASS=HAMLET>
      Hamlet: Then I would you
      were so honest a man.
  </BODY>
</HTML>
```

So, use the **STYLE** *element* to apply styles to all of a type of element. Save the **STYLE** *attribute* for occasional stylistic changes you want to make to an element.

COMBINING SELECTOR TYPES

So far, three kinds of selectors have been described in this chapter: Type selectors, ID selectors, and class selectors. Often, different selector types are combined to form more complex selectors. By combining selectors, you can more accurately target elements that you want to give a certain presentation. For example, by combining a type selector and a class selector, an element must fulfill both requirements: It must be of the right type *and* the right class in order to be influenced by the style rule. Figure 4.7 shows one example.

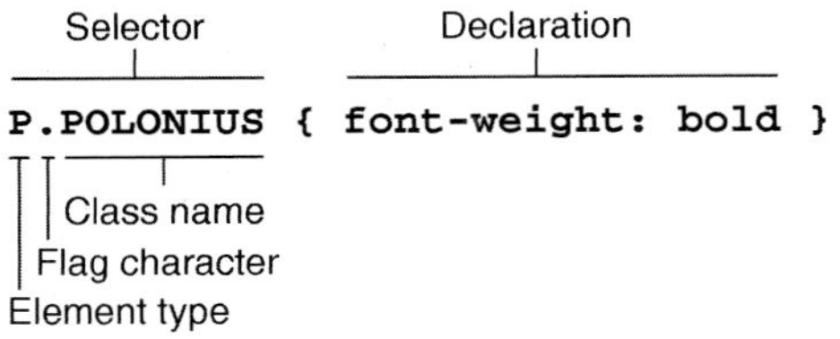

Figure 4.7 A combined type and class selector.

```
Selector              Declaration
  |                        |
P.POLONIUS { font-weight: bold }
| |       |
| | Class name
| Flag character
Element type
```

In English, this selector reads, "**P** elements with class name POLONIUS." That is, an element must be of the right type (**P**), and it must also be of the right class (POLONIUS). Compare the previous example with this selector:

```
.POLONIUS { font-weight: bold }
```

The latter example omits the element type and starts off with the flag character. By doing so, it selects all elements with the right class, no matter what type the element is.

We see more examples of how to combine different kinds of selectors later in this chapter.

SIMPLE CONTEXTUAL SELECTORS

A *contextual selector* is a selector that takes into account the context in which the style is to be applied. That is, the specified style is applied to an element only if the element is in the specified context. An element's context is formed by its ancestor elements and the elements that precede it. In this section, we look only at the ancestors. The section, "Advanced contextual selectors," describes how other contexts can be added to a selector.

Suppose you were to write these two rules:

```
H1 { color: red }
EM { color: red }
```

These rules will work fine. **H1** headings will turn red, and so will **EM** elements. Now, suppose you have this code in your document:

```
<H1>This headline is <EM>very</EM> important.</H1>
```

You want to emphasize "very" but because both the **EM** and the **H1** are set to red, you will lose the emphasis provided by **EM**. You want both **EM** and **H1** to stay red for the document as a whole, but for **EM** elements inside **H1**, you need to come up with some other way to emphasize "very." You still want to use the **EM** element. How do you do it?

Using a contextual selector, you can specify a rule that applies only to **EMS** that are inside **H1** elements. No other **EM** elements are affected. Consider this rule:

```
H1 EM { color: blue }
```

In English, this rule says: "For any **EM** that is inside **H1**, make it blue (and not red like the previous rule specified)." Thus, the **EM** will be made blue only in the context of an **H1**. In all other contexts, it will be red as usual. Hence, the name contextual selector.

Contextual selectors are made up of two or more simple selectors separated by white space. Any type, class, or ID selector is a simple selector. Also, combinations of type and class selectors, as described in the previous section, are regarded as simple selectors.

EXTERNAL INFORMATION: PSEUDO-CLASSES AND PSEUDO-ELEMENTS

In CSS1, style is normally based on the tags and attributes found in the HTML source. This works fine for many design scenarios, but it doesn't cover some common design effects designers want to achieve.

Pseudo-classes and pseudo-elements were devised to fill in some of these gaps. Both are mechanisms that extend the expressive power of CSS. In CSS1, using pseudo-classes, you can change the style of a document's links based on whether and when the links have been visited, or based on how the user interacts with the document. Using pseudo-elements, you can change the style of the first letter and first line of an element, or add elements that were not present in the source document. Neither pseudo-classes nor pseudo-elements exist in HTML; that is, they are not visible in the HTML code. Both mechanisms have been designed so that they can be further extended in future versions of CSS; i.e., fill in more gaps.

This section describes the pseudo-classes to format hyperlinks and the pseudo-elements to set properties on the first letter and first line of a paragraph. Other pseudo-classes and pseudo-elements are introduced in the sections, "Advanced pseudo-classes," and "Advanced pseudo-elements."

The anchor pseudo-classes

In HTML, there is only one element that can be a hyperlink: the **A** (anchor) element. In document formats written in XML, there can be others. An *anchor pseudo-class* is a mechanism by which a browser indicates to a user the status of a hyperlink in the document the user is viewing.

A browser typically displays a link in a document in a different color from the rest of the text. Links that a user hasn't visited will be one color. Links the user has visited will be another color.

There is no way for an author to know whether a user has visited a link; this information is known only to the browser. However, you can set in the style sheet the colors that indicate the status of links. This is done by including an anchor pseudo-class in the selector (see Figure 4.8).

Figure 4.8 Anatomy of a rule with an anchor pseudo-class.

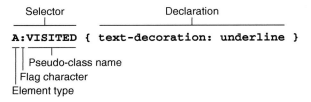

There are several things to note in Figure 4.8:

- The selector is a combination of a type selector and a pseudo-class selector. Because only **A** elements can have anchor pseudo-classes in HTML, the **A** could have been omitted, but the selector arguably looks nicer.
- The flag character is a colon (:). Both pseudo-classes and pseudo-elements use the colon as the flag character.

All links in a document (that is, all **A** elements with an **HREF** attribute) are automatically classified as either visited (`:visited`) or unvisited (`:link`).

Initially, a link is in pseudo-class "link." If the link has been visited recently, the browser puts it into pseudo-class "visited." (How recent the visit has to be is up to the browser.) The names of pseudo-classes and pseudo-elements are case-insensitive.

Here are some examples:

```
A:link { color: red }       /* unvisited link */
A:visited { color: blue }   /* visited link */
```

The first-letter and first-line pseudo-elements

Pseudo-elements allow you to set styles on a subpart of an element's content. Like pseudo-classes, pseudo-elements don't exist in the HTML code. Pseudo-elements have been introduced to allow for designs that would otherwise not have been possible.

Two of these pseudo-elements are "first-letter" and "first-line." The effects of these elements are not related to the structure of the HTML document. Rather, the effects are based on how the element is formatted. They enable you to impose styles on the first letter of a word and on the first line of a paragraph, respectively, independent of any other styles. Both can only be attached to block-level elements (that is, elements with their **display** property set to block; see Chapter 6, "The fundamental objects").

These effects are not new. Traditional printers have been using them for centuries, and you will often find them in contemporary magazines. A common usage is to increase the size of the first letter or make the first line use uppercase letters. However, you can also set the properties for color, background, text decorations, and case transformation, among others. See Figure 4.9 for an example.

According to the CSS1 specification, CSS1 browsers are not required to support pseudo-elements. CSS2.1 makes no such exception, but you may encounter browsers that do not support the first-letter and first-line pseudo-elements.

A pseudo-element has the general form shown in Figure 4.10.

L e 23 juin, le Palace a ér million de francs, à Pie propriétaires de nomb parisiennes. Or le premier ɑ ancien président de chambre Paris, «encore en fonctions le date de l'ouvertᵘʳⁿ de la ɦⁿᶜᵉ́

Figure 4.9 The beginning of an article showing a "drop-cap."

Figure 4.10 Anatomy of a rule with a type selector, a class selector, and a pseudo-element.

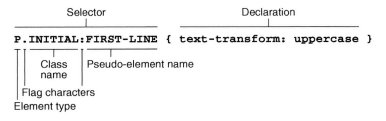

73

A pseudo-element selector is almost always used in combination with other selectors. This because you seldom want pseudo-element formatting on all elements in your document. Here, the pseudo-element selector is combined with two other selectors: a type selector (**P**) and a class selector (.initial). The resulting selector reads, "the first line of **P** elements with class name initial." This rule is the first step on the way to create a style sheet that replicates the style of magazine articles such as *TIME*. Let's put this rule into a complete document:

```
<HTML>
  <TITLE>The style of TIME magazine</TITLE>
  <STYLE TYPE="text/css">
    P.initial:first-line {
      text-transform: uppercase }
  </STYLE>
  <BODY>
    <H1>A sample article</H1>
    <P CLASS=initial>The first line
      of the first paragraph in a TIME
      magazine article is printed in
      uppercase letters.
    <P>The text in the second paragraph
      has no special formatting.
  </BODY>
</HTML>
```

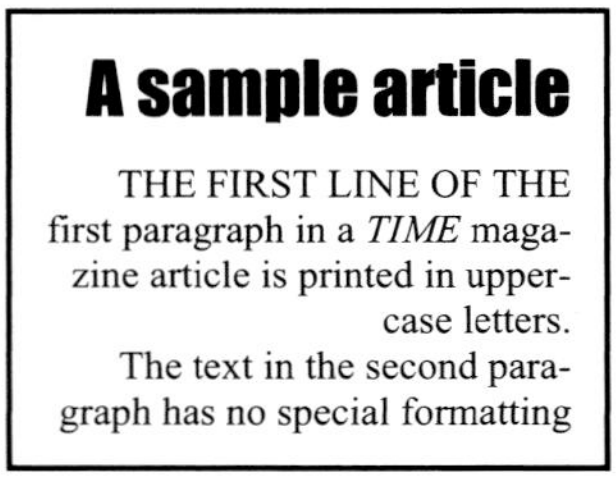

It doesn't make any difference how long the line is or how many words are on it. Whatever text happens to fall on the first line is displayed in uppercase. See Figure 4.11. Because browser windows can be resized, there is no way to know how many words will be on the first line of a paragraph, so using a pseudo-element is the only way to achieve this effect.

The style sheet for *TIME* magazine is still missing a key design feature: the drop-cap initial letter. A drop-cap initial is a common trick in typography: The first letter of a text is enlarged and "dropped" into the formatted paragraph. We can attach style rules to the first letter of an element by using, you guessed it, the "first-letter" pseudo-element:

```
P.initial:first-letter { font-size: 200% }
```

The selector in this example reads, "The first letter of **P** elements with class name initial." That is, the style rule applies to the first letter of lines that were affected in the previous example. The whole rule says, "The first letter of **P** elements with class name initial should have a

---

A sample article

THE FIRST LINE OF THE first paragraph in a *TIME* magazine article is printed in uppercase letters. The text in the second paragraph has no special formatting

Figure 4.11 Rendering of the first *TIME* example.

font size two times bigger than the surrounding text." Formatted, the text now looks like what's shown in Figure 4.12.

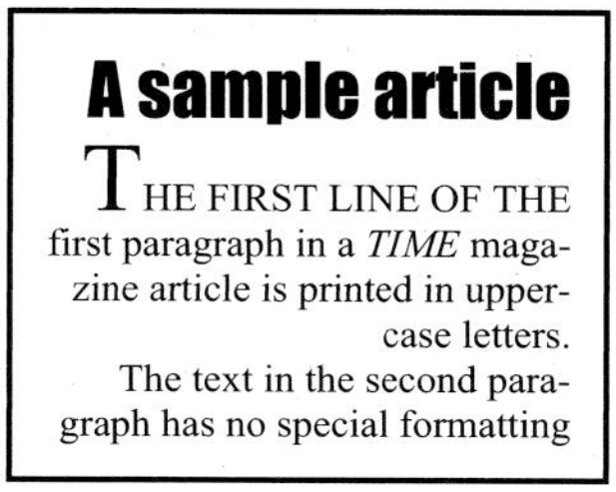

We're almost there! The first letter now has the right size, but not the right position; it's not "dropped" into the formatted paragraph. By making the first letter "float" (discussed in Chapter 8, "Space around boxes"), we achieve the drop-cap effect. The HTML example becomes

A sample article

T HE FIRST LINE OF THE first paragraph in a *TIME* magazine article is printed in upper-case letters. The text in the second paragraph has no special formatting

Figure 4.12 Rendering of the *TIME* example with a large initial.

```
<HTML>
  <TITLE>The style of TIME magazine</TITLE>
  <STYLE TYPE="text/css">
    P.initial:first-line {
      text-transform: uppercase }
    P.initial:first-letter {
      font-size: 200%; float: left }
  </STYLE>
  <BODY>
    <H1>A sample article</H1>
    <P CLASS=initial>The first line
      of the first paragraph in a TIME
      magazine article is printed in
      uppercase letters.
    <P>The text in the second paragraph
      has no special formatting.
  </BODY>
</HTML>
```

Our sample document is formatted as in Figure 4.13.

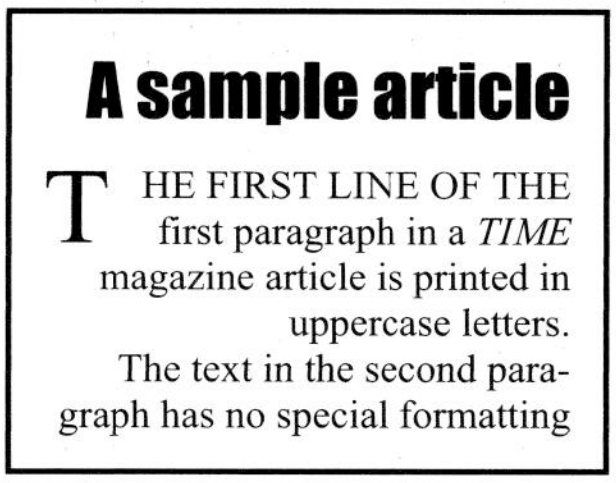

A sample article

T HE FIRST LINE OF THE first paragraph in a *TIME* magazine article is printed in uppercase letters. The text in the second para-graph has no special formatting

Figure 4.13 Rendering of the *TIME* example with a drop-cap ini-tial.

DIV AND SPAN

Before we discuss the advanced selectors, we must talk about two HTML elements. **DIV** (division) and **SPAN** (a span of words) have been added to HTML partly to support style sheets. We delayed describing them until now because they are mostly used in combination with the **CLASS** attribute.

The **CLASS** attribute is a powerful feature of CSS. Using it, you can, in effect, create new elements in HTML. Creating new elements through the **CLASS** attribute is much easier than convincing browser vendors and maintainers of the HTML specification that a new tag is needed and beneficial for everyone.

By using the **DIV** and **SPAN** elements, you can create your own ele-ments. The reason there are two elements for this is that **DIV** is a block-level element, while **SPAN** is inline. For example, if you are a poet, you have no way to mark your products as poems in HTML. For this, you would like to have a new **POEM** tag. It's unlikely that **POEM** will become an HTML element in the near future, but the **DIV** element, in combination with the **CLASS** attribute, offers you an alternative:

```
<DIV CLASS=POEM>
  Roses are red, <BR>
  violets are blue, <BR>
  if you're into poetry, <BR>
  DIV is for you!
</DIV>
```

In this way, you can preserve semantics (the fact that the previous text is a poem) through the use of the **DIV** element. In the style sheet, you can set a certain style for the "poem" element:

```
DIV.POEM { font-family: cursive }
```

Using the **SPAN** element, you can make new inline elements:

```
<DIV CLASS=POEM>
  <SPAN CLASS=FLOWER>Roses</SPAN> are red, <BR>
  <SPAN CLASS=FLOWER>violets</SPAN are blue, <BR>
  if you're into poetry, <BR>
  DIV is for you!
</DIV>
```

The new "flower" element can be addressed in the style sheet:

```
SPAN.FLOWER { font-family: fantasy }
```

The complete HTML example thus becomes as follows:

```
<HTML>
  <TITLE>A poem</TITLE>
  <STYLE TYPE="text/css">
    DIV.POEM { font-family: cursive }
    SPAN.FLOWER { font-family: fantasy }
  </STYLE>
  <BODY>
    <DIV CLASS=POEM>
      <SPAN CLASS=FLOWER>Roses</SPAN> are red, <BR>
      <SPAN CLASS=FLOWER>violets</SPAN are blue,<BR>
      if you're into poetry, <BR>
```

```
        DIV is for you!
    </DIV>
  </BODY>
</HTML>
```

This code can be displayed as shown in Figure 4.14.

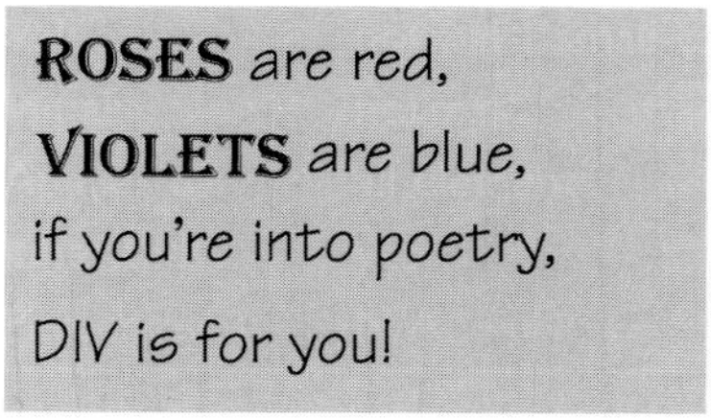

Figure 4.14 The effect of the "poem" and "flower" elements.

ROSES are red,

VIOLETS are blue,

if you're into poetry,

DIV is for you!

ADVANCED ATTRIBUTE SELECTORS

The **CLASS** and **ID** attributes are easy to use, but sometimes, it is impossible to add them to the document. For example, if you are writing a style sheet for a set of documents that you are not allowed to edit, you have to write selectors that make use of whatever attributes and context there are. If the documents use attributes consistently, it may be possible to select elements based on them.

CSS2.1 has three different advanced attribute selectors, plus two selectors that are designed for multilingual documents and that select elements based on the language of their contents.

Selecting on the presence of an attribute

A selector that matches elements based on whether they have a certain attribute is constructed by putting the attribute name in square brackets:

```
[COMPACT] { font-weight: bolder }
TABLE[BORDER] { border: thin solid }
```

The first rule matches all elements that have a **COMPACT** attribute; the second matches all **TABLE** elements that have a **BORDER** attribute. The actual value of the attributes is not important, as long as the attribute is present. Here is another example, combining type selectors, contextual selectors, and advanced attribute selectors:

```
TABLE[BORDER] TD { border: medium ridge }
```

Note that in HTML, the names of attributes, like the names of elements, are case-insensitive. You can write BORDER and border. But, in document formats that are written in XML, the names of attributes and the names of elements are case-sensitive. In style sheets for XML-based documents, BORDER and border are *not* the same.

Selecting on the value of an attribute

A selector that matches on the value of an attribute is written like this:

```
[ALIGN="left"] { text-align: left }
```

This matches all elements that have an **ALIGN** attribute with the value left.

In HTML, some attribute values are case-sensitive and others are not. Rather than list which is case-insensitive, we recommend that you try to write the attribute values in the selectors with the same case as they appear in the source document. This is especially important because in XML, *all* attribute values are case-sensitive.

However, the rule of thumb for HTML attributes is that attributes that accept a limited set of keywords, such as the **ALIGN** and **RULES** attributes, are case-insensitive, while attributes that accept many different values, such as **HREF** and **ALT**, are case sensitive. Thus, [ALIGN="left"] and [ALIGN="LEFT"] are the same, but [ALT="Diagram"] and [ALT="diagram"] are not. In case of doubt, consult an HTML book or the official HTML specification.

Selecting on a single word in the value of an attribute

Some attributes may accept space-separated lists of values. The **CLASS** attribute is an example, as is the **REL** attribute of **A** elements. Attributes, such as the **ALT** attribute, that typically have a short sentence as value, can also be regarded as a space-separated list of values.

A selector that matches single words from such attributes is written as follows:

```
[REL~="home"] { color: green }
```

This matches elements such as <A REL="home"> or <... REL="up home"...>. In fact, the class selector can be expressed this way. The following two rules are equivalent:

```
.note { text-decoration: underline }
[CLASS~="note"] { text-decoration: underline }
```

Although you can use this selector with attributes like **ALT**, which contain short phrases, you have to be careful. The selector [ALT~="Yes"] matches the element <IMG ALT="Yes and No"...>, but not the element <IMG ALT="Yes, and No"...> because of the comma that is attached to the word.

Selecting on the language of an element

Documents are usually written in some human language, at least the documents for which a style sheet makes any sense. Some documents are written in a combination of languages; for example, an English article with French citations, or a manual in four languages.

There are at least two reasons why a selector for language is necessary. The first is the case where you have a set of documents that must all have the same style sheet, but where some documents are in a different language. Although most of the style rules can be the same, certain styles must be different for each language; for example, the quotation marks (see Chapter 6). The second reason is the case of multilingual documents, which are documents that contain text in more than one language.

A browser can get language data from two places. One is from the headers that are sent along with the document (but outside the document) when a Web server transfers the document to the browser. The HTTP protocol for transferring information between servers and clients has a special field for the language of the document. This is the default language of the document. An English article with quotations in Russian would be labeled as English, not Russian.

The other place is in attributes on each element. All HTML elements may have a **LANG** attribute. In XML-based documents, the attribute is called **XML:LANG**, but otherwise, it is exactly the same.

The value of the **LANG** attribute and of the HTTP header has a certain structure: It contains a two-letter language code (see Table 4.1) and optionally further precisions as to what region of the world (another two-letter code), or which dialect. Here are some examples:

- en – English
- en-uk – British English
- en-us – American English
- fr-argot – French slang
- i-navajo – Navajo

Navajo (an American-Indian language) doesn't have a two-letter code in the ISO (International Organization for Standardization) list of languages. Instead, it uses a code that is registered with IANA (Internet Assigned Numbers Authority).

The selector that checks for a language has the following form:

```
[LANG|="en-uk"] { background: rgb(90%,90%,0%) }
[LANG|="en-us"] { background: rgb(90%,90%,90%) }
[LANG|="en"] { color: blue }
```

The first matches elements that have an attribute LANG="en-uk" or LANG="en-uk-..." where the dots stand for arbitrary codes. The third rule matches everything the first two match, plus LANG="en". The result is that every element that is in English (and their child elements, if they don't override it) will have blue text against either a yellow background (for British English) or a light gray one (for American English).

CSS2.1 also provides a language selector based on a pseudo-class. It is written like this:

```
P:lang(nl) { font-style: italic }
```

This works differently from the attribute selector because it selects all elements (all **P** elements in this case) that are in a certain language, not just those that have a **LANG** attribute. An element is considered to be in a certain language if

- It has a **LANG** attribute for that language.
- It doesn't have a **LANG** attribute but its parent is in that language.
- It is the root element, and the HTTP header specifies that language.

aa	Afar	eu	Basque	kk	Kazakh	om	Oromo (Afan)	sw	Swahili
ab	Abkhazian	fa	Persian	kl	Greenlandic	or	Oriya	ta	Tamil
af	Afrikaans	fi	Finnish	km	Cambodian	pa	Punjabi	te	Tegulu
am	Amharic	fj	Fiji	kn	Kannada	pl	Polish	tg	Tajik
ar	Arabic	fo	Faeroese	ko	Korean	ps	Pashto (Pushto)	th	Thai
as	Assamese	fr	French	ks	Kashmiri	pt	Portuguese	ti	Tigrinya
ay	Aymara	fy	Frisian	ku	Kurdish	qu	Quechua	tk	Turkmen
az	Azerbaijani	ga	Irish	ky	Kirghiz	rm	Rhaeto-Romance	tl	Tagalog
ba	Bashkir	gd	Scots Gaelic	la	Latin	rn	Kirundi	tn	Setswana
be	Byelorussian	gl	Galician	ln	Lingala	ro	Romanian	to	Tonga
bg	Bulgarian	gn	Guarani	lo	Laothian	ru	Russian	tr	Turkish
bh	Bihari	gu	Gujarati	lt	Lithuanian	rw	Kinyarwanda	ts	Tsonga
bi	Bislama	ha	Hausa	lv	Latvian (Lettish)	sa	Sanskrit	tt	Tatar
bn	Bengali (Bangla)	hi	Hindi	mg	Malagasy	sd	Sindhi	tw	Twi
bo	Tibetan	hr	Croatian	mi	Maori	sg	Sangro	uk	Ukrainian
br	Breton	hu	Hungarian	mk	Macedonian	sh	Serbo-Croatian	ur	Urdu
ca	Catalan	hy	Armenian	ml	Malayalam	si	Singhalese	uz	Uzbek
co	Corsican	ia	Interlingua	mn	Mongolian	sk	Slovak	vi	Vietnamese
cs	Czech	ie	Interlingue	mo	Moldavian	sl	Slovenian	vo	Volapuk
cy	Welsh	ik	Inupiak	mr	Marathi	sm	Samoan	wo	Wolof
da	Danish	in	Indonesian	ms	Malay	sn	Shona	xh	Xhosa
de	German	is	Icelandic	mt	Maltese	so	Somali	yo	Yoruba
dz	Bhutani	it	Italian	my	Burmese	sq	Albanian	zh	Chinese
el	Greek	iw	Hebrew	na	Nauru	sr	Serbian	zu	Zulu
en	English	ja	Japanese	ne	Nepali	ss	Siswati		
eo	Esperanto	ji	Yiddish	nl	Dutch	st	Sesotho		
es	Spanish	jw	Javanese	no	Norwegian	su	Sudanese		
et	Estonian	ka	Georgian	oc	Occitan	sv	Swedish		

Table 4.1 ISO two-letter language codes (ISO 639)

The following HTML fragment illustrates the effect of the LANG pseudo-class. The document has elements in two languages: English and French. The start tags of the elements that would match `:lang(fr)` are shown in bold:

```
<BODY LANG="en">
  <H1>English title</H1>
  <P>This is a paragraph in English, that leads
    up to the quotation:
  <BLOCKQUOTE LANG="fr">
    <P>Ici commencent les lignes en français.
      Il y a même un mot en <B>gras.</B>
    <P>Encore un peu de français.
  </BLOCKQUOTE>
  <P>And here it is back to English again.
</BODY>
```

ADVANCED CONTEXTUAL SELECTORS

The context of an element consists of all the element's ancestors and all elements that precede it in the document. It is not possible to look at elements that follow an element because browsers often need to be able to decide on the style of an element before the rest of the document comes in. The most common contextual selector is the one that was explained earlier, in the section, "Simple contextual selectors." It only checks whether an element is inside some other element, without regard for how far removed that ancestor is.

Two other contextual selectors, the child selector and the sibling selector, give precise control over the relation between the element to select and its context. In combination with the first-child pseudo-class explained next, these can be used to trace out a path from some element to the element you want to select.

The child selector

To select an element under the condition that its parent matches some other selector, you can use a rule like the following:

```
DIV.chapter DIV.warning > P { text-indent: 0 }
```

This rule selects any **P** elements whose parent matches DIV.CHAPTER DIV.WARNING; in other words, all **P** elements that are children of a **DIV** element with class warning that is inside a **DIV** element of class "chapter." This may be quite different from the following:

```
DIV.chapter > DIV.warning P { text-indent: 0 }
```

The sibling selector

Sometimes what determines the style of an element is not so much its parent or other ancestors, but the element that precedes it. A typical example is the indentation of the first line of a paragraph. This book uses that device to make it easier to spot where one paragraph ends and the next one begins.

The rule is that an indent is only used between paragraphs; in other words, not on a paragraph that follows a heading, a list, or something else that is already visually distinguished. Expressed in CSS, the rule becomes

```
P + P { text-indent: 2em }
```

This matches a **P** if it is preceded by another **P**, and both have the same parent.

Here is a triplet of rules that sets the font size of **H1** and **H2** elements: By themselves, they are set to fairly large letters, but when an **H2** immediately follows an **H1**, it is made smaller. You might do this, for example, because such **H2**s function as subtitles:

```
H1 { font-size: xx-large }
H2 { font-size: x-large }
H1 + H2 { font-size: medium }
```

ADVANCED PSEUDO-CLASSES

In addition to the two anchor pseudo-classes that were previously described, CSS2.1 has four more pseudo-classes. Three of them allow dynamic effects: The style changes when the user does something. The fourth pseudo-class selects elements that are the first children of their parent.

User-interaction: the active, hover, and focus pseudo-classes

CSS2.1 can describe a few dynamic effects. They typically give the users of a document extra visual feedback on the purpose of various elements. For example, you can change the color of an **A** element when the mouse moves over it, or you can change the shape of the mouse pointer itself to give an extra visual clue that the **A** element is active and that something more would happen if the user actually clicked instead of just moved the mouse.

Because they are dynamic, these dynamic effects attract the user's attention more than static displays of colors and text. But, they can be easily overdone, and many people don't like it when their attention is constantly drawn to new areas when all they do is slightly move the mouse. So, be careful with these features.

The three pseudo-classes that select elements based on the user's interaction with them represent three common states for elements in an interactive document. They can be applied to the source anchors of hyperlinks, to elements in forms, and in documents with scripts often to other elements. (But, in that last case, extra care is called for because users don't expect elements outside a form to be active.) The three states are the following:

- hover – The mouse or some other pointing device "hovers" over the element. The user hasn't clicked or otherwise activated the element, but is in a position that he or she *could* click. For example, to change the background of a hyperlink when the mouse enters the element's box, you might use this rule:

  ```
  A:link:hover, A:visited:hover {
    background: yellow }
  ```

- active – The element has been activated, and some action is being performed, but is not yet complete. The typical application is again for hyperlinks, to indicate that the user's request to fetch a new page has been accepted, but that the page hasn't arrived yet:

  ```
  A:active { color: white; background: black }
  ```

- focus – When elements accept keyboard input, such as the **INPUT** and **TEXTAREA** elements of HTML, at most, one of them can accept input at any time. The user has to explicitly select the element he or she wants to send characters to. Depending on the browser, that is done by clicking or using the Tab key. The element that currently has the input focus is often indicated with a border-like outline. The CSS rule for that might be as follows:

  ```
  :focus { ouline: solid medium black }
  ```

The browser may only support a limited number of properties for these pseudo-classes. For example, you should not expect all browsers to be able to change the font size of the active pseudo-class because this would mean the browser has to reformat the entire document when you click a link. It's safe to assume that you can change colors and add/remove underlining because these are purely local changes. But, any rule that may change the size of something (for example, font or margin) may be ignored by the browser.

Counting elements: the first-child pseudo-class

The contextual rule for siblings previously described (in "The sibling selector") selects elements that have a certain preceding element. The opposite, selecting an element because it has no preceding element, is provided by the first-child pseudo-class. For example:

```
DIV.bio > P:first-child { font-weight: bold }
```

This selects **P** elements that are children of bio elements, but only if they are the first child. Combining child selectors, sibling selectors, and the first-child pseudo-class leads to very precise selectors. They can sometimes even take the place of an ID selector (refer to "The **ID** attribute"), if there is no possibility of adding an **ID** attribute to the document.

This example picks out the third list item of every **UL** list:

```
UL > LI:first-child + LI + LI {
   font-style: italic }
```

When it's applied to this HTML fragment:

```
<UL>
  <LI>horses
  <LI>dogs
  <LI>cows
    <UL>
      <LI>Greta IV
      <LI>Berta II
      <LI>Berta III
    </UL>
</UL>
```

it causes "cows" and "Berta III" to be italic (see Figure 4.15).

Figure 4.15 Using contextual selectors to put the third item of every **UL** list in italic.

- horses
- dogs
- *cows*
    - Greta IV
    - Berta II
    - *Berta III*

ADVANCED PSEUDO-ELEMENTS

The first-line and first-letter pseudo-elements select a part of an element (discussed in the section, "The first-letter and first-line pseudo-elements"). The before and after pseudo-elements go further: They actually add new parts to an element. Here are a few examples. (The full discussion can be found in Chapter 6.)

The before and after pseudo-elements are used together with the **content** property, which determines what text goes into the pseudo-element. The first example adds the word "Note" in front of every paragraph of class "note":

```
P.note:before { content: "Note." }
```

If the element to which the pseudo-element is added is itself a block element, the pseudo-element can also be made a block. In other words, it is possible to add a paragraph. The following example adds a centered line "The end" between two horizontal rules at the end of the document:

```
BODY:after {
  content: "The end";
  display: block;
  border-top: solid thin;
  border-bottom: solid thin }
```

THE "ANY" SELECTOR

The final type of selector in CSS2.1 is a selector that simply selects all elements. It can be used to set a property on all elements, but that is a rare occurrence. It can also be used in combination with the child selector to count ancestors. Here is an example of the "any" selector used on its own:

```
* { cursor: auto }
```

This resets the shape of the mouse pointer to the browser's default. This quickly undoes all changes to the mouse cursor. If the style sheet that comes with a document makes it difficult to find the hyperlinks, this might be a useful rule to have in a user's style sheet.

Another place where the "any" selector might come in handy is in selectors that must match only at a certain depth in the document tree. For example, to select all paragraphs except those that are children of the **BODY** element, this rule will do this:

```
BODY * P { font: medium "gill sans", sans-serif }
```

This matches **P** elements that are descendants of any element that is a descendant of **BODY**. Therefore, it excludes **P** elements that are children of **BODY** itself.

A final way to use the "any" selector is for purely aesthetic reasons. If you like all of your selectors to start with an element name, you can use the * in places where the element name doesn't matter:

```
*[BORDER] { border: solid }
*.POLONIUS { font-weight: bold }
*:hover { color: inherit; background: inherit }
```

In these cases, the "any" selector is used merely to avoid starting a selector with a flag character. It is a matter of taste.

Table 4.2 summarizes all selectors in CSS2.1.

Pattern	Matches
*	Any element.
E	Any E element (*i.e.*, element of type "E").
F E	Any E element that is a descendant of an F element.
F > E	Any E element that is a child of an F element.
F + E	Any E element that immediately follows an F element.
.class	Any element with class "class."
#id	The element with ID "id."

Cascading Style Sheets

Pattern	Matches
:first-child	Any E element that is the first child of its parent.
:link	Any element that is an unvisited hyperlink.
:visited	Any element that is a visited hyperlink.
:active :hover :focus	Any element that is "activated" by the user; respectively: (1) an action has started but not completed; (2) the mouse "hovers" over the element; (3) the element is ready to receive keyboard input.
:active	Any element that is "activated" by the user, e.g., by clicking it.
:hover	Any element that the mouse pointer "hovers" over.
:focus	An element that is ready to receive keyboard input.
:lang(C)	Any element whose content is in (human) language C.
[att]	Any element with an "att" attribute.
[att="val"]	Any element with an "att" attribute with value "val."
[att~="val"]	Any element with an "att" attribute that includes the word "val."
[att|="val"]	Any element with an "att" attribute of the form "val-..."
x, y	Grouping: any element that matches x *or* y.
E:first-letter	The first letter of any (block) element E.
E:first-line	The first line of any (block) element E.
E:before	The text inserted at the start of any E element.
E:after	The text inserted at the end of any E element.

Table 4.2 Overview of the building blocks of selectors.

Chapter 5

Fonts

Specifying typesetting properties is one of the most common uses of style sheets. Such properties include a font's size, its width, its weight (is it light or bold?), and its posture (does it slant or stand upright?).

Getting the fonts you want with HTML is difficult because HTML was designed without any concept of fonts. In HTML, the appearance of the page is the result of the browser's inserting styles it thinks are appropriate. It does this using the HTML structural information in your document. The lack of control over fonts in HTML has led to documents containing pictures of text instead of text. By making pictures of text, designers get total control over fonts. They can pick and choose between any font they have on their own machine and don't have to worry about which fonts are available on the user's machine. The downside of using images is that documents become big and download slowly.

CSS has been designed to give designers the influence over fonts they request without having to resort to images. This is done by setting values on a set of font properties that are defined in CSS. In previous chapters, you saw examples of these properties. For example, the **font-style**, **font-weight**, and **font** properties were used in Chapter 2, "CSS." In this chapter, you find the full definition of all font properties and the values they can take. Also, there are more examples of how they can and should be used in style sheets.

This chapter introduces you to typesetting terminology before moving on to describing the CSS font properties. Along the way, we also describe the units of measurements used by the font properties. These units are also used by other properties, so pay attention!

TYPESETTING TERMINOLOGY

Typesetting terminology is a difficult field. No universally accepted system for classifying fonts exists, and many of the terms in use mean different things to different people. Traditional printing terminology and that used in desktop publishing and Web design don't always agree.

The word "type" is derived from the Greek word *typos*, which means "impression" and "shape." Today, "type" refers to letters and other symbols that create words and sentences.

A *typeface*, sometimes called *face*, is all type of a single design and style. All letters and symbols within a typeface share some common characteristics so that they visually fit together. For example, the vertical stems of letters within a typeface typically have the same thickness.

Several typefaces that share the same basic design form a *type family*. The different typefaces in a type family can vary in *style* by certain attributes, including weight (degree of boldness versus lightness), width (such as narrow versus expanded), and posture (straight versus slanted). Among the most common type families are Helvetica, Arial, and Palatino. Times New Roman (TR) is the name of another popular type family. *TR Regular, TR Italic, TR Bold,* and *TR Bold Italic* are typefaces within the TR type family. Figure 5.1 shows the TR family and a sample of each typeface.

Figure 5.1 Four typefaces of the Times New Roman type family.

Aa Bb Cc TR Regular
Aa Bb Cc TR Italic
Aa Bb Cc TR Bold
Aa Bb Cc TR Bold Italic

The most common type families usually have at least these four styles: *regular* (also called "roman"), *bold* (also known as "boldface"), *italic*, and *bold italic*. The roman style often forms the basic and most commonly used typeface within the family because, in many type families, it is appropriate for running text. However, all type families have their own version of roman, even those whose appearance is inappropriate for running text. Furthermore, not every type family has variations, while other families have many typefaces with these or other characteristics, such as being narrow, expanded, or condensed.

The traditional definition of a *font* is one typeface in one size. For example, a 10pt TR Regular is one font, a 12pt TR Regular is another font, and so is a 14pt TR Regular. These differ only in their sizes, and each is considered to be a font by the traditional definition. Other fonts could be 10pt TR Bold, 10pt TR Italic, and 10pt TR Bold Italic. These differ only in their style, weight, or both.

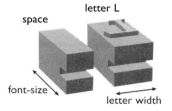

Figure 5.2 Metal type. Small lead or brass blocks all the same height (the font size) but different widths, each with a raised mirror image of a letter, are assembled on rails to form lines. Spaces bear no letter image. The lines are arranged and locked into a galley to form the pages. After inking, the page is printed onto a sheet of paper.

This definition of font comes from the time when each size and variation of a typeface were cast in lead (Figure 5.2) and stored separately from other fonts so that they wouldn't get mixed up. This also meant the number of fonts was relatively limited (even large printers only had room for so many different fonts). With the introduction of photocomposition (a type technology) and digital computers, type can be scaled by small amounts easily, thus the number of fonts is potentially much greater. So, the consideration of size in the definition of font is no longer useful, and the terms font, typeface, and face are all used synonymously, as is the case in this book. So, we consider TR Italic to be a font, TR Bold to be a font, etc., with no consideration of the size of type.

CLASSIFYING FONT FAMILIES

Font families are often classified into a few general categories. The number and names of categories vary from one typographic tradition to another. Here are the questions CSS asks when classifying a font family:

- Does it have *serifs* (defined shortly) or is it *sans serif*?
- Is it proportional-spaced (variable-width) or monospaced (fixed width)?
- Was it designed to resemble handwriting?
- Is it intended primarily for decorative purposes rather than for use in running text and headings?

We discuss each of these in the next several subsections.

Serif or sans serif?

A *serif* is a short cross-stroke that some letters have. A font that has serifs is called *serif*. A font that has no serifs is called *sans serif* (sans is French for "without"). Serifs can differ in appearance, ranging from short feathery strokes to slab-like square strokes. Figure 5.3 shows examples from several serif and sans serif families. Both sans serif and serif fonts work well for text and for headings.

Figure 5.3 (a) Serif fonts; (b) sans serif fonts.

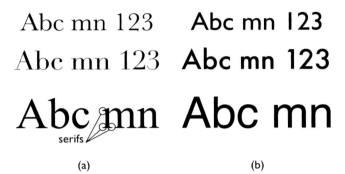

(a)   (b)

Proportional-spaced or monospaced?

In a variable-width (or *proportional-spaced*) font, each letter takes up just the amount of space it needs. An "I," being naturally skinny, takes up less space than the naturally fatter "M." In a fixed-width (or *monospaced*) font, each letter takes up the same amount of space regardless of its width. For example, an "I" and an "M" take up the same amount of space even though they are obviously of different widths.

Proportional-spaced fonts may be either serif or sans serif and may generally be used both for text and headings. Monospaced fonts are often called *typewriter type*. This is because, for a long time, typewriters could produce only monospaced type. Monospaced fonts may be used for both text and headings; however, they are usually reserved for special usages, such as to mimic the effects of a typewriter or to portray computer code. Figure 5.4 shows examples of proportional-spaced and monospaced type.

Figure 5.4 (a) Proportional-spaced fonts; (b) monospaced fonts.

(a) Aa Bb Ii Mm 0123 !?
The quick brown fox jumps over the lazy dog
(b) Aa Bb Ii Mm 0123 !?
The quick brown fox jumps over the lazy dog

Does it resemble handwriting?

A font designed to resemble handwriting is called *cursive*. Cursive characters are usually rounder than serif or sans serif type; they do not have serifs; and they usually slant to the right. They may also be connected, like handwriting usually is, although this is not necessary. Many italic versions of serif fonts look cursive. They differ from cursive fonts in that a serif font has a roman version, while a cursive form does not. Cursive fonts are often effective when you want to convey a personal touch because much of it resembles handwriting. Figure 5.5 shows examples of cursive and italic fonts.

Figure 5.5 (a) Cursive fonts; (b) italic fonts.

This is a cursive font
(Apple Chancery)

This is a cursive font
(Brush Script)

This is an italic font
(Garamond italic)

This is an italic font
(Didot italic)

(a)

(b)

Is it mainly for decorative purposes?

Some fonts are seldom used for large amounts of text because their appearance is too unique to be read easily in large amounts. Typically, they are reserved for display and, to some extent, headline purposes. Some don't even have full alphabets; they just have capital letters. They may be strangely decorated, irregular in shape, or very fancy. Figure 5.6 shows examples of fantasy font families.

Figure 5.6 Some fantasy font families.

CHARLEMAGNE Giddyup HERCULANUM
ROSEWOOD Viva Comic Sans MS
COPPERPLATE IMPACT Blippo Old Town
Sinaloa Futura Poster

On the basis of these factors, CSS classifies font families into five categories:

- sans-serif
- serif
- monospace
- cursive
- fantasy

In CSS, these are known as generic font families. To specify that a document should be printed with a font from a generic font family – or from a specific font family, such as *Helvetica* – the **font-family** property is used.

THE FONT-FAMILY PROPERTY

The **font-family** property lets you specify the font families that will be used in your documents. Here is the formal definition of the property:

FF Op Sa IE Pr

•   •   •   •   •

Name:	font-family
Value:	[*<specific-family>* ,]* [*<specific-family>* | *<generic-family>*]
Initial:	UA specific
Applies to:	all elements, except replaced elements
Inherited:	yes
Percentages:	N/A

Each CSS property has a "data sheet" like the one just shown, which describes key characteristics of the property. Also, on the left, there is a "button bar" that gives you an overview of how widely supported the property is. Throughout this book, you can find definitions like this for each new CSS property that is introduced. Learning what the different fields represent saves you time when encountering new properties or reviewing old ones. The following sidebar describes how to read the property definitions.

Even when you learn to read the property data sheet, you need to read the textual description of the property to understand how the property changes a document's presentation.

HOW TO READ PROPERTY DATA SHEETS

The "button bar" to the left of a property definition indicates how major browsers support each property. The browser categories are FF (FireFox, version 1), Op (Opera, version 8), Sa (Safari), and IE (Microsoft Internet Exporer for Windows, version 6). Also, the Prince formatter, which converts HTML and XML documents to PDF files, is listed as Pr (Prince, version 4.1). The buttons have the following meaning:

○ The property is not supported by the browser.

◑ The property is partially supported by the browser.

● The property is, for most practical purposes, fully supported by the browser.

Name: This is the first field in the formal definition. It simply lists the name of the property.

Value: This field specifes the possible values of the property. You may find one or many values. Words written in italics refer to a group of values that are described elsewhere, upright words are literal keywords. If a property offers many possible values or many possible complex combinations of values, you may find square brackets, vertical bars, and other symbols in this area. The appendix called "Reading property value definitions" describes in detail how to read the special symbols.

We know from experience, however, that many designers do not feel comfortable reading formal grammars, but they still write excellent style sheets. Instead of reading this field, you can learn about the possible values by reading the text and examples that follow the data sheet.

Initial: This field gives the *initial value* of the property. If the property is inherited, this value is given to the first element of the document (which is **HTML** in HTML). Otherwise, it is the value that the property will have if there are no style rules for it in the style sheets. Initial values make life easier for designers because they most often make sense and don't need to be changed. The initial value can be either a specific value for a property or "UA-specific," which means that CSS does not define an initial value. Instead, it leaves that definition to the "UA" or *User Agent;* that is, the browser (or other program) that processes CSS on behalf of the user.

Applies to: This field describes what kinds of elements the property applies to. All elements have all properties, but some properties have no effect on some types of elements. For example, **font-family** has no effect if the element is a replaced element (such as an image).

Inherited: This field indicates whether the value of the property is inherited from a parent element. For a review on inheritance, see Chapter 2 which gives examples of **font-familiy** values inheriting from parent to child elements.

Percentages: This field indicates how percentage values should be interpreted on this property. We talk more about how percentages work in the description of the **font-size** property. If the line reads "N/A" (not applicable), this means that the property does not accept percentages as values.

The **font-family** property accepts a list of font families as value. The font families are separated with commas, and there are two different kinds:

- Specific font families (for example, `Arial` or `Courier`)
- Generic font families (one of `serif`, `sans-serif`, `monospace`, `cursive`, `fantasy`)

For example, a document that is to be displayed in Times might have a style sheet that looks like this:

```
BODY { font-family: Times }
```

A document that is to be displayed in Garamond, if possible, and Times if Garamond is not available, would have a style sheet like this:

```
BODY { font-family: Garamond, Times }
```

where Garamond and Times are both family names.

It's important to remember the comma when you specify a list of font families. Some font-family names have spaces in them (for example, "New Century Schoolbook"), and the space character is therefore not sufficient for separating different font families. In addition, you may use quotation marks around family names, as in this example rule:

```
BODY { font-family: "new century schoolbook", serif }
```

The quotation marks are necessary if the name contains characters other than letters, digits, dashes, and spaces. For example, if a font were named "Dollar$," the browser might get confused by the dollar sign.

The value can also be the name of a generic font family — instead of or in addition to the specific font families. Use of generic font families is a partial solution to the problem of dealing with unavailable fonts. A browser may not have any of the fonts listed in the value. To ensure that something is displayed in the worst case of no match, you can add a generic font family, such as `serif`, to the list. In this case, if the browser does not have any of the given families, it has to use any font it has that has serifs. Here are the generic names:

- `serif`
- `cursive`
- `sans-serif`
- `fantasy`
- `monospace`

Look familiar? They correspond to the font categories defined earlier in this chapter. Here's an example rule that includes a generic family name:

```
BODY { font-family: Garamond, Times,
  "New Century Schooolbook", serif }
```

In this example, the browser first checks to see if it has Garamond. If it doesn't, it checks for Times. If it doesn't have Times either, it tries New Century Schooolbook. And, if that fails, too, it uses any fonts it has in a serif style that it can use to display the document.

The use of generic font families is encouraged. Each browser has a list of fonts that it can display. Those lists usually differ among browsers. However, all browsers must understand the previous five category names. Hence, when a requested font is not available on a particular browser, and you told the browser which category the font is in, the browser is expected to substitute a font from the same category. Although the resulting translation may be a bit rough, it is usually a font that looks at least somewhat like the intended one. Figure 5.7 shows sample fonts from the five generic type families.

Figure 5.7 Examples of the five generic font families.

serif   serif

sans-serif   **sans-serif**

monospace   monospace

cursive   *cursive*

fantasy   **fantasy**

Don't put quotes around the generic name! The generic family names are special keywords in CSS, not real font families. If you write `font-family: "serif"`, the browser thinks you mean a font named "serif."

Design tips using font families

Good document design generally involves using just two or three different font families. When there are more, finding ones that look good together soon becomes a problem. Unless you are a skilled graphics designer, restricting your creative urges to two or three families gives your document a professional look. Unless you want a document that looks like a Ransom letter...

A typical, time-proven scheme is to set all text in a serif font and the headings in a sans serif font. Popular choices are Times Roman and Helvetica, respectively, or their clones, such as Times New Roman and Arial. You may want to use a monospace font for some text if you are writing about computer software. For example, code is often set in a monospaced font, as may be filenames, function names, method names, and so on. The rest of the variation in your document should be created by using different font styles, weights, and sizes within the same two or three families.

People writing multilingual documents, in which they may be using two or more alphabets, know that it is difficult to find two fonts that look well together, let alone three or more. Some alphabets, such as Thai and Devanagari (which is a script from India), have very different conventions for a letter's baseline and, therefore, its height and depth. For example, a 12pt Devanagari font may look too big next to a 12pt Latin font. But, because only a few multilingual fonts exist, there is often not much choice. Figure 5.8 shows a sample of Bitstream Cyberbit, a family with more than 8,000 characters. Bitstream made the normal style and weight available for free; for italic and bold, you'll have to pay. See www.bitstream.com.

Figure 5.8 Sample of Bitstream Cyberbit family, which has over 8,000 characters.

abpmnABCD1234&!àá
âÈÉËþýßÆÞðĐşıŞğĞ™
¾«“”•חוגבךרשתאΰαβγ
πϱςΓΔΘΙΛώύίΖήΠЯбв
ИЙЛюэБЖЮثجحخذنก
ขฃคฅあきげち世丟两€

Restraint is the key to good design. There are so many possibilities in CSS that it is easy to overdo and spoil your design.

FONT METRICS

Fonts are typically measured in a unit specific to the printing industry called the *point*. A point (abbreviated "pt") is the traditional printer's and typographer's unit for specifying the size of fonts, the spacing between adjacent lines, and the thickness of rules, among other things. It is still used a lot, although some countries and publishers now prefer to use the metric system, specifically, the millimeter (mm) and centimeter (cm). There are three variants of the point:

- The continental European point (the Didot point = 0.376065mm)
- The Anglo-American point (the pica point = 0.351461mm)
- Another Anglo-American point (defined as 1/72in. = 0.352778mm)

CSS uses only the last one. It does so because that point's value is in between the other two values. Also, it conforms to the point size used in PostScript printers, which is the most common type of printer.

To understand how type is sized, you first need some information about what makes up a letter. The *x-height* is the size of the body, or main part, of the letter and is approximately equal to the height of the x of the font. The *ascender* is that part of the lowercase letter that extends above the x-height. The *descender* is that part of the lowercase letter that extends below the x-height.

Type sits on an imaginary horizontal line called the *baseline*. For example, notice this line of type you now read. All of it sits on a base-line. Figure 5.9 shows the parts of a letter sitting on a baseline.

Figure 5.9 Parts of a letter.

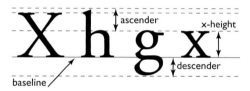

The size of type is usually obtained by measuring from roughly the top of its ascenders to the bottom of its descenders. (In the days of metal type, the font size was the size of the letter body; refer to Figure 5.2.) The measurement is expressed in points. The difference of a point is more noticeable in smaller sizes than in larger sizes. Text type, which is type used for running text, is generally 14pt or less. Common sizes are 10pt and 12pt. Display type, which is the type used for headings, is generally bigger than 14pt.

Although different fonts may be of the same point size, they may appear to be different sizes. This is typically because the x-heights of fonts vary. Some fonts may have a large x-height, while others in comparison have a small x-height. Because type of one size has just so much height it can work with, a large x-height is often combined with short descenders and ascenders, while a small x-height is combined with long descenders and ascenders. So, the visual impression of size that a font makes is largely caused by the font's x-height in combination with the size of its ascenders and descenders. As Figure 5.10 shows, Times Roman has a relatively large x-height and therefore relatively short descenders and ascenders in comparison to Bernhard Modern, which has a relatively small x-height and relatively long descenders and ascenders. Notice that the Times Roman sample appears bigger than the Bernhard Modern sample even though both are the same point size.

Figure 5.10 Because of differences in x-heights, the Times Roman sample (a) looks bigger than the Bernhard Modern sample (b) even though both are the same point size.

Because of differences in x-heights, the Times Roman sample (a) looks bigger than the Bernhard Modern sample (b) even though both are the same point size.

Because of differences in x-heights, the Times Roman sample (a) looks bigger than the Bernhard Modern sample (b) even though both are the same point size.

(a)   (b)

This relationship is important because it is one factor that affects the readability of your font on a user's screen. A font with a large x-height is often easier to read in smaller sizes than one with a small x-height. As the font size increases, this difference lessens.

LENGTH UNITS

The point unit is the traditional measurement of length in typography, but not always the best for Web design. CSS accepts a range of different units, which fall into three categories:

- Absolute units – This category includes the point unit previously described as well as other units (mm, cm, in, pc) that describe physical distances that can be measured with a measuring band.
- Relative units – These units describe distances relative to other distances. The em unit, described in Chapter 3, "The amazing em unit and other best practices," is the foremost member of this group, which also includes the ex unit.
- The pixel unit – The pixel unit, as defined in CSS, forms a group of its own since it has some unique characteristics. On normal computer screens, the pixel unit does what you expect. On printers and other high-resolution devices, it does what you hope!

The three groups and their units are described in more detail next. Common for all the units is the way they are combined with numbers to form values. Here are some examples: 12pt, 0.9in, 2.54cm, -3px.

To form a value, a number is combined with a unit. The number can be a whole number (0, 1, 2...), a fractional number (0.5, 2.57, 1.04...), or a negative number (-1, -3.14, -0.25...). If the integer part of the fractional number is 0, it can be omitted (.25, -.61). The unit of measure is added directly after the number with no space between the number and the unit. All units are two-letter abbreviations with no period at the end.

Properties may restrict the numbers and lengths they accept. For example, the **font-size** property cannot be set to a negative length. All CSS properties that accept lengths also accept the number 0 without a unit of measure. (If a length is 0, it doesn't matter whether it is points or inches.)

Absolute units

An *absolute unit* is a unit of measure that specifies a fixed length, which is a length that can be measured with a measuring band. The units are as follows:

- Millimeter: mm
- Centimeter: cm (1cm = 10mm)
- Inch: in (1in = 25.4mm)
- Point: pt (72pt = 1in)
- Pica: pc (1pc = 12pt)

The mm and cm units come from the metric system of measurements. The other units are all defined as fractions of an inch. A *pica* is 12 points. Six picas equal 1 inch.

Absolute units have limited usefulness because they cannot be scaled. In general, they should be used only if you know the physical properties of the output medium. For example, if you write a style sheet for a document you know will only be printed on A4-sized paper, absolute units may be the correct choice. In most cases, however, you are better off using relative units.

Relative units

A *relative unit* is a unit of measure that specifies a value that is relative to the font size. There are two relative units in CSS: em and ex. Usually, the font size they refer to is the font size of the element itself. (The only exception is the **font-size** property, which we discuss later in this chapter, for which the value scales to the font size of the element's parent.) Relative units have an advantage over absolute units in that they scale automatically. When you choose a different font, all properties that were expressed in em or ex don't have to be changed.

The em unit was heavily promoted in Chapter 3, and we will not repeat all the good arguments for using the em unit here, but merely state the facts. In CSS, the em is exactly equal to the font size (i.e., the height of the font). For example, in a 12pt font, the em is 12pt wide, while in a 15pt font, the em is 15pt wide. (There are other historical definitions of em that we don't go into. We chose for CSS the one that appeared to be the most convenient.)

The ex unit is also relative to the font size but in a different way. It is called "ex" because it is defined as the x-height (see Figure 5.11). The em can be set explicitly in CSS1, but the ex is a characteristic of the font, so it cannot be set explicitly. This means you can determine how big it is only by inspecting the font. For example, Times Roman has a relatively large ex (x-height) compared to Baskerville. So, even though a 12pt Times Roman and a 12pt Baskerville both have an em of 12pt, their ex values will vary because their x-heights vary. Times Roman's will be somewhat larger than Baskerville's. (Figure 5.11 illustrates this.) An ex is usually around 0.45em, but may be as large as 0.58em (in Verdana) or as small as 0.28em (in some cursive fonts).

Figure 5.11 Times Roman and Baskerville with the same em values have different ex values.

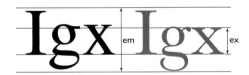

The pixel unit

The term *pixel* is derived from Picture Element. The pixel is the smallest element on a video-display screen, such as a computer monitor or a television. It also applies to the output from certain types of printers, such as laser printers. The pixel unit in CSS is based on pixels, but is slightly more refined than the name implies.

On current generation computer screens, the pixel unit behaves as you expect it to. Consider these two rules:

```
H1 { border-width: 4px }
H2 { border-width: 3px }
```

In this example, the width of the border surrounding **H1** elements is set to 4 pixels and the border around **H2** elements is set to 3 pixels. On a normal computer screen, these values are used as specified. That is, the border around **H1** elements will actually be 4 pixels wide, and the border around **H2** elements will be 3 pixels wide. Another seemingly obvious fact is that the **H1** border will be exactly 1 pixel thicker than the **H2** border.

When we try to print the document, things get more complicated. Typically, the resolution – the density of pixels – on a laser printer is much higher than the resolution on a computer screen. Therefore, a four-pixel border on a laser printer appears much thinner than a four-pixel border on a computer screen. CSS deals with this problem by saying that pixel measurements should always appear as they would on a computer screen. When printing, the browser should therefore replicate pixels so that, for example, the borders will be roughly as thick as they would on a computer screen.

For example, a 600dpi laser printer has six times more pixels per inch than a typical computer monitor does. Most often, however, the paper that it prints is held closer to the eyes than a computer screen, so to get the same perceived effect on screen and on paper, the laser printer could use a square of four by four pixels to emulate one screen pixel.

Pixels are a useful unit of measure because, on any medium, it is guaranteed that a difference of one pixel will actually be visible. On the other hand, the difference between 0.5em and 0.6em may disappear on a computer screen because the screen cannot show differences of less than 1 pixel.

PERCENTAGES AS VALUES

Many properties that accept a number or a length as a value also accept a percentage, such as 50%, 33.3%, and 100%. Although not a unit of measure, percentages offer similar advantages that relative units do; that is, they automatically scale.

What the percentage is a percentage of – that is, what it is relative to – depends on the property. Usually, it is a percentage of the value that the property has in the parent element. For example, an **H1** with a font size of 80% means the font is 80 percent of the font size of its parent (often the **BODY** element).

KEYWORDS AS VALUES

Keywords are not units of measure, but some have connotations of being relative. In this case, they have the same advantage as relative units and percentages in that they can be scaled. For example, the keywords bolder and lighter for the **font-weight** property are clearly relative: They are relative to the font weight of the parent. The same applies to larger and smaller for the **font-size** property, which we get to next.

THE FONT-SIZE PROPERTY

The **font-size** property specifies the size of the font:

FF   Op   Sa   IE   Pr
•   •   •   •   •

Name:	font-size
Value:	*<length>* | *<percentage>* | *<absolute-size>* | *<relative-size>*
Initial:	medium
Applies to:	all elements
Inherited:	yes
Percentages:	relative to parent's font size

This property has four possible types of values:

- Length
- Percentage
- Absolute size
- Relative size

The first two types are general types of values that can be used on many CSS properties. The last two types are sets of keywords that are particular to the **font-size** property.

The "length" value

When a property accepts length values, all units described in the "Length units" section can be used. This includes absolute units (mm, cm, in, pt, pc), relative units (em, ex), and the pixel unit (px). Here are some examples:

```
BODY { font-size: 12pt }
PRE { font-size: 0.4mm }
H1.chapter { font-size: 16px }
```

Traditional paper-based design specifies the size of a font in absolute units, most often in points, but when working with Web pages, the use of absolute units for specifying sizes is not advised because, for example, quality differences in screens will make some sizes difficult to read, and the font size you request may not be available on a particular browser. (Scaling may cause them not to align perfectly with the screen pixels.) It's better to use one of the relative units instead:

```
H1 { font-size: 1.2em }
```

On all properties except **font-size**, the em unit refers to the font size of the element itself. This makes it possible to make the border as thick as the size of the font, for example. However, when used on the **font-size** property, the em unit has to refer to something else. So, instead of referring to the font size of the element itself, the em unit refers to the font size of its parent. In the previous example, the font size of **H1** elements is set to 1.2 times the font size of its parent. A similar example is given in Chapter 3, "The amazing em unit and other best practices" (where the em unit is the hero).

The "percentage" value

On the **font-size** property, using percentages is equivalent to using the em unit. In this case, because the em is the font size of the parent element, a value of 120% is exactly the same as a value of 1.2em. Another context-dependent method for specifying the font size is thus to use percentages. A percentage value gives an element the size of the parent's font times the percentage. Thus, 120% gives a size that is 20 percent more than the size of the parent element, while 80% gives a size that is 80 percent of the parent element's size. For example, if the parent element size is 12pt, a 120% value results in a size of 14.4pt, while an 80% value results in a size of 9.6pt. Here is an example:

```
H1 { font-size: 120% }
```

This example is equivalent to the previous example using the em unit.

The "absolute-size" value

The *absolute-size* value is an index to a table of font sizes that is computed and kept by the browser. These sizes are expressed as keywords, as follows:

- `xx-small`
- `x-small`
- `small`
- `medium`
- `large`
- `x-large`
- `xx-large`

These sizes form an increasing range. For computer screens, the CSS2 specification suggests a number of different sizes (e.g., the large size should be about 1.2 times as big as the medium, and the small size should be about 0.9 times as big as the medium). That is, if the medium version of a font is 10pt, the large version would be about 12pt. Different media may use or need different scaling factors. Figure 5.12 gives the table's keywords and a representative example of each.

Figure 5.12 Comparison of the values of the size table.

`xx-small`	abcdefghijklmnopqrstuvwxyz
`x-small`	abcdefghijklmnopqrstuvwxyz
`small`	abcdefghijklmnopqrstuvwxyz
`medium`	abcdefghijklmnopqrstuvwxyz
`large`	abcdefghijklmnopqrstuvwxyz
`x-large`	abcdefghijklmnopqrstuvwxyz
`xx-large`	abcdefghijklmnopqrstu...

Here's an example usage of the absolute value of the **font-size** property:

```
H1 { font-size: xx-small }
```

The "relative-size" value

The *relative-size* value lets you specify the size in a context-dependent manner. The value has two keywords: `larger` and `smaller`. The keywords are interpreted relative to the table of font sizes mentioned in the previous section and the font size of the element's parent element.

Specifying one of these keywords is a safe way to provide for context-dependent size changes. For example, suppose the parent element has a font size of medium. If you then set the **font-size** property on the child element to larger, that is, larger than medium, the resultant size of the child is large, which is the next value in the table of size values. Here's the code for doing this:

```
BODY { font-size: medium }
H2 { font-size: larger }
P { font-size: smaller }
```

BODY has a font size of medium. **H2**, as a child element of **BODY**, is one size larger than **BODY**; that is, large. **P** is one size smaller than **BODY**, which is small.

THE FONT-STYLE PROPERTY

The **font-style** property lets you specify an oblique or italic style within the current type family.

FF	Op	Sa	IE	Pr			
•	•	•	•	•	Name:	font-style	
					Value:	normal │ italic │ oblique	
					Initial:	normal	
					Applies to:	all elements	
					Inherited:	yes	
					Percentages:	N/A	

This property has three keyword values:

- normal – The normal style of the font (often known as "roman," "regular," or sometimes "upright"). This is the default value.
- italic.
- oblique.

Italic and oblique styles are similar, but not the same. Sans serif families usually consider the two to be the same. Both are a variant that looks slanted to the right. For some families, that is how they are produced: by mechanically slanting the roman letters. Usually, however, that doesn't lead to beautiful letters, and for most fonts, the italic and roman forms are designed separately.

Serif families usually distinguish between the two. The italic form looks different from the oblique form. The two differ in the shape of their serifs and often look like completely different letter forms. Oblique refers to a version that looks like slanted roman. Oblique serif fonts are rare. Figure 5.13 compares roman, oblique, and italic style.

Figure 5.13 Sans serif roman, oblique, and italic (top); serif roman, oblique, and italic (bottom).

	roman	oblique	italic
sans-serif	ifa	*ifa*	*ifa*
serif	ifa	*ifa*	*ifa*

Font designers have used all kinds of names for their fonts without much consistency. Two other names that usually refer to what we described as oblique are *inclined* and *slanted*. Fonts with "Oblique," "Inclined," or "Slanted" in their names are usually labeled "oblique" in a browser's font database and are selected by the oblique value. Other names that usually refer to what we described as italic are *cursive* and *kursiv*. Fonts with "Italic," "Cursive," or "Kursiv" in their names are usually labeled "italic" in a browser's font database and are selected by the italic value.

If a type family has only an oblique style font, that font will be used as the italic as well. However, if you ask for oblique and the family has only an italic variant, you won't get the italic as a substitute for the oblique. Instead, the next family in the list is tried to see if it contains an oblique variant.

Here are example rules using the **font-style** property:

```
H1, H2, H3 { font-style: italic }
P { font-style: oblique }
H1 EM { font-style: oblique }
```

THE FONT-VARIANT PROPERTY

The **font-variant** property lets you specify a small-caps style within the current font family.

FF	Op	Sa	IE	Pr
●	●	●	●	○

Name:	font-variant
Value:	normal ǀ small-caps
Initial:	normal
Applies to:	all elements
Inherited:	yes
Percentages:	N/A

This property has two values:

- `normal`
- `small-caps`

A small-caps font style, despite its name, does not really consist of small capital letters. It is an entirely differently shaped letter that resembles capital letters. They are slightly smaller and have slightly different proportions. Figure 5.14 compares small-caps and regular capital letters. The first line of the figure shows a true small-caps font. The second line shows uppercase letters from a roman font that have been reduced by 80 percent to simulate small-caps.

Figure 5.14 (a) A true small-caps font; (b) the same font, but with the small-caps characters simulated from capitals. The font used in the example is BaseNine.

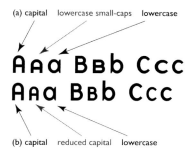

Notice that the stems of the small-caps are the same width as the stems of the lowercase letters around them, while the reduced uppercase letters are too thin. The small-caps are also wider than the reduced uppercase letters.

The value `normal` selects a font that is not a small-caps font, while `small-caps` selects a small-caps font. In the absence of a small-caps font, the browser may try to create one from an available normal font by scaling down and then stretching some uppercase letters. As a last resort, the browser may even use a normal font's uppercase letters without reducing them. On the screen in low resolutions and on low-grade printers, the difference between this adaptation and true small-caps is difficult to discern. On paper or a higher quality output device, where the resolution is normally much higher, the difference is noticeable.

If no small-caps style exists, and the browser hasn't been configured to fake one, it tries the next family in the list of font families to see if it has a small-caps style. The following is an example rule that sets the **font-variant** property value:

```
H3 { font-variant: small-caps }
```

THE FONT-WEIGHT PROPERTY

The **font-weight** property specifies the weight of the desired font within the current family.

FF	Op	Sa	IE	Pr		
•	•	•	•	•		

Name:	font-weight
Value:	normal | bold | bolder | lighter | 100 | 200 | 300 | 400 | 500 | 600 | 700 | 800 | 900
Initial:	normal
Applies to:	all elements
Inherited:	yes
Percentages:	N/A

This property has nine levels of weight:

- The nine values 100 to 900 form an ordered sequence, where each number indicates a weight that is at least as dark as its predecessor (100 is the lightest).
- normal is the same as 400.
- bold is the same as 700.

Two of the values, bolder and lighter, select a weight that is relative to the parent's weight.

The **font-weight** property is a superset of what is available for most families. Few families have the equivalent of all nine different weights. Hence, many of the CSS weight values result in the same font. On the other hand, some families, such as the Adobe's Multiple Master fonts, have an almost unlimited range. For those families, the browser selects nine of the possible weights and assigns them to the nine values.

Numerical values are used because we felt that descriptive words, other than `normal` and `bold`, could be potentially confusing. This is because no universal naming system for fonts exists. For example, a font that you might consider bold could be described, depending on the font, as Roman, Regular, Book, Medium, Semi-Bold, Demi-Bold, or numerous other names. These names are generally meaningful mainly within the family that uses them and differentiate fonts within that family. Outside that family, a name may have a different meaning. So, you cannot necessarily gauge the weight of a font from its name. In CSS1, the value `normal` (400) will have the weight that is normal *for the specified font*. What it means for another font may differ.

Figure 5.15 gives examples of the nine weights. These are only samples. Exactly what you get if you select a value of, say, 300 depends on the font you use, but Figure 5.15 helps you get some idea of how the weights vary.

Figure 5.15 Numerical values of the **font-weight** property.

100 Font weight sample
200 Font weight sample
300 Font weight sample
400 Font weight sample
500 Font weight sample
600 **Font weight sample**
700 **Font weight sample**
800 **Font weight sample**
900 **Font weight sample**

The following are descriptions of the nine numerical values:

- 100 – This is the lightest weight. Not many fonts have weights lighter than 400 ("normal"). Those that do, for which the browser would select the 100 value, often have "Thin," "Light," or "Extra-light" in their names. But font names are inconsistent in their descriptions, so we suggest that you don't rely on them. Let the browser figure out the weight of a font.

- 200 – This is not usually any different from 100. However, it is included because some fonts, such as the Multiple Master fonts, have many weights.
- 300 – This is slightly heavier than the 100 and 200.
- 400 – This is available for all fonts. It corresponds to the normal keyword that the property offers. You can choose either the number or keyword.
- 500 – This is slightly bolder than 400, but not by much. Some fonts have a weight called Medium, which is just a little bolder than the normal weight; 500 would result in that weight. If there is no such font, 500 will be the same as 400.
- 600 – This is slightly bolder than 500. A weight name of Demi-bold or Semi-bold would correspond to the 600 weight.
- 700 – This is available for most fonts. It corresponds to the bold keyword that the property offers. You can choose either the number or keyword.
- 800 – This is heavier than the usual bold. Fonts that have such a weight may have "Extra-bold," "Black," or "Heavy" in their names. Other possibilities are Poster and Ultra.
- 900 – This is the heaviest weight available in a font. Fonts with this weight often have rather strange names, such as Nord or Ultima. Or they may have cryptic numbers, often the case with Multiple Master fonts. Most fonts on the typical computer don't go beyond bold (700), so choosing either 800 or 900 results in the same effect as choosing 700.

The bolder and lighter values select a weight that is relative to the parent's weight. For example, consider this style sheet:

```
P { font-weight: normal } /* same as 400 */
H1 { font-weight: 700 } /* same as bold */
STRONG ( font-weight: bolder }
```

In this example, a **STRONG** element that appears in either the **P** or **HI** element will be bolder than its parent. However, the weight of **STRONG** when it appears in the **P** element may be less than its weight in the **HI** element. This is because the parent elements' weights differ.

In this case, we say "may" because, as previously mentioned, the font used also plays a role in how bold type looks.

For more information on how fonts are assigned to the numerical scale for each font, we recommend you check the CSS specifications.

THE FONT PROPERTY

The **font** property lets you specify, in one action, all the other font properties previously described plus **line-height** (which we discuss in Chapter 7, "Space inside boxes").

FF Op Sa IE Pr

Name:	font
Value:	[[<font-style> ‖ <font-variant> ‖ <font-weight>]? <font-size> [/ <line-height>]? <font-family>] ∣ caption ∣ icon ∣ menu ∣ message-box ∣ small-caption ∣ status-bar
Initial:	see individual properties
Applies to:	all elements
Inherited:	yes
Percentages:	allowed on <font-size> and <line-height> only

The **font** property is the first of the so-called *shorthand properties* we describe in detail. Shorthand properties let you set a group of properties that naturally belong together. The font properties described in this chapter (**font-style**, **font-variant**, **font-weight**, **font-size**, and **font-family**) form one such group, and the **font** property sets all of them in one statement. Also, the **line-height** property (described in Chapter 7) is set by the **font** property, but note that **font-stretch** and **font-size-adjust** (described next) are not included in this group because they were added in CSS2.

The **font** property is one of the most common CSS properties, and a simple example of its use was given in Chapter 2. Here is another example:

```
H1 { font: 1.3em sans-serif }
```

The font property requires that you always specify a font size and a font family; all other values are optional. The previous example is equivalent to writing the following:

```
H1 {
   font-style: normal;
   font-weight: normal;
   font-variant: normal;
   font-size: 1.3em;
   line-height: normal;
   font-family: sans-serif;
 }
```

Except for **font-size** and **font-family**, all properties in this example are set to their initial values. Because the browser does this automatically, it is normally not necessary to set them. Still, if you write your style sheets "by hand," using a normal text editor rather than a dedicated tool, you may appreciate the brevity of shorthand properties.

In principle, all values that are legal on the individual properties are also legal on the **font** property. There are restrictions, however, on the order the values must come in. First comes the **font-style**, **font-weight**, and **font-variant** values, in any order. These are optional and are set to their initial values if they are omitted. Then comes the **font-size** value, which is required. It may optionally be followed by a "/" and a **line-height** value. Finally comes the **font-family** value, which is required.

The syntax resembles a shorthand common in traditional typography (for example, "12/14 Times bold italic"). Here is an example of how to write a rule that reflects this shorthand:

```
P { font: italic bold normal 12pt/14pt Times, serif }
```

For demonstration purposes, we set every property, including **font-variant**, which has its initial value of normal. Specifying initial values is not necessary. The browser automatically uses the initial values for those properties not explicitly set. For example:

```
P { font: italic bold large palatino, serif }
```

This sets all properties except **font-variant** and **line-height**, whose initial values will be used. In other words, it is equivalent to the following set of rules:

```
P {
   font-style: italic;
   font-weight: bold;
   font-variant: normal; /* default */
```

```
    font-size: large;
    line-height: normal; /* default */
    font-family: palatino, serif;
}
```

Here are some more examples:

```
P { font: italic 12pt/14pt bodoni, bembo, serif }
P { font: normal small-caps 120%/120% fantasy }
P { font: x-large/100% "new century schoolbook", serif }
P { font: message-box }
```

The keyword `message-box` in the last rule refers to the font used in user interface dialog boxes. The rule sets all six properties to the values used in dialog boxes. The system font keywords are

- `caption` – The font used for captioned controls (for example, buttons, drop-downs, etc.).
- `icon` – The font used to label icons.
- `menu` – The font used in menus (for example, dropdown menus and menu lists).
- `message-box` – The font used in dialog boxes.
- `small-caption` – The font used for labeling small controls.
- `status-bar` – The font used in window status bars.

System fonts may only be set as a whole; that is, the font family, size, weight, style, etc., are all set at the same time. These values may then be altered individually. For example;

```
BODY { font: message-box;
    font-size: x-large }
```

THE TEXT-DECORATION PROPERTY

The **text-decoration** property does not specify a font property, although it seems to fit best in this chapter because it affects type. The property is used to add underlining, overlining, strike-out, or a blinking effect to the text.

FF	Op	Sa	IE	Pr
•	•	•	•	•

Name:	text-decoration
Value:	none | [underline || overline || line-through || blink]
Initial:	none
Applies to:	all elements
Inherited:	no (but see the following text)
Percentages:	N/A

The value is either none, meaning no decoration, or any combination of the following:

- underline – An underline is added below the text.
- overline – An overline is added above the text.
- line-through – A horizontal line is inserted through the text (also known as strike-out).
- blink – The text is made to blink.

In many browsers, underlining is used with the **A** element to mark the status of hyperlinks. The default style sheet for those browsers includes a rule like this:

```
A:link, A:visited, A:active { text-decoration: underline }
```

You cannot specify the exact position and thickness of the decorations. Many fonts come with indications of the preferred thicknesses of an overline, underline, and line-through and their distances from the base-line, and the browser tries to use those thickness and distance values. Otherwise, it computes appropriate values based on the size of the font. The color of the lines will be the same as the color of the text.

You have a similar lack of precise control over the blink decoration. The blinking text is shown in its own colors about half of the time; how it looks the other half is not specified. It may be invisible or it may be shown in a different color so that the two colors show alternately. Most browsers blink at a rate of approximately half a second on and half a second off. Not all browsers can blink, and, of course, blink has no effect when the document is printed.

The **text-decoration** property is not inherited. However, a decoration on a parent will *continue* in child elements. The effect of this continuation differs from the effect that would result if we were to give the child element its own decoration. For example, suppose you added this rule to your style sheet:

```
EM { text-decoration: underline }
```

In the following, the underline decoration affects all the **EM** element, even the child element, **STRONG**:

```
Some <EM>very, <STRONG>very</STRONG> important
things</EM> resulted from this effort.
```

The result would look like this:

Some <u>very, **very** *important things*</u> resulted from this effort.

The color of the decoration (if any) also continues across child elements. Thus, even if **STRONG** had a different color value, its underline would still have been black.

The reason **text-decoration** is not inherited has to do with possible future additions to this property. For example, suppose the decoration were a fancy border (see Figure 5.16). The **EM** rule in the style sheet would change from text-decoration: underline to, say, text-decoration: deco-border (note, this value is not yet available in CSS). The child element is included as part of the decoration of its parent. Figure 5.16(b) shows the effect if the child element were to inherit the fancy box value of its parent. The child would have a fancy border of its own in addition to that of its parent.

Figure 5.16 (a) The decoration continues across the embedded element; (b) the embedded element has its own decoration.

(a) Some (very, **very** important things) resulted from this effort.

(b) Some (very, (**very**) important things) resulted from this effort.

THE TEXT-TRANSFORM PROPERTY

The **text-transform** property, like the **text-decoration** property, does not specify a font. However, it best fits this chapter because it affects the case of text.

FF	Op	Sa	IE	Pr		
•	•	•	• .	◑		

Name:	text-transform
Value:	capitalize | uppercase | lowercase | none
Initial:	none
Applies to:	all elements
Inherited:	yes
Percentages:	N/A

This property has four values:

- capitalize
- uppercase
- lowercase
- none

The capitalize value capitalizes The First Letter Of Each Word, To Give An Effect Like This. Uppercase converts everything to UPPERCASE LETTERS LIKE THESE; lowercase does the opposite. None neutralizes an inherited value. These effects are often used in headings and titles but seldom in running text.

Here are some example usages:

```
H1 { text-transform: uppercase }
H1 { text-transform: capitalize }
```

The rules for converting from uppercase to lowercase and vice versa depend on the language used and on the browser. For example, the Dutch have a special letter that is usually written "ij," although it is really a single letter. So a word like ijstijd would be capitalized as IJstijd. Turkish has a dotless ı as well as a dotted i, the former capitalizes to an equally dotless I, the latter to a dotted İ.

The property is also useful for converting acronyms, such as NATO, BASIC, PIN, and NASA to small-caps, as in, NATO, BASIC, PIN, and NASA. Acronyms in standard uppercase letters look too large. So in the next example, we use small-caps instead. We use **font-variant** to change the font to small-caps. But, we don't use the uppercase version of small-caps because our intent is to make the acronym look smaller, as shown earlier in the paragraph. So, we use the lowercase version of small-caps (text-transform: lowercase) to achieve the right effect:

CSS:	/* no CSS rules */	.acronym {
		    font-variant: small-caps
		}
			.acronym {
			    font-variant: small-caps;
			    text-transform: lowercase
			}

For-mat-ted result:	Success for NASA	Success for NASA	Success for NASA
	(a)	(b)	(c)

Figure 5.17 Converting acronyms from standard uppercase letters into lowercase small-caps: (a) the acronym in standard uppercase letters; (b) the acronym in uppercase small-caps – this is not the effect we want; (c) the acronym in lowercase small-caps – this is the effect we want.

```
ACRONYM {
    text-transform: lowercase;
    font-variant: small-caps;
}

Success for <ACRONYM>NASA</ACRONYM>
```

There is often confusion about the effects of **text-transform**'s uppercase and **font-variant**'s small-caps. However, as stated earlier in this chapter, selecting a small-caps font doesn't change the characters. A text transform, on the other hand, does. **Font-variant** selects a font, but **text-transform** doesn't. There is still a connection between them, however.

The fact that small-caps relies on the availability of a small-caps font also means that it can fail if there is no such font available. For example, if the style sheet reads:

```
P {
    font-family: "Zapf Chancery", cursive;
    font-variant: small-caps;
}
```

the small-caps fails because the Zapf Chancery family doesn't have a small-caps variant. The browser may be able to synthesize one by taking the capitals and reducing them in height, but if it is not able to do that, it shows the P in all capitals instead, exactly as if the rule had read text-transform: uppercase. In other words, uppercase is a fall-back strategy for browsers that don't have access to small-caps fonts.

THE DIRECTION AND UNICODE-BIDI PROPERTIES

To make the World Wide Web truly worldwide, browsers must be able to display pages in many languages. Western languages – of which English is an example – are written from left to right. Other languages – for example, Hebrew and Arabic – are written from right to left. So far, so good. However, pages written in right-to-left (rtl) languages often include content written left-to-right (ltr). In Arabic, for example, numbers are written ltr just like in English and lines therefore contain both ltr and rtl content. This is called bi-directional content, or "bidi" for short. Bidi is a fascinating topic, that tends to interest people who are interested in fonts.

Two CSS properties give authors fine-grained control over bidi: **direction** and **unicode-bidi**. Web authors normally do not need to use them because characters are automatically placed in their normal direction. If, however, you need to make exceptions to the rules that govern bidi content, these properties are your solution. If this unlikely event occurs, we suggest you read the full definition of these properties in the CSS 2.1 specification. For reference purposes, we include the formal definition of the properties.

FF	Op	Sa	IE	Pr		
●	●	●	●	○	Name:	direction
					Value:	ltr | rtl
					Initial:	ltr
					Applies to:	all elements
					Inherited:	yes
					Percentages:	N/A

FF	Op	Sa	IE	Pr		
●	●	◑	●	○	Name:	unicode-bidi
					Value:	normal | embed | bidi-override
					Initial:	normal
					Applies to:	all elements
					Inherited:	no
					Percentages:	N/A

MORE INFORMATION ABOUT FONTS

The Internet offers a lot of information about fonts. A good place to start is the Open Directory's collection of typography links, which is at URL http://dmoz.org/Arts/Graphic_Design/Typography/.

Chapter 6

The fundamental objects

When a document displays on a user's screen, what shows up is not the underlying HTML code. Instead, it is the browser's interpretation of that code. In the absence of any explicit instructions to the contrary, the browser displays the document using a set of default parameters. In HTML, for example, the browser puts **P** elements in separate blocks of text and **LI** elements in blocks with a label on the side, but it does not create a separate block for **EM** elements.

You can affect the basic shape of elements onscreen by using the **display** property. With this property, you can specify that each element be displayed onscreen as one of the following:

- A block of text – For example, paragraphs and headings are usually (but not always) displayed as a text block.
- As part of a line of text – For example, inline elements such **EM** and **SPAN**.
- A list item, a block with a label (number or bullet) on the side – For example, an **LI**.
- A "run-in" header – A header that starts a new block of text but doesn't have a line break after it (see the section, "The run-in value").
- A compact label in the margin, such as the **DT** element in some types of list.
- A cell or row in a table (table layout is explained in Chapter 17, "Tables").

In this chapter, we show you how to use the **display** property to influence the form of elements onscreen. You may think that a heading will always be displayed in its own block or that a list item will always be part of a stepped-out list, with list item on top of list item, but this is not the case. By changing the **display** property, you can create entirely different effects. We give you some examples of how this is done.

In this chapter, we also discuss two related properties:

- **List-style** property (actually a set of four properties), which enables you to create lists with different types of numbers or bullets
- **White-space** property, which lets you control how tabs, newlines, and extra white spaces are handled

This chapter also explains how to insert extra text before and after elements. This is useful if the standard list bullets and numbers are not sufficient, but it can do much more.

THE BOX MODEL

An HTML or XML document consists of elements inside other elements. For example, an **EM** can be inside a **P**, which is inside **BODY**, which is inside **HTML**. In earlier chapters, we showed this as a tree structure, which is a model that helps when we deal with inheritance. This arrangement also could be visualized as a box model, whereby smaller boxes fit inside increasingly larger boxes, as illustrated in Figure 6.1.

Figure 6.1 The box model.

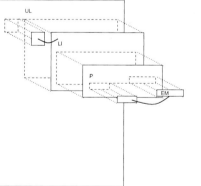

```
<UL>
<LI>
   <P>Text of the first
   item in the list has
   <EM>a few emphasized
   words</EM> in the
   middle.</P>
<LI>...
```

- Text of the first item in the list has *a few emphasized words* in the middle

- ...

The box model can depict the structure of an HTML document. The outermost box is the **HTML** element. The last box contains either text, such as "a few emphasized words" in Figure 6.1, or nothing, such as an empty element like **BR**. In between is everything else – **BODY**, **P**, **HI**, **DIV**, **IMG**, etc. A block-level element, such as **DIV** and **P**, is normally shown as a box on its own. An inline element, such as **EM** and **SPAN**, may be broken into several small boxes, if it is broken across lines. **LI** is commonly displayed as a box with a marker called a *label* – a bullet or number – on the side. The size and position of each element is relative to the enclosing box.

Although in CSS, it looks as if the style properties are added to elements, what happens in fact is that the browser creates a parallel structure: For each element in the source, an object, called a *formatting object*, gets all the properties. The **display** property determines the type of object and thus the type and number of boxes that are created.

The fact that there is a difference between the elements and the formatting objects created from them can safely be ignored by CSS users, but people creating browsers encounter the objects. Formatting objects also plays a role when you deal with highly complex design tasks, where simply formatting the document is not enough, and the document must be transformed in some other way. In that case, you have to switch to a language other than CSS, for example, XSL. XSL has the same formatting objects and the same properties as CSS, but it also provides ways to create more than one formatting object per element and to rearrange the order of the formatting objects. XSL is also more difficult to use.

THE DISPLAY PROPERTY

The **display** property determines whether an element is displayed as a block, inline, list item, or other type of element.

FF   Op   Sa   IE   Pr
◑   ●   ●   ◑   ◑

Name:	display
Value:	inline | block | list-item | run-in | inline-block | marker | table | inline-table | table-row-group | table-header-group | table-footer-group | table-row | table-column-group | table-column | table-cell | table-caption | none
Initial:	inline
Applies to:	all elements
Inherited:	no
Percentages:	N/A

The **display** property has many possible values, but the most common are block and inline. The table values are explained in Chapter 17; the others are explained in the following sections.

The "block" value

An element with a block value starts and ends on a new line. For example, the start tag <h1> starts a box that contains the **H1** element and the end tag </h1> ends the box. Here are some examples from HTML:

```
P { display: block }
H1 { display: block }
DIV { display: block }
```

The "inline" value

An element with an "inline" value does not start and end on a new line. It is displayed in a box set on the same line as the previous content. The dimensions of the box depend on the size of the content. If the content is text, it may span several lines, and there will be a box of text on each line. Familiar examples are **EM**, **STRONG**, and **SPAN**:

```
EM { display: inline }
STRONG { display: inline }
SPAN { display: inline }
```

All elements have a value for the **display** property in the browser's default style sheet and, for HTML, that is usually the one you want, so you don't often have to use the **display** property yourself. But occasionally, you may want to make an **LI** inline or a **SPAN** block. Or you may want to set an element back to its normal display type if you cascade off a style sheet that changes the display of an element.

For XML-based documents, the situation is different. The browser probably doesn't have a default style sheet for them, and thus all elements will be "inline" unless you write **display** properties for them.

The "list-item" value

An element with a "list-item" value is displayed as a box with a label. This value typically applies to the **LI** element of HTML. A series of **LI**s with this value forms either an **OL** or **UL** list.

The **LI** may or may not have a visible label: a bullet or number that appears to the left of the list item. The characteristics of the label are set with the **list-style** property, which is dicussed in the section, "More about lists."

The "none" value

To completely hide an element from view, you can set **display** to none. The element is not displayed at all. An example is a document with questions and answers interleaved: First, you display the document with the answers hidden and after you try to answer the questions, you change to a different style sheet that shows the answers. The first style sheet could contain something like this:

```
.answer { display: none }
```

No boxes are created – not for the element itself and not for its children, either.

The "run-in" value

Although headings of sections are normally displayed in a block of their own, such as the heading above this section, it is also possible to put them on the first line of the first paragraph in the section. The effect looks like this:

The run-in value. Although headings of sections are normally displayed in a block of their own, it is also possible to put them on the first line of the first paragraph in the section.

This is called a *run-in header*. The effect is achieved with two style rules such as the following:

```
H3 { display: run-in }
H3:after { content: ". " }
```

The **content** property and the :after pseudo-element are explained in detail later in this chapter. They are used here to insert a period and a space after the run-in header.

An element can only be displayed run-in if the next element is a block or an inline element. If there is, for example, a list item or a table after the heading, the run-in heading is displayed as a normal block instead.

The "inline-block" value

The inline-block value was added to CSS in the 2.1 edition, but it is already well supported by browsers. The name of the value may first seem like a contradiction in terms — it can't be both inline *and* block-level? Well, sort of. An element with this value is treated as an inline element seen from the outside, but the content inside the box is formatted as a block-level element. Visually, this makes sense (see Figure 6.2).

USING THE DISPLAY PROPERTY

Each HTML element has a default value for the **display** property, but the value can be changed in your style sheet to achieve different effects. An inline element can be "block," a block-level element can be "inline."

For example, instead of placing **LI** elements in separate blocks below each other with the list-item value, you could string them together in a running sentence and separate them by commas or semicolons. You would do this using the value inline.

Figure 6.3 (a) shows a typical **UL** list. The **UL** has its **LI**s set to list-item. The labels (bullets) are set via the **list-style** property, which is discussed in the next section.

Figure 6.2 Lines within lines.

HTML code:	<DIV>Reading between the lines <SPAN>(nudge, nudge)</SPAN> is more cumbersome when there are many lines to read between.</DIV>	
CSS code:	```DIV SPAN { display: inline-block; font-size: 0.6em; width: 3em; }```	```DIV SPAN { display: inline; }```
For-matted result:	Reading between the lines (nudge, nudge) is more cumbersome when there are many lines to read between.	Reading between the lines (nudge, nudge) is more cumbersome when there are many lines to read between.
	(a)	(b)

Figure 6.3 (b) shows the same list, but now with all items following each other on the line – so-called "inline." In this case, the **LI** elements have the value `inline` and there are no labels.

Figure 6.3 Using `list-item` (a) and `inline` (b) to format lists.

HTML code:	```<UL> <LI>item one, <LI>item two, <LI>item three, <LI>item four. </UL>```	
CSS code:	```LI { display: list-item; list-style: disc; }```	```LI { display: inline }```
Format-ted result:	• item one, • item two, • item three, • item four.	item one, item two, item three, item four.
	(a)	(b)

In another example, you can change the **IMG** element, which is normally inline, to become a block-level element. Figure 6.4 (a) shows a paragraph with an inline image in it. In Figure 6.4 (b), the **IMG** element has been set to be block-level and the image takes up a line of its own.

Figure 6.4 (a) An image with the value `inline`; (b) an image with the value `block`.

HTML code:	<P>Text of a paragraph that is interrupted <IMG SRC="http://www.image.file"> by this image.	
CSS code:	IMG { display: inline }	IMG { display: block }
Format-ted result:	Text of a paragraph that is suddenly interrupted by an image.	Text of a paragraph that is suddenly interrupted by an image.
	(a)	(b)

MORE ABOUT LISTS – THE LIST-STYLE PROPERTIES

List items may or may not have a label. If they do, the label is usually a bullet: for example, ● ○ □; or a series of numbers (for example, I, II, III or 1, 2, 3). Lists also may be *nested,* i.e., there can be lists within lists, with each list level having a different type of number or bullet. Labels may be displayed as follows:

- Outside the box that encloses the LI
- To the left of the first line of the LI inside the box

The **list-style** properties specify whether a list-item has a label, what kind of label (if the list item has one), and where it is placed. As mentioned earlier in this chapter, a list may be either stepped-out or run-in, depending on the display property value you choose. The style and position of labels apply only to list items with the **display** property value of `list-item`.

List-style is the most convenient property to use because it sets all aspects of the label together, but you can also use **list-style-type**, **list-style-image**, and **list-style-position** to set individual aspects of the label.

THE LIST-STYLE-TYPE PROPERTY

The **list-style-type** property sets whether there is a label and, if so, its appearance.

FF	Op	Sa	IE	Pr		
●	●	●	◑	◑	**Name:**	list-style-type
					Value:	disc | circle | square | decimal | decimal-leading-zero | lower-roman | upper-roman | lower-alpha | lower-latin | upper-alpha | upper-latin | lower-greek | armenian | georgian | none
					Initial:	disc
					Applies to:	elements with **display** property value "list-item"
					Inherited:	yes
					Percentages:	relative to parent's font size

You can set the style of the label by specifying either a keyword or a URL. The property has nine values that are keywords. They can be divided into groups as follows.

To set the label to a predefined symbol:

- disc (●) – this is the default
- circle (○)
- square (□)

To set the label to a number:

- decimal (1, 2, 3,...)
- decimal-leading-zero (01, 02, 03,...)
- lower-roman (i, ii, iii,...)
- upper-roman (I, II, III,...)
- lower-alpha/lower-latin (a, b, c,...)
- upper-alpha/upper-latin (A, B, C,...)
- lower-greek (classical Greek numbers: α, β, γ)
- armenian, georgian (traditional numbering systems using the Armenian and Georgian scripts, respectively)

The final keyword, none, suppresses the label.

However, none does not suppress the counting in a numbered list. If the next list item has a visible label, it will be two numbers higher than the item before the invisible label. For example, suppose you have a list of three list items and the value of the second item is set to none. The first item will be numbered 1 and the last item will be numbered 3, even though there is no visible number 2 next to the second item. It will look like this:

1 Item with **list-style-type**: decimal
   Item with **list-style-type**: none
3 Item with **list-style-type**: decimal

The following are several examples of rules that set labels:

```
OL { list-style: lower-alpha }     /* a b c d... */
OL { list-style: lower-roman }     /* i ii iii... */
UL UL { list-style: square }       /* square bullet */
LI.nolabel { list-style: none }    /* no label */
UL UL.compact { list-style: circle } /* circle */
```

THE LIST-STYLE-IMAGE PROPERTY

Instead of a number or a predefined symbol, you can also use a (small) image as the label. That is done with the **list-style-image** property.

FF Op Sa IE Pr
●   ●   ●   ●   ○

Name:	list-style-image
Value:	<url> | none
Initial:	none
Applies to:	elements with **display** property value "list-item"
Inherited:	yes
Percentages:	N/A

For example:

```
UL { list-style-image:
   url("http://www.example.com/star.png") }
```

Which might look like this:

★ the first item
★ the second item
★ the third item

If there is a **list-style-image** other than none, it will be used as the label, instead of the **list-style-type**. However, if for some reason, the browser is unable to download or display the image, it will use the **list-style-type** again.

THE LIST-STYLE-POSITION PROPERTY

The **list-style-position** property specifies the position of the list item label: inside or outside the list box.

FF   Op   Sa   IE   Pr
•   •   •   •   •

Name:	list-style-position
Value:	inside | outside
Initial:	outside
Applies to:	elements with **display** property value "list-item"
Inherited:	yes
Percentages:	N/A

This property has two values:

- inside
- outside – This is the default.

Outside places the label outside the list-item box aligned with the first line of text. Inside places the label inside the list item box aligned with the first line of the text. The latter value creates a more compact list. Figure 6.5 compares the results of the two methods, along with the code that produced the results.

THE LIST-STYLE PROPERTY

The **list-style** property is a shorthand means of setting both the label and its position at the same time. Its values are the legal values of the **list-style-type**, **list-style-image**, and **list-style-position** properties. The following are examples:

```
UL { list-style: disc inside }
OL OL { list-style: circle outside }
```

When you set a URL, it's a good idea to also set a keyword so that if the image cannot be displayed, the browser can display the symbol indicated by the keyword; for example:

```
UL.files {
   list-style: url("images/file.png") square }
```

HTML code:	<UL> <LI>A list with labels on the inside. The text forms a box and encloses the label as well as the text. The label is the first thing inside that box. <LI>The second item in this list. Notice how the text aligns under the label, not under the first word of the first line, thus making the list look more compact. </UL>	
CSS code:	```UL { list-style-position: outside }```	```UL { list-style-position: inside }```
Formatted result	• First item of a list with labels on the outside. Note that the label is positioned at the same height as the first line of the text, outside the text block. • The second item in this list. Notice also how the text aligns under the first word of the first line, not under the label.	• A list with labels on the inside. The text forms a box and encloses the label as well as the text. The label is the first thing inside that box. • The second item in this list. Notice how the text aligns under the label, not under the first word of the first line, thus making the list look more compact.
	(a)	(b)

Figure 6.5 (a) A list with labels outside the box; (b) a list with labels inside the box.

Using the **list-style** properties, you can create nested lists with a different numbering style at each level. Suppose you want to create a set of three nested lists. The labels of the first list are decimal: 1, 2, 3, and so on. The labels of the first nested list are upper-alpha: A, B, C, and so on. The labels of the second nested list are upper-roman: I, II, III, and so on. You would write three rules, two of which use contextual selectors:

```
OL { list-style: decimal }
OL OL { list-style: upper-alpha }
OL OL OL { list-style: upper-roman }
```

Here is the resulting list:

1 First item of the first list
2 Second item of the first list
3 Third item of the first list; start of the first nested list

A First item of the first nested list
B Second item of the first nested list; start of the second nested list

    I First item of the second nested list
    II Second item of the second nested list
    III Third item of the second nested list

C Return to the first nested list; back to uppercase letters

4 Back to the first list; back to decimal numbers
5 Fifth and last item of the first list

Note how the numbers align. You cannot change the alignment of the numbers. Nor can you specify the distance between the number and the text. You can, however, control the distance of the text from the left margin by using the **margin-left** property, which we describe in Chapter 8, "Space around boxes."

GENERATED TEXT, COUNTERS, AND QUOTES

Sometimes, text needs to be added that is not in the original source. Examples are texts like "Figure 7" or "Chapter XI," quote marks that are automatically inserted around citations, but also the list bullets and numbers of the previous section.

List bullets and numbers are the most common and are the easiest to specify. Numbering for list items is implicit: There is no explicit mention of a counter in the style sheet. But sometimes, the **list-style** properties are not enough (for example, when lists must be numbered as A1, A2, etc.). For those cases, CSS provides explicit counters. The same explicit counters are also used to number chapters, sections, figures, tables, and so on.

Fixed texts, such as the word "Figure" in "Figure 7," can be inserted together with the counters, or even on their own. A typical case is the insertion of the word "Note:" in front of all paragraphs that constitute notes.

Quotation marks are a special case. Although it is possible to just insert quote marks as fixed texts, in many cases, it is desirable to use different quote marks based on whether the quote is nested inside some other quote or not. CSS has a property **quotes** that automatically track the nesting level of quotations and inserts the quote marks for that level.

The :before and :after pseudo-elements and the content property

One example where you might want to use the style sheet to insert text is in the case of notes. Say you have a paragraph with class "note" that looks like this in the source document:

```
. . .
<P CLASS="note">Steps 22 to 24 should be repeated
for each B-channel.
. . .
```

The way this should look in the formatted output is like this:

Note: Steps 22 to 24 should be repeated for each B-channel. [end of note]

The text "Note:" is inserted at the start, and "[end of note]" at the end. Here are the style rules to achieve this:

```
P.note:before {
   content: "Note: ";
   font-weight: bold }
P.note:after {
   content: " [end of note]" }
```

:before and :after are *pseudo*-elements. They refer to "elements" that do not exist in the source document. You can think of them as elements that, had they existed, would have been just after the start tag and just before the end tag:

```
<P CLASS="note">
  <:before>Note: </:before>
  Steps 22 to 24 should be repeated
  for each B-channel.
  <:after> [end of note]</:after>
</P>
```

The **content** property specifies the text that is in the pseudo-element. This property can only occur in rules for the :before and :after pseudo-elements because all other elements already have content.

FF	Op	Sa	IE	Pr
●	●	●	○	●

Name:	content
Value:	[normal | *<string>* | *<counter>* | open-quote | close-quote | no-open-quote | no-close-quote]+
Initial:	normal
Applies to:	:before and :after pseudo-elements
Inherited:	no
Percentages:	N/A

The initial value of the **content** property is normal, which means that the corresponding pseudo-element contains no content so no box is generated. The property only becomes interesting when the values is set to a sequence of text strings and/or counters and/or quote marks. For example:

```
BLOCKQUOTE:before {
  content: open-quote "quote " counter(bq) ". " }
BLOCKQUOTE:after {
  content: close-quote }
```

The next sections explain the keywords for the quote marks and the counters.

The :before and :after pseudo-elements are inline elements by default. They are put just before the first content of the element, or just after the last content. But sometimes, you may want to put them on a separate line, in a block of their own. If their parent element is a block element, the :before and :after pseudo-elements may themselves also be block elements. That is done with the **display** property. For example, to end an HTML document with the words "The End" centered on a line by themselves, all that is required is

```
BODY:after {
  content: "The End";
  display: block;
  text-align: center;
  margin-top: 1em }
```

The **margin-top** is thrown in to add a little space between the last line of the document and the words "The End."

Generating quote marks

FF	Op	Sa	IE	Pr
●	●	○	○	○

Name:	quotes
Value:	[*<string>* *<string>*]+ | none | inherit
Initial:	browser dependent
Applies to:	all elements
Inherited:	yes
Percentages:	N/A

The simplest way to add quotes elements, such as **BLOCKQUOTE** and **Q**, is with a rule like Q:before {content: '"'}. However, most designers want to change the double quotes to single quotes if the **Q** occurs inside another citation. You can usually do that with contextual selectors (Q Q:after {...}), but CSS2 has an easier solution.

The solution has two parts. The first part is to declare all the quote marks you want to use at each nested level of quotations. A good place to put them is on the **BODY** element in HTML, or on the document's root element in XML-based documents:

```
BODY { quotes: '"' '"' "«" "»" }
```

This defines that the sequence of quote marks for progressively nested levels of quotations is ". . ." for the first citation and «. . .» for the second level of quotations and beyond. After declaring the quotes, all that remains is to write the rules that say which elements get quotes, without saying which quotes, because that will be automatically handled:

```
BLOCKQUOTE:before, Q:before { content: open-quote }
BLOCKQUOTE:after, Q:after { content: close-quote }
```

Now a **BLOCKQUOTE** that is not inside another **BLOCKQUOTE** gets the ". . ." quotes, and if a **Q** or another **BLOCKQUOTE** occurs inside it, it automatically gets the «...» quotes because the browser counts how many quotes have been opened.

Mark	Hex-code	Description
"	\22	Straight double quotation mark
'	\27	Straight single quotation mark ("apostrophe")
"	\201C	Left double quotation mark ("double high 6")
"	\201D	Right double quotation mark ("double high 9")
'	\2018	Left single quotation mark ("single high 6")
'	\2019	Right single quotation mark ("single high 9")
«	\AB	Left-pointing double angle quotation mark ("left guillemets")
»	\BB	Right-pointing double angle quotation mark ("right guillemets")
‹	\2039	Single left-pointing angle quotation mark
›	\203A	Single right-pointing angle quotation mark
„	\201E	Double low-9 quotation mark

Table 6.1 Common quote marks and their hex-codes.

If you look closely at the rule for the **quotes** property in the previous example, you probably find that your keyboard does not have all the necessary keys. The program that you use to type in the style sheets may have special functions for generating them, but if it doesn't, there are other ways to put them in the style sheet. For example, even the simplest text editor allows you to write the rule like this:

```
BODY { quotes: '\201C' '\201D'
  '\2018' '\2019'  '\2039' '\203A' }
```

It may not be immediately clear that \201C is the left double quotation mark ("), but when you are in a bind, this may be the only way out. Table 6.1 shows the most common quote marks and their hex-codes.

Most programs give you the straight quote marks (". . ." and '. . .') when you type the corresponding keys on the keyboard. But look carefully because some programs interpret the keys differently.

Different typographic traditions prefer different quotation marks. Here are some examples in different languages, using the quotes from Table 6.1.

English:

When I read: "The double angle quotation marks are also called 'guillemets'," I knew that they must be French.

```
BODY { quotes: '"' '"' ''' ''' }
```

Dutch:

In een geschiedenisboek las ik: „Van Speyk wilde van overgeven niet horen. 'Dan liever de lucht in,' zei hij."

```
BODY { quotes: '„' '"' ''' ''' }
```

German:

Er sagte: ›Wie wär's mit »Gutentag«?‹

```
BODY { quotes: '›' '‹' '»' '«' }
```

French:

Dans un interview, Emmanuel a expliqué : « Je ne peux pas dire "Oui, je sais comment cela ce passe." Tout cela est ecrit. »

```
BODY { quotes: '«' '»' '"' '"' }
```

In high-quality French typesetting, the guillemets and the single angle marks have half a space between them and the quoted words. The hex-code for a "thin space" (which is half the width of a normal space) is 2009, so you can make French graphic designers happy if you change that last example to the following:

```
BODY { quotes: '«\2009' '\2009»' '"' '"' }
```

In fact, if you look closely, you can see that the French example actually did use this rule; for French, it just looks better. If the half space is not supported by your software, the French will be almost as happy with a non-breaking space:

```
BODY { quotes: '«\A0' '\A0»' '"' '"' }
```

A final note about the "thin space," for people interested in the details. Typography is always a bit more subtle than you think, and the thin space isn't exactly equal to half a normal space, or at least not always, although it is close enough for our purposes. On most systems, a thin space is equal to 1/6 of an em, which works out to be close to half of a normal space for most fonts. But, it depends a bit on the font. For proportional fonts, the normal space is usually between 0.30 and 0.36em (so the thin space is between 46 and 56 percent of the normal space), but for monospace fonts, a space may be as wide as 0.5em (and a thin space is thus no more than 33 percent of a normal space).

Counters

If the numbering provided by the **list-style** property is not enough, you have to resort to explicit counters. For numbering chapter and section titles or tables, there is no other way. Three things can happen to counters: They are used somewhere, they are incremented, or they are reset to zero.

Using counters is only possible in the **content** property. For example, to number notes, you could do the following:

```
P.note:before {
  content: "Note " counter(note) ". " }
```

This inserts the fixed texts "Note" and ". " before every note paragraph, with the value of the "note" counter in between.

For incrementing counters, there is the **counter-increment** property. So, if the note counter must be incremented every time there is a note paragraph, the rule would be as follows:

```
P.note { counter-increment: note }
```

This is enough to number all notes in the document. But sometimes, the style calls for a more sophisticated way of numbering (for example, if notes must be numbered within chapters only). Then, every new chapter must reset the counter to zero. If we assume that chapters start with an **H1** element, this rule suffices:

```
H1 { counter-reset: note }
```

FF	Op	Sa	IE	Pr		
○	●	○	○	●	Name:	counter-increment
					Value:	none | <counter-name>+
					Initial:	none
					Applies to:	all elements
					Inherited:	no
					Percentages:	N/A

FF	Op	Sa	IE	Pr
○	●	○	○	●

Name:	counter-reset
Value:	none | *<counter-name>*+
Initial:	nonen
Applies to:	all elements
Inherited:	no
Percentages:	N/A

counter-increment and **counter-reset** become more difficult if more than one counter needs to be incremented or reset. For example, if the **HI** element resets not only the note counter, but also the counter for subsections and for figures, the rule would have to be similar to this:

```
H1 { counter-reset: note subsection figure }
```

This means you have to be careful when cascading several style sheets together. If one rule said H1 {counter-reset: figure} and later on, there is a style rule H1 {counter-reset: note}, the value of the **counter-reset** property will be just note, and the figure counter will not be reset.

Here is an example that numbers chapters and sections as 1., 1.1, 1.2, . . . 2., 2.1, etc.:

1. Life on the ground

. . .

1.1 Black and red ants

. . .

1.1.1 Ant heaps

. . .

1.1.2 What ants eat

. . .

The style rules that produce this are as follows:

```
H1:before {
  content: counter(chapter) ". ";
  counter-reset: section;
  counter-increment: chapter }
H2:before {
  content: counter(chapter) "." counter(section);
  counter-reset: subsection;
  counter-increment: section }
```

```
H3:before {
  content: counter(chapter) "." counter(section)
    "." counter(subsection);
  counter-increment: subsection }
```

Styles for counters

By default, counters are shown as decimal numbers: 1, 2, 3, ... But, just like list numbers, counters can also use roman numerals, letters, or various non-Western numbering styles. This style is indicated by adding a style keyword after the counter name:

```
counter(chapter, upper-roman)
```

This produces chapter numbers I, II, III, IV, ... All the styles that are available for **list-style** can also be used inside counter. For example, if the appendices of an article have to be numbered "Appendix A," "Appendix B," "Appendix C," etc. and the appendices all start with <H1 class="appendix">, this rule makes that possible:

```
H1.appendix:before {
  content: "Appendix "
    counter(app, upper-alpha) " ";
  counter-increment: app }
```

Self-nesting counters

Numbering schemes such as 1, 1.1, 1.2, 1.2.1, . . . are common. To number the section headings in HTML this way is not difficult. There will be a counter associated with each of **H1**, **H2**, **H3**, to **H6**. But sometimes, things have to be numbered that can nest to arbitrary depth. In HTML, **H6** is as far as you can go with subsections, but lists, for example, can nest to any depth, and all of them are called **OL** and **LI**.

CSS handles that by automatically creating a new counter when an element resets a counter that is already in use. For example, to create lists that look like this:

1 first item in first list
2 second item in first list
2.1 first item in first sub-list
2.2 second item in first sub-list
2.2.1 first item in sub-sub-list

2.2.2 second item in sub-sub-list
2.3 third item in sub-list
2.4 fourth item in sub-list
3 third item in first list

and that can go on to any depth, it is enough to create one counter, say
item-nr, and reset it on every **OL** element. The first **OL** creates the
first item-nr, the second **OL** creates a new item-nr, etc. Each
counter can only be used on element at the same depth on the document tree, or deeper, than the element that reset it. Therefore, the last
item in this list uses the counter created by the topmost **OL**; all the others are "out of scope."

But, how do you insert the number 1.1 into the formatted output? A
declaration like

```
content: counter(item-nr) "." counter(item-nr)
```

does not work, because both counters refer to the same instance of the
"item-nr" counter. Instead, CSS provides a variation of the counter
function, spelled counters with an "s." The correct rule, then, is as follows:

```
LI:before { content: counters(item-nr, ".");
   counter-increment: item-nr }
OL { counter-reset: item-nr }
```

The second argument of counters is the fixed text to put between the
numbers. At the first level, the number will be 1, at the second, 1.1, at
the third, 1.1.1, etc.

Of course, counters also accept a style argument. If the numbers
should be C.B.D, or III.II.IV, the value becomes counters(item-nr,
".", upper-alpha) or counters(item-nr, ".", upper-
roman).

THE WHITE-SPACE PROPERTY

The **white-space** property specifies how tabs, newlines (also known
as line breaks), and extra white space in an element's content are handled.

FF	Op	Sa	IE	Pr
●	●	◐	◐	●

Name:	white-space
Value:	normal | pre | nowrap | pre-wrap | pre-line
Initial:	normal
Applies to:	block elements
Inherited:	yes
Percentages:	N/A

An HTML document may contain unwanted tabs, newlines, and additional white spaces (more than the normal one white space between words). These can be called collectively *white-space characters*. Usually, you'll want those extra white-space characters to be ignored. The browser does this automatically for you and lays out the text in a way that fits the window. It throws away any extra white spaces at the beginning and end of a paragraph and *collapses* (combines) all tabs, newlines, and extra white space between words into single white-space characters. In addition, as the window is resized by the user, the browser reformats the text as needed to fit it in the new window size.

For some elements, you may have specifically formatted the text in such a way that includes extra white-space characters. You don't want those characters thrown away or collapsed. HTML offers two simple ways to control white space: the **PRE** element (which we discussed in Chapter 1, "The Web and HTML") and *non-breaking space*. Here is a simple example that shows how non-breaking space can be used:

```
<P>There will be   three spaces before the
word "three" no matter what the value of the display
property is. Also, there will never be a line break
between "be" and "three."
```

This results in a presentation like this one:

> There will be   three spaces before the word "three" no matter what the value of the display property is. Also, there will never be a line break between "be" and "three."

However, if you want more control over white space characters, you need to use the **white-space** property, and the rest of this chapter describes its various values.

The value "normal" of the **white-space** property causes all extra white-space characters in the element to be ignored or collapsed. This is the default behavior for all HTML elements, except the **PRE** element. The behavior of the **PRE** element is described by the pre value of the **WHITE-SPACE** property. All browsers, therefore, use this rule internally:

```
PRE { white-space: pre }
```

The left margin note: *If you wonder why tabs are interpreted in this strange way, it has to do with the traditional way tabs are displayed on computer terminals. Especially in the first pages on the Web, the* **PRE** *element was mostly used for displaying computer code; that's why it made sense to interpret a tab as a jump to the next multiple of eight.*

The pre value causes all extra white space to be retained and newlines to cause line breaks. It also causes tabs to be converted into spaces according to a certain formula. The tab is replaced by from 1 to 8 spaces so that the last one is at a column that is a multiple of 8. For example, suppose there are 52 characters to the left of the tab. The browser inserts 4 spaces to reach the nearest multiple of 8, that is, 56. So, the next character after the tab ends up as the 57th character of the line. This effect is all right when you use a monospaced (fixed-width) font, but it looks strange when it's used with a proportional-spaced (variable-width) font. Here is how it looks with a monospaced font:

```
These words have been aligned    with
tabs so that     the letters align   nicely?
```

And this is with a proportional font. The number of spaces that are inserted is the same, but that doesn't cause the words to be aligned:

These words   have been aligned   with

tabs so that   the letters align   nicely?

The **PRE** value also suppresses justification. We discuss justification in Chapter 7.

Figure 6.6 compares the results of the normal and pre values on an example paragraph of text.

Although the value pre can make text look strange it can be a very useful value in other cases. Here is an example that uses the **PRE** element and a **CLASS** attribute to create an element that is specialized for simple poems:

```
<HEAD>
  <TITLE>A poem</TITLE>
  <STYLE>
    PRE.poem {
      white-space: pre;
      font-family: serif
    }
```

HTML code:	`<P> This is a paragraph`
	`with some    random             tabs`
	`        and       lots of        spaces. (It may`
	`    have     been`
	`the result of    some hasty copying and`
	`        pasting.)`	

CSS code:	`P {white-space: normal}`	`P {white-space: pre}`

Format-ted result:	This is a paragraph with some random tabs and lots of spaces. (It may have been the result of some hasty copying and pasting.)	This is a paragraph
		with some random tabs
		     and lots of spaces. (It may
		  have been
		the result of some hasty copying and
		     pasting.)

	(a)	(b)

Figure 6.6 The result of formatting the example paragraph with two values for the **white-space** property. In (a) with value "normal"; in (b) with value "pre."

```
    </STYLE>
    </HEAD>
    <BODY>
      <H1>A poem</H1>
      <PRE CLASS="poem">
In this little poem
all white space counts
      therefore this line
      and also this
were indented with four spaces
exactly as much
as between this word      and this.</PRE>
    </BODY>
```

Here is the result:

A poem
In this little poem
all white space counts
      therefore this line
      and also this
were indented with four spaces
exactly as much
as between this word   and this.

The **white-space** property has three other values that are not widely used, but are useful when you need them: nowrap, pre-wrap, and pre-line. The last two of these were added in CSS 2.1.

The nowrap value collapses extra white space like normal, but it won't automatically break lines that are too long. Line breaks occur only when there is a <br> in the text. The example paragraph would be all on one line, which is too long to show on this page.

The pre-wrap value behaves like the pre value except that additional line breaks are inserted whenever necessary by the browser. This avoids losing content on the sides when, for example, the browser window is narrow.

The pre-line value behaves like the normal value except that line breaks in the text are honored. So, if you dislike putting **BR** elements in you code, but would like to insert line breaks at will, this value may be useful.

Chapter 7

Space inside boxes

Extra space in and around elements on a page can enhance your presentation and help get your message across to the reader. Along with influencing color (Chapter 10, "Colors") and fonts (Chapter 5, "Fonts"), influencing spacing has been high on the wishlists of Web-page designers.

Before CSS, there were three ways to control space in HTML:

- *Elements* – Recall that browsers normally throw away white space characters: newlines, tabs, and extra white spaces (any more than the usual one space between words). However, inside the **PRE** element, these characters are preserved with their original meanings. By using **PRE**, designers have used white space characters to achieve, for example, a crude multicolumn layout. Other HTML tags also have been used in unexpected ways. For example, some designers rely on empty **P** elements or **BR** elements to increase vertical spacing and on **BLOCKQUOTE** to indent paragraphs. Often, the results are different in different browsers.

- *Images* – Recall from Chapter 1, "The Web and HTML," that we talked about the use of images as substitutes for text. Text has often been rendered as an image, because, in this way, every pixel can be controlled. Also, to make minor spacing adjustments, some designers insert transparent images into the text. For example, they indent a paragraph by placing five 1-pixel images at the beginning of each paragraph. However, using images has a downside: They are not scalable from one screen resolution to another, they are not very accessible, and they make the page download slower.

- *Tables* — The use of tables is the most recent and most "advanced" method for controlling space in HTML. Tables offer layout capabilities beyond CSS1 (although not beyond CSS2). Unlike images, they are scalable from one screen resolution to another. The downside of tables is that the HTML markup is complicated. Tables also take longer to render and are bad for accessibility. We talked about the use of tables also in Chapter 1.

Occasionally, there may still be no other way to realize a certain effect. However, these methods do not offer the depth of functionality for influencing space in your documents that CSS does. By using CSS, you can greatly expand your control of spacing in and around block-level elements and replaced elements. In this chapter, we show you how you control spacing inside a box: between letters, between words, and between lines. In the next chapter, we deal with spacing around the box: margins, padding, and floating boxes.

SPACE INSIDE BLOCK-LEVEL ELEMENTS

You can affect the space inside a block-level element by changing the amount of space between letters, words, lines, or paragraphs and by varying the alignment of text. Six properties help you influence space inside paragraphs:

- **text-align**
- **text-indent**
- **line-height**
- **word-spacing**
- **letter-spacing**
- **vertical-align**

These, plus the font properties discussed in Chapter 5, give you significant amount of control over your document's appearance.

Among these six properties, **text-align**, **text-indent**, and **line-height** are used most often because they are the primary means of expressing the character of the text and of safeguarding readability. The other three, **word-spacing**, **letter-spacing**, and **vertical-align**, are usually used only to achieve special, localized effects. In the following sections, we discuss each of the six properties.

THE TEXT-ALIGN PROPERTY

The **text-align** property sets the way the lines are adjusted horizontally between the left and right margins of the element.

FF Op Sa IE Pr
●   ●   ●   ●   ●

Name:	text-align
Value:	left | right | center | justify | <string>
Initial:	UA-specific
Applies to:	block-level elements
Inherited:	yes
Percentages:	N/A

This property has four values:

- left — Lines are aligned at the left margin; the right margin is ragged (uneven). Sometimes called *left-justified*.
- right — Lines are aligned at the right margin; the left margin is ragged. Sometimes called *right-justified*.
- center — Lines are individually centered in the middle of the box; both the right and left margins are ragged.
- justified — Lines are aligned on both the left and right margins; text is spread out between the margins as evenly as possible. Sometimes called *fully justified*.

Figure 7.1 shows each type of alignment.

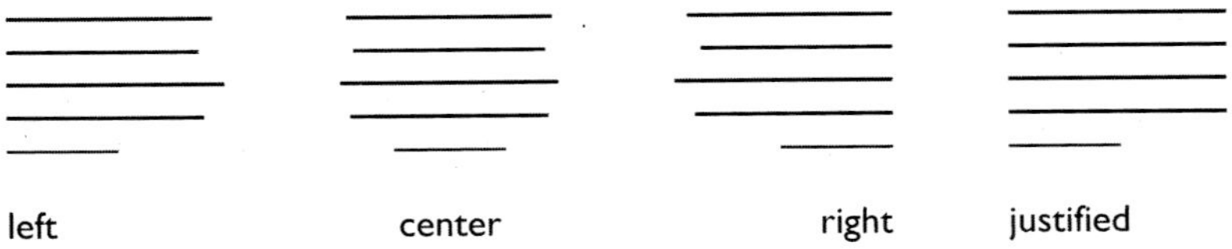

Figure 7.1 The four types of horizontal alignment with **text-align**.

left   center   right   justified

Here's an example rule for changing the alignment of a **P** element from the default to center:

```
P { text-align: center }
```

The **text-align** property is inherited, so you can set the alignment of the entire document by using the **BODY** element as follows, where we change the alignment from the default to justify:

```
BODY { text-align: justify }
```

Note: Alignment of text is relative to the width of the element, not the width of the canvas. For example, the text of an element with **text-align** set to center will be centered between the margins of the element, regardless of where the element is positioned on the canvas. Hence, the text may not appear centered on the canvas.

RIGHT ALIGNING TEXT

The most common alignments are left, justified, and centered. Right aligning text – placing it against the right margin – is seldom done in languages that are written and read from left to right, such as English, at least not for long stretches of text. It is too difficult to read in large amounts. Its use is usually reserved for titles, cells in a table, and special design effects. Examples of these three are shown in Figure 7.2.

Another use for right is the closing signature in a letter. The traditional layout of letters in many languages is for a signature to be aligned against the right margin. Here's how you would code this. Figure 7.2(d) shows the result.

```
<STYLE>
  P.date, P.closing, P.signature {
    text-align: right }
  P.opening, P.closing { margin-top: 1.2em }
  P.opening { margin-bottom: 1.2em }
</STYLE>

<P CLASS="date">Nice, March 3, 1999
<P CLASS="opening">Dear reader,
<P>We hope you enjoyed reading the book so far.
But don't stop now! There is more to come. We close
this letter with a European-style, right-aligned
closing:
<P CLASS="closing";>With kind regards,<BR>
The authors
```

Figure 7.2 Examples of right-aligned text: (a) a right-aligned heading; (b) a table with right-aligned text in the first column; (c) right-aligned "side-heads;" (d) a letter with a right-aligned date and signature.

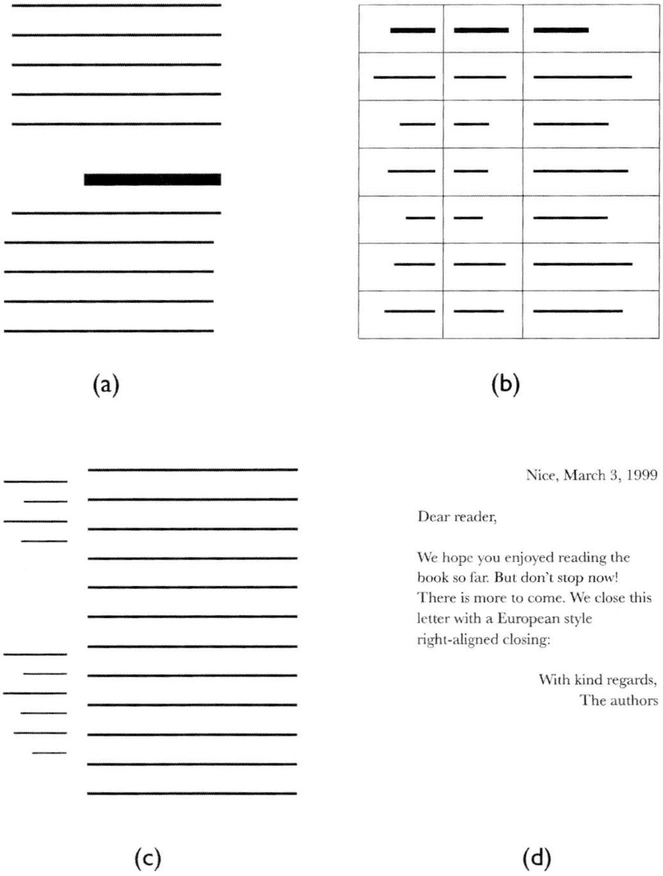

(a)

(b)

(c)

(d)

Nice, March 3, 1999

Dear reader,

We hope you enjoyed reading the book so far. But don't stop now! There is more to come. We close this letter with a European style right-aligned closing:

With kind regards,
The authors

JUSTIFYING TEXT

Justified text is text that is spaced out from the left to right margin so that the texts fills the space between the margins. For the value `justify`, CSS does not specify how text is stretched, or spaced out, as part of distributing it between the margins. Some implementations stretch only the spaces between the words. Others may stretch the spaces between the letters as well. Yet others may occasionally shrink spaces instead (and thus put more words on a line). Which method is used depends on the browser and on the language in which the text is displayed.

HTML has a special *entity* for manually hyphenating words: ­ ("soft hyphen"). When you insert it in the middle of a word, like this: hy­phen­ate, a browser may break the word at the position of the entity. If the word is not broken, the entity remains invisible. Unfortunately, at the time of writing (end of 2004), there are still browsers that insert a hyphen for every ­ without breaking the word.

In languages with long words, you may want to avoid justifying lines, unless the lines are relatively long. Long words are often stretched out to fill the line, sometimes resulting in too much space between the letters. You may have noticed this effect in newspapers, in which full justification can create rivers of white running down through a column of type. One alternative is to use hyphens. CSS2 doesn't support hyphenation. Future versions of CSS may allow you to control hyphenation. At that time, justifying such languages would be feasible, although perhaps at the trade-off of splitting words. In the meantime, you can manually insert hyphens if you want to achieve a better-looking justified appearance.

Not all browsers support justify. Those that don't usually supply a replacement, typically left in Western languages.

THE TEXT-INDENT PROPERTY

The **text-indent** property specifies the indentation of the first line of a paragraph. In a left-to-right language, such as English or French, the indentation is added to the left of the first line. In a right-to-left language, such as Arabic or Hebrew, it is added to the right of the first line.

FF	Op	Sa	IE	Pr
•	•	•	•	•

Name:	text-indent
Value:	*<length>* | *<percentage>*
Initial:	0
Applies to:	block-level elements
Inherited:	yes
Percentages:	refer to parent element's width

This property has two values:

- A length – An absolute or relative number.
- A percentage – A percentage of the width of the paragraph; for example, 10% means indent the first line by 10 percent of the width of the paragraph.

text-indent is an inherited property. Only the computed value is passed on. That is, the amount of indentation is computed once for the parent element and the *result* is inherited by all of its children. The value is not computed again in its child elements even if they have a different font size. For example, if the current font size of the parent element is 10pt and the amount of indentation is set to 2em, child elements will inherit an indent of 20pt, no matter what their own font size is (10pt × 2 = 20pt). Negative values are allowed, although some browsers may not be able to display them.

USING THE TEXT-INDENT PROPERTY

Indenting first lines is more common in fiction than in technical texts. Some people consider it old-fashioned, although a large indent may look quite modern again. At the same time, a too-large indent can hamper readability.

Perhaps the best and most common reason for choosing to indent the first line is that it is a good way to indicate the start of a paragraph. That's why we used it in this book. Also, when used in this way, you can save space within the document. Without the indent, paragraphs must have extra space between them so that one paragraph can be distinguished from another. This adds to the length of the document. See Figure 7.3(b), which was achieved using this rule:

```
P { text-indent: 1em }
```

Interesting effects can be achieved with *negative* indents. A negative indent causes the first line to stick out, outside the bounding box of the paragraph. Some newspapers use this effect to distinguish commentaries from news articles, or to give a distinct visual appearance. Figure 7.3(c) shows a negative indent, achieved using this rule:

```
P { text-indent: -1em }
```

However, you have to be careful when using negative indents; otherwise, unexpected effects may result. Figure 8.5 in Chapter 8, "Space around boxes," shows an example of a negative indent that is too large: part of the first word ends up outside the window. This resulted from input like this:

```
BODY { margin-left; 2em }
P { text-indent: -4em }
```

Similarly, an effect that may actually be desirable from a design perspective is when the first word overlaps something that is to the left of the text, such as a floating image. Code like this could produce that result:

```
P { text-indent: -4em }
IMG { float: left; margin: 2em }
```

This effect is shown in Figure 7.3(d).

text-indent indents only the first line of any element. However, some elements have a first line that is actually inside another element. In this case, **text-indent** may not be able to indent the first line. Here's an example of how this works. A style sheet with these specifications

```
DIV { text-indent: 2em }
P { text-indent: 0em }
```

and a document with this text

```
<DIV><P>A nonindented paragraph...</DIV>
```

results in the paragraph not having any indentation. This is because the first line of **DIV** occurs *inside* another element, **P**, which has a **text-indent** of 0. The 0em value of **P** overrides the 2em value of **DIV**.

On the other hand, an element may appear to consist of several paragraphs, but it is actually a paragraph that is interrupted by another element. It will still have only one first line and, hence, only that first line will be indented by **text-indent**. For example, suppose you were to specify this style sheet:

```
P { text-indent: 2em }
```

and interrupt a paragraph element with a **BR** element; this would be the result:

```
<P>This is a paragraph
broken by another element.
<BR><BR>
This line is not indented.
```

    This is a paragraph broken by another element.

This line is not indented.

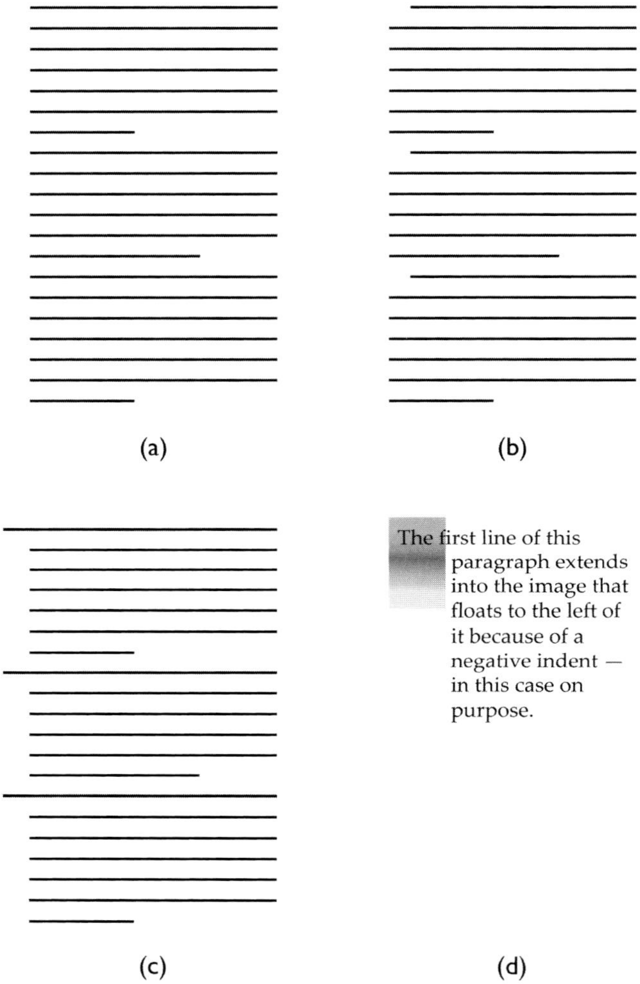

Figure 7.3 Using the
text-indent property to indent
paragraphs: (a) a nonindented
paragraph; (b) a regular indented
paragraph; (c) a negative indented
paragraph; (d) a negative indent
with a large indent that was done
intentionally to achieve a particular design effect.

(a)

(b)

The first line of this
paragraph extends
into the image that
floats to the left of
it because of a
negative indent —
in this case on
purpose.

(c)

(d)

THE LINE-HEIGHT PROPERTY

The **line-height** property specifies how far apart the lines in a paragraph are. Or more precisely, it specifies the *minimum* distance between
the baselines of the adjacent lines.

Figure 7.4 shows schematically what the **line-height** specifies.

Figure 7.4 What the

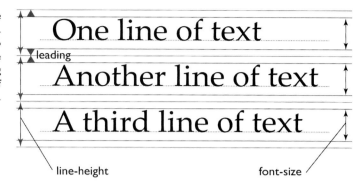

Figure 7.4 What the **line-height** property measures. The added space in addition to the font size is often called the *leading*. In CSS, half of the leading is inserted above the text and half of it below.

FF Op Sa IE Pr

Name:	line-height
Value:	*<number>*	*<length>*	*<percentage>*
Initial:	UA-specific
Applies to:	all elements
Inherited:	yes
Percentages:	relative to the font size of the element itself

This property has three values:

- number
- length
- percentage

The length value is either an absolute value (e.g. 1cm, 0.5in, 15mm, 20pt, 2.3pc) or a relative value (e.g. 1.2em). A common absolute value for **line-height** is 12pt for a 10pt font.

The number and percentage values, as well as a length value with an em unit, operate similarly to each other, with an important difference. In principle, all three are interpreted as relative to the font size; if we assume a font size of 10pt, a line height of 1.2 means the line height is set to 12pt (1.2 times the font size). A percentage value works similarly: If the value is set to 120%, the resulting line height of a 10pt font is again 12pt (120% × 10pt). In the same manner, a value of 1.2em means 1.2 × 10 = 12pt.

However, they differ in how they handle inheritance. A line height specified as a number is computed for the parent *and for each child*. The line height corresponding to the percentage and the em is computed once and the *result* is inherited by all children. (This is true for all prop-

% a em

erties that allow a percentage or em unit as the value.) Of the three methods for calculating the value, the number method is preferred.

Figure 7.5(a) shows the effect of using the percentage value. Figure 7.5(b) shows the effect on the same text using the number value. In (a), the paragraph has a line height of 120% times the font size of the body (10pt), which computes to a line height of 12pt. The quote is printed in a smaller font, but the line height is not changed. The value of 12pt is inherited, which may be what the author wanted, but then again, it may not be. In Figure 7.5(b), the paragraph has a line height of 1.2 times its own font size, which again computes to 12pt. The quote is printed in a smaller font, but this time, the line height is changed with it because the line height is inherited as a factor, not as a fixed size.

A rule of thumb in calculating line height is to start with a value that is 20 percent more than the font size, either a number value of 1.2 or a percentage of 120%. From there, you can then adjust to create whatever effect you seek.

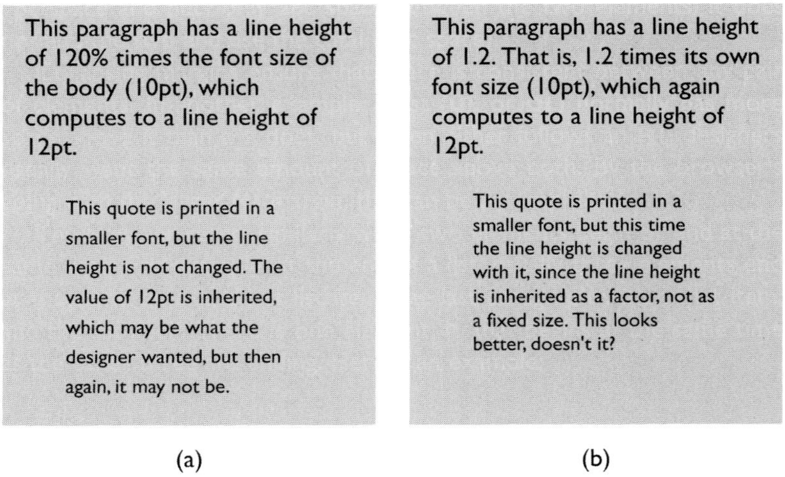

Figure 7.5 (a) The effect of setting the **line-height** of the body with a percentage; (b) setting the same **line-height**, but with a number.

This paragraph has a line height of 120% times the font size of the body (10pt), which computes to a line height of 12pt.

> This quote is printed in a smaller font, but the line height is not changed. The value of 12pt is inherited, which may be what the designer wanted, but then again, it may not be.

(a)

This paragraph has a line height of 1.2. That is, 1.2 times its own font size (10pt), which again computes to a line height of 12pt.

> This quote is printed in a smaller font, but this time the line height is changed with it, since the line height is inherited as a factor, not as a fixed size. This looks better, doesn't it?

(b)

```
<STYLE>
  BODY { font-size: 10pt; line-height: 120% }
  BLOCKQUOTE { font-size: 8pt }
</STYLE>
<BODY>
<P>This paragraph has a line height of 120% times
the font size of the body (10pt), which computes to a
line height of 12pt.
<BLOCKQUOTE>
<P>This quote is printed in a smaller font, but
the line height is not changed. The value of 12pt is
```

```
inherited, which may be what the designer wanted, but
then again, it may not be.
</BLOCKQUOTE>
</BODY>
```

and

```
<STYLE>
  BODY { font-size: 10pt; line-height: 1.2 }
  BLOCKQUOTE { font-size: 8pt }
</STYLE>
<BODY>
<P>This paragraph has a line height of 1.2 times
its own font size, which again computes to 12pt.
<BLOCKQUOTE>
<P>This quote is printed in a smaller font, but
this time the line height is changed with it, since the
line height is inherited as a factor, not as a fixed
size. This looks better, doesn't it?
</BLOCKQUOTE>
</BODY>
```

USING THE LINE-HEIGHT PROPERTY

The line height has a large effect on the character and the readability of text. Specifying a line height is often not just a matter of plugging in a standard value. Many factors go into deciding how large or small a line height should be for a given situation. These factors include the font's size, its appearance (e.g., fancy versus plain), its x-height, the lengths of its ascenders and descenders, and the length of the line of text.

For example, large line heights are sometimes used in advertisements, where a profoundly modern look is called for, even if the result reduces readability. In comparison, titles, which are typically a larger font and usually short in length, often look better with a smaller line height. A font with relatively long ascenders and a small x-height introduces a lot of visual space between lines, so you can use a smaller line height. In contrast, relatively short ascenders and large x-height can seem to reduce the visual space between lines. Thus, you can use a larger line height.

On the other hand, small line heights may force lines too close together, thereby interfering with readability. Longer lines often need extra space between them to guide the eyes on their way back from the end of one line to the start of the next. Shorter lines can often tolerate a smaller line height. An effect similar to double spacing can be achieved by setting the line height to 2.0. This is too much for most cases, but it is sometimes required.

Because this property specifies the *minimum* distance between the baselines of the lines, an inline element with a larger line height or an inline image may cause lines to be farther apart than expected.

THE WORD-SPACING PROPERTY

The **word-spacing** property enables you to adjust the amount of spacing between words. Each font has a normal word spacing – the amount of space that is put between words – that should be used in the "ideal" situation (ideal according to the font's designer). Browsers try to use this value. However, you may sometimes want to achieve certain effects with your text by expanding or shrinking the word spacing.

FF	Op	Sa	IE	Pr
●	●	●	●	○

Name:	word-spacing
Value:	normal | *<length>*
Initial:	normal
Applies to:	all elements
Inherited:	yes
Percentages:	N/A

There are two values:

- normal – Word spacing is left up to the browser. This is the default.
- Length – Either an absolute or relative value.

Any length value is added to the normal word spacing; thus, 0 and normal mean the same thing.

word-spacing is an inherited property. The amount of word spacing is computed once for the parent element and the *result* is inherited by all of its children. The value is not computed again for its child elements even if they have a different font size. For example, if the current font size of the parent element is 10pt and the word spacing is set to 1em, its child elements will inherit a word spacing of 10pt no matter their font size.

The value can be negative, provided the resulting amount of word spacing is not negative. What happens if the original word spacing minus the set value of **word-spacing** is less than 0 is undefined. Some browsers act as if the resulting space is 0; others may actually overlap the words.

Here are example rules of the use of the **word-spacing** property:

```
H1 { word-spacing: 15mm }
P { word-spacing: 0.4em }
```

In the first case, the space between words will be increased by 15mm and in the second case, the space will increase by 0.4em.

USING THE WORD-SPACING PROPERTY

To make the text appear slightly more open or dense, or to waste or gain some space, use the **word-spacing** property to specify the amount of space to be added or subtracted from the normal word spacing. Figure 7.6 shows an example of text with normal word spacing and the same text with extra word spacing and less word spacing. Increasing or decreasing the distance between words should be done in moderation. Generally, only small changes should be made if your intention is to improve readability.

Figure 7.6 Three different levels of word spacing: (a) normal; (b) more than normal word spacing; (c) less than normal word spacing.

(a) A text with some word spacing
```
(word-spacing: normal)
```

(b) A text with some word spacing
```
(word-spacing: 0.25em)
```

(c) A text with some word spacing
```
(word-spacing: -0.125em)
```

Justifying a line with **text-align** set to justify often causes the word spacing to stretch or shrink. Text is justified starting from the adjusted word spacing. A browser may use any of many different algorithms to justify text, but the better algorithms ensure that the average space in the paragraph is close to the adjusted word spacing. You may want to adjust the word spacing to improve the text's appearance.

THE LETTER-SPACING PROPERTY

The **letter-spacing** property lets you adjust the amount of spacing that occurs between letters. Similarly to word spacing, each font has a normal *letter spacing* — the amount of space between letters — that should be used in the "ideal" situation (as determined by the font's designer). Although browsers try to use this value, you may sometimes want to achieve certain effects with your text by expanding or shrinking the letter spacing.

FF	Op	Sa	IE	Pr		
●	●	●	●	○	Name:	letter-spacing
					Value:	normal | *<length>*
					Initial:	normal
					Applies to:	all elements
					Inherited:	yes
					Percentages:	N/A

This property has two values:

- `normal` — Letter-spacing is left up to the browser. This is the default.
- Length — Either absolute or relative.

letter-spacing is an inherited property. The actual value is passed on. That is, the amount of letter spacing is computed once for the parent element and the *result* is inherited by all of its children. The value is not computed again for its child elements even if they have a different font size. For example, if the current font size of the parent element is 10pt and the letter spacing is set to 0.5em, its child elements will inherit a letter spacing of 5pt regardless of their font size.

The value can be negative, but browsers may have limitations on how far negative the value can be. Some browsers act as if the resulting space is 0; others may actually overlap the letters.

Here are examples of using the **letter-spacing** property:

```
BLOCKQUOTE { letter-spacing: 0.04in }
P { letter-spacing: 0.1em }
```

In the first case, the space between letters will be increased by 0.04in. and in the second case, the space is increased by 0.1em.

USING THE LETTER-SPACING PROPERTY

As with word spacing, increasing or decreasing the distance between the letters in a word should be done with moderation. Begin with small amounts if your intention is to improve readability.

Adjusting the letter spacing is seldom done in running text. When it is used, it is often because tradition calls for it. For example, a publisher producing a "critical edition" (a book comparing different versions of another book) often demands that letter spacing be used in certain types of footnotes. Professional designers often frown on the use of letter spacing for anything other than titles because it interferes with the spacing between the letters of a font. The font's designer has usually carefully determined the optimal distance between each pair of letters – ab, bo, bi, Bl, and so on – to achieve a uniform look for all pairs. Some pairs, such as VA, require less space between them, otherwise they look too spaced. Simply adding or subtracting a fixed amount of space is likely to give less-than-pleasing results. Increasing the spacing may cause nonuniform distribution of white space. Decreasing the spacing may cause some letters to touch each other while others don't. Also, if the shapes of certain combinations of letters don't match very well, the font designer may have provided ligatures to replace them. However, when a nonzero **letter-spacing** value is requested, those ligatures must be abandoned, and you end up with a displeasing match of characters.

Justification may also affect letter spacing. With the normal value, the browser is free to change the letter spacing to justify text. By setting letter spacing explicitly to 0 or another length value, you prevent the browser from doing this. A 0 value means the letter spacing will not be changed, while any other length value means the browser must change the letter spacing by that exact amount.

Figure 7.7 shows examples of two fonts, each with normal letter spacing, less than normal letter spacing, and more than normal letter spacing.

Figure 7.7 Examples of **letter-spacing**, using Helvetica and Times as examples: (a) normal text; (b) positive letter spacing; (c) negative letter spacing. As the examples show, letter spacing is useful for uppercase, but much less for lowercase text.

(a)
A normal line of text – AND UPPERCASE
A normal line of text – AND UPPERCASE

(b)
A stretched line of text – AND UPPERCASE
A stretched line of text – AND UPPERCASE

(c)
A condensed line of text – AND UPPERCASE
A condensed line of text – AND UPPERCASE

You may sometimes want to adjust the letter spacing to achieve a certain dramatic effect. For example, stretching a word is an alternative way of emphasizing it. This was commonly done in the nineteenth century, especially in German books, primarily because the font used in them didn't have an italic variant. (Onscreen, there are many other ways to emphasize text besides italicizing it; for example, by using color.) Figure 7.8 shows text in German Fraktur font with the word "emphasizing" stretched to draw attention to it.

Figure 7.8 Example of stretching a word for emphasis. This used to be common with the German Fraktur font, which is shown here.

Stretching a word can sometimes be used as an alternative way of e m p h a s i z i n g it. It used to be a quite common device in the nineteenth century, especially in German books. One of the main reasons being that the font they used did not have an italic variant.

Today, explicit letter spacing is still used in titles; often extreme values are used to achieve extreme effects. Figure 7.9 shows examples.

Figure 7.9 Examples of letter spacing: (a) 1em; (b) 0.7em; (c) -0.25em for the word "NARROW" and 0.3em for "WIDE."

(a)
New! bubble gum that lasts *l o n g e r . . .*

(b)
T O O L A T E

(c)
This new wall-to-wall carpet will fit in NARROW and also in W I D E rooms

THE VERTICAL-ALIGN PROPERTY

The **vertical-align** property lets you raise or lower letters, as well as images, above or below the baseline of text.

FF Op Sa IE Pr
•   •   •   •   •

Name:	vertical-align
Value:	baseline | sub | super | top | text-top | middle | bottom | text-bottom | <percentage>| <length>
Initial:	baseline
Applies to:	inline elements
Inherited:	no
Percentages:	refer to the line height of the element itself

Text is normally aligned on an invisible baseline. The bottoms of the letters are on the baseline no matter what the style, weight, or even size of the letters. Sometimes, a letter or a word has to be raised above the baseline or lowered below the baseline. This is the case with abbreviations that must be superscripted, such as N° (numero), Mme (Madame), and Mlle (Mademoiselle) and for simple mathematics that must be superscripted or subscripted, such as y^2 or x_i.

vertical-align applies to inline elements, including replaced elements (images) that are inline. These images can be put on the baseline, centered vertically between lines, aligned with the top of the letters, or any of several other possibilities.

This property has three types of values: a keyword, a length, and a percentage. Six of the eight available keywords are relative to the parent:

- `baseline` – Aligns the baseline of the child element with the baseline of its parent. This is the default. An element without a baseline, such as an image or object, has its bottom aligned with the parent's baseline.
- `sub` – Subscripts the element, that is, aligns the baseline of the element with its parent's preferred position for subscripts. That position normally depends on the font of the parent. If the font does not explicitly define those positions, the browser chooses a "reasonable" (browser-specific) position.
- `super` – Superscripts the element, that is, aligns the baseline of the element with its parent's preferred position for superscripts. That position normally depends on the font of the parent. If the font does

not explicitly define those positions, the browser chooses a "reasonable" (browser-specific) position.

- `text-top` – Aligns the top of the element with the top of its parent's tallest letters. Some people prefer this way of aligning instead of using the value "super."
- `middle` – Aligns the vertical midpoint of the element (typically an image) with the baseline plus half the x-height of its parent element, that is, the middle of the parent's lowercase letters. More precisely, the element is centered on a line 0.5ex above the baseline.
- `text-bottom` – Aligns the bottom of the element with the bottom of its parent's font.

Here are some example rules using these values of the **vertical-align** property:

```
SUP { vertical-align: super; font-size: 7pt }
SUB { vertical-align: sub; font-size: 7pt }
SPAN.index { vertical-align: sub }
IMG.initial { vertical-align: middle }
```

Figure 7.10 shows examples of the various alignments that can be obtained using these six values of the **vertical-align** property.

Figure 7.10 Different ways to vertically align the triangle: (a) baseline; (b) sub; (c) super; (d) text-top; (e) middle; (f) text-bottom.

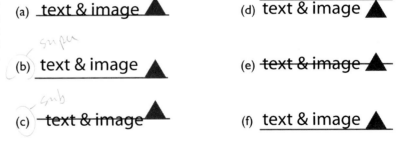

The "top" and "bottom" keywords

The last two keywords, `top` and `bottom`, have definitions that look no more difficult than those of the six just described. The element with **vertical-align** set to `top` will have its top aligned with the top of the tallest thing on the line. The value `bottom` aligns the bottom of the element with the bottom of the lowest thing on the line. Sounds easy enough, doesn't it? Ah, but there's a snake in the grass.

An object that is aligned top or bottom can only be aligned with things that aren't themselves aligned top or bottom, or undefined situations may arise. Figure 7.11 shows an example: Images 1 and 2 are aligned top and bottom, respectively, but they are aligned to the top and bottom of the text, not to each other, even though they are taller than the text. If they would be aligned to each other, there would be a question as to whether image 1 was aligned to the top of 2 or 2 to the top of 1, and, moreover, where they would be relative to the text.

By the way, there doesn't actually have to be text on the line. The vertical alignment is done as if there was some text with the font size of the paragraph, in addition to whatever else there is on the line.

Figure 7.11 Images 1 and 2 are aligned top, resp., bottom.

The value as a percentage or length

Apart from using the keywords, you may also specify a percentage or length as a value that indicates by how much the element is to be raised or lowered. A value of 50% means the element will be raised by half the element's line height (all elements have a **line-height** property, even images). Negative values lower the element similarly. Here is an example:

```
He climbed higher,
<SPAN STYLE="vertical-align: 50%">
and higher,</SPAN>
<SPAN STYLE="vertical-align: 100%">
and higher still...</SPAN>
<SPAN STYLE="vertical-align: -100%">
until he fell</SPAN>
<SPAN STYLE="vertical-align: -200%">
down!</SPAN>
```

He climbed higher, and higher, and higher still...

until he fell

down!

THE CURSOR PROPERTY

The last property of the chapter is **cursor**. It does not affect space inside boxes, but it describes box-centric behavior: what type of cursor to use when the pointer is inside a box.

FF	Op	Sa	IE	Pr
◑	◑	◑	●	○

Name:	cursor
Value:	[[<*url*> ,]* [auto | crosshair | default | pointer | move | e-resize | ne-resize | nw-resize | n-resize | se-resize | sw-resize | s-resize | w-resize | text | wait | help | progress]]
Initial:	auto
Applies to:	all elements
Inherited:	yes
Percentages:	N/A

The values of the property are described here along with suggested cursor images:

+	crosshair	A simple crosshair (e.g., short line segments resembling a plus sign).
	default	The platform-dependent default cursor. Often rendered as an arrow.
	pointer	The cursor is a pointer that indicates a link.
	move	Indicates something is to be moved.
	e-resize	Indicates that the eastern edge is to be moved.
	ne-resize	Indicates that the north-eastern edge is to be moved.
	nw-resize	Indicates that the north-western edge is to be moved.
	n-resize	Indicates that the northern edge is to be moved.

↖	`se-resize`	Indicates that the south-eastern edge is to be moved.
↙	`sw-resize`	Indicates that the south-western edge is to be moved.
↕	`s-resize`	Indicates that the southern edge is to be moved.
↔	`w-resize`	Indicates that the western edge is to be moved.
I	`text`	Indicates text that may be selected.
⧗	`wait`	Indicates that the program is busy and the user should wait.
⬉	`help`	The program is performing some processing, but the user may still interact with the program.

The initial value of the property is `auto`, which lets the browser choose which cursor to use. Also, a URL pointing to an external cursor can be specified.

The property accepts a comma-separated list of values. For example, to change the cursor inside **BLOCKQUOTE** elements, you can use this code:

```
blockquote {
    cursor: url(http://www.example.com/text.ico), text
}
```

If a browser does not support downloadable cursor, the predefined `text` cursor will be used.

Chapter 8

Space around boxes

In this chapter, we discuss properties that affect spacing around block-level elements. Recall from Chapter 6, "The fundamental objects," that we talked about the box model. In accordance with that model, a block-level element – such as a paragraph or heading – is drawn inside an imaginary rectangular bounding box that fits tightly around the text, as illustrated in Figure 8.1. (The dashed line is for illustration purposes only and does not show up on the screen.)

Figure 8.1 A paragraph within a bounding box.

A block of text (such as this paragraph) forms a "box," as shown by the dashed line around this text.

Outside the bounding box are three "belts" that can be manipulated in a style sheet:

*   **margin**
*   **padding**
*   **border**

Figure 8.2 shows how these belts are layered around a paragraph.

The next three sections discuss the properties that let you adjust the margins, padding, and borders of block elements. Then, we discuss additional properties that let you fine-tune the spacing of elements:

*   **width**
*   **height**
*   **float**
*   **clear**

Figure 8.2 Example block-level element with three belts around it. The dashed lines only indicate the boundaries of the belts and are not visible on the screen.

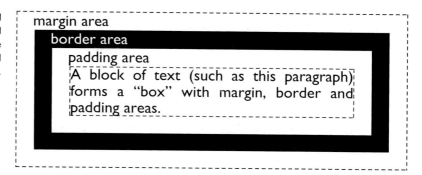

MARGINS AND THE MARGIN PROPERTIES

One of the most common ways to specify spacing in your document is to adjust the margins. A *margin* is the space between the element's bounding box and the bounding box of any adjacent element. There are five margin properties; four let you set the margins for the left, right, top, and bottom margins individually or in any combination: **margin-left**, **margin-right**, **margin-top**, and **margin-bottom**.

The fifth one – **margin** – is a shortcut by which you can set all four margins in one step.

FF	Op	Sa	IE	Pr
●	●	●	◗	●

Name:	margin
Value:	[*<length>* | *<percentage>* | auto] {1,4}
Initial:	0
Applies to:	all elements
Inherited:	no
Percentages:	refer to width of containing block

FF	Op	Sa	IE	Pr
●	●	●	◗	●

Name:	margin-top, margin-right, margin-bottom, margin-left
Value:	*<length>* | *<percentage>* | auto
Initial:	0
Applies to:	all elements
Inherited:	no
Percentages:	refer to width of containing block

margin can have between one and four values, the other four margins can have only a single value. The properties have three possible types of values. The default is 0, and negative values are acceptable:

- Length – Either an absolute or relative value.
- Percentage – A percentage of the width of the block-level element that contains this element, usually the parent element; for example, 10% means leave a space as large as 10% of the width of the parent element.
- auto – The auto value is discussed in detail in the section, "The whole story on width computation" later in this chapter.

These properties affect all content of an element (for example, all the lines of a paragraph). To set the margin for only the first line of a paragraph, see the section, "The text-indent property" in Chapter 7, "Space inside boxes."

Figure 8.3 shows example rules for using the **margin-left**, **margin-right**, **margin-top**, and **margin-bottom** properties.

Figure 8.3
(a) Initial situation, all margins zero.
(b) Setting the left margin: margin-left: 3em.
(c) Setting the right margin: margin-right: 25%.
(d) Setting the top margin: margin-top: 5pt.
(e) Setting top and bottom: margin-top: 1.2em; margin-bottom: 1.2em.
(f) Setting left and right margins: margin-left: 5mm; margin-right: 5mm.
(g) Negative margins: margin-left: 1cm; margin-right: -1cm.

[a] The artist is the creator of beautiful things. To reveal art and conceal the artist is art's aim. The critic is he who can translate into another manner or a new material his impression of beautiful things.

[b] The highest as the lowest form of criticism is a mode of autobiography. Those who find ugly meanings in beautiful things are corrupt without being charming. This is a fault.

[c] There is no such thing as a moral or an immoral book. Books are well written, or badly written. That is all.

[d] The nineteenth century dislike of realism is the rage of Caliban seeing his own face in a glass.

[e] The nineteenth century dislike of romanticism is the rage of Caliban not seeing his own face in a glass. The moral life of man forms part of the subject-matter of the artist, but the morality of art consists in the perfect use of an imperfect medium.

[f] No artist desires to prove anything. Even things that are true can be proved. No artist has ethical sympathies. An ethical sympathy in an artist is an unpardonable mannerism of style. No artist is ever morbid. The artist can express everything.

[g] Thought and language are to the artist instruments of an art. Vice and virtue are to the artist materials for an art. From the point of view of form, the type of all the arts is the art of the musician. From the point of view of feeling, the actor's craft is the type. All art is at once surface and symbol. Those who go beneath the surface do so at their peril.

OSCAR WILDE

USING THE MARGIN PROPERTY

By using the **margin** property, you can set all four margins at once. Here's how it works:

- If only one value is set on this property, that value applies to all four sides.
- If two values are set, the first is for top and bottom, the second is for right and left. For example, suppose the value is 3em 2em; in that case, the top and bottom are set to 3em, and the right and left are set to 2em.
- If three values are set, the first is the top, the second are the right and left, and the third is the bottom margin.
- If four values are set on this property, the order they are applied is top, right, bottom, and left.

The following are examples of rules for using the **margin** property in these various ways:

```
/* All margins will be 2 em */
BODY { margin: 2em }

/* The top and bottom margins will be 1 em, and
   the right and left margins will be 2 em. */
BODY { margin: 1em 2em }

/* The top margin will be 1 em, the right and left
   will be 2 em, and the bottom margin will be 3 em. */
BODY { margin: 1em 2em 3em }

/* All margins will be set, and values will be
   applied in top/right/bottom/left order. */
BODY { margin: 1em 3em 5em 7em }
```

COMMON USES OF THE MARGIN PROPERTIES

One common use of the margin properties is to indent a paragraph from the left and right margins to set it apart from the rest of the text. An example is a quotation. The following code shows how you can do this:

```
BLOCKQUOTE { margin-left: 4em; margin-right: 4em }
```

This code applies to all quotations in the entire document.

Another use of the **margin** property is to provide space between paragraphs to visually distinguish them from each other. Here's the code for inserting space above and below paragraphs using the margin properties:

```
P { margin-top: 0.5em; margin-bottom: 0.5em }
```

Figure 8.4 shows a comparison of paragraphs before and after the extra space is added.

Figure 8.4 Adding space above and below paragraphs to distinguish paragraphs from each other; (a) with zero margins; (b) with 0.5em top and bottom margins.

The first of three paragraphs without any spacing in between. Both the top and bottom margins are zero.

The second paragraph is directly below the first one.

The third paragraph follows the second, again without any space above it to separate it from the second one.

(a)

The first of three paragraphs with some space in between them. The top and bottom margins are now 0.5em.

The second paragraph is now much easier to read.

The third paragraph is again separated from the second one.

(b)

Note: Another way to visually distinguish paragraphs is to indent the first line. We explained how to do this in Chapter 7, when we talked about the **text-indent** property. When **text-indent** is used, space above and below paragraphs is usually not necessary. Some people like to do it anyway, but it's a bit of an overkill.

You can also set negative margin values, although some browsers may not be able to handle them. You want to be careful when setting negative values; otherwise, unexpected effects may result. Figure 8.5(a) shows an example of a negative margin that is too large – part of the text ends up outside the window. This resulted from input like this, where the text indent was set to −4em:

```
BODY { margin-left: 2em }
P { text-indent: -4em }
```

Figure 8.5(b) shows a potentially useful negative margin. In this case, we adjust the top margin by −50px:

```
<STYLE>
  H2.overlap {
     margin-top: -0.6em;
     font-style: italic;
  }
</STYLE>
<H1>Rare flowers>
<H2 CLASS="overlap">-an introduction</H1>
```

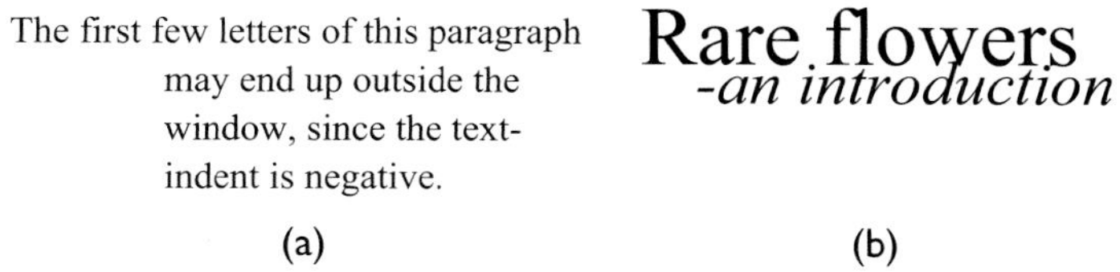

Figure 8.5 Using negative indents with the margin properties: (a) a large negative indent; (b) a negative top margin used to achieve a specific design effect.

The first few letters of this paragraph may end up outside the window, since the text-indent is negative.

(a)

Rare flowers
-an introduction

(b)

Although the five margin properties allow flexible spatial control, there is no way to control the appearance of margins. Margins are transparent, which means that whatever is underneath shows through. Figure 8.6 shows a child element with a 3em margin on all four sides whose parent has a patterned background. Notice how the pattern shows through and crowds the child element.

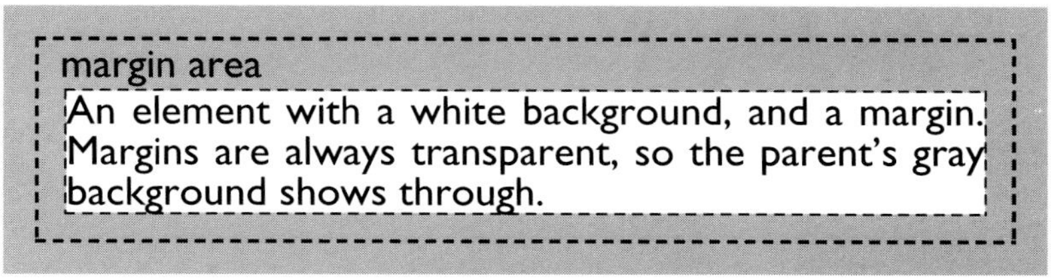

Figure 8.6 An element with a white background and a 3em margin. The margins are transparent, so the parent's gray background shows through in the margin area.

margin area
An element with a white background, and a margin. Margins are always transparent, so the parent's gray background shows through.

To control the appearance of the area immediately around an element, you use the padding and border properties, which we discuss in the next two sections.

THE PADDING PROPERTIES

The padding properties describe how much space to insert between an element and its margin, or if there is a border, between an element and its border. (We discuss borders next.) There are five padding properties, and you set the length of the padding with one of them. Four let you set the amount of padding to insert on the left, right, top, and bottom individually: **padding-left**, **padding-right**, **padding-top**, and **padding-bottom**.

The fifth one – **padding** – is a shortcut by which you can set all four padding values in one step.

All these properties can be described by the following definition, except that only **padding** can have up to four values, the others can have only one.

FF	Op	Sa	IE	Pr		
●	●	●	●	●	Name:	padding
					Value:	[<length> | <percentage>] {1,4}
					Initial:	0
					Applies to:	all elements
					Inherited:	no
					Percentages:	refer to width of containing block

FF	Op	Sa	IE	Pr		
●	●	●	●	●	Name:	padding-top, padding-right, padding-bottom, padding-left
					Value:	<length> | <percentage>
					Initial:	0
					Applies to:	all elements
					Inherited:	no
					Percentages:	refer to width of containing block

The properties can have one of two types of values. The default is 0, and the values cannot be negative:

- Length – Either an absolute or relative value.
- Percentage – A percentage of the width of the block-level element in which this element is contained; usually the parent element; for example, 10% adds padding that is as wide as 10% of the width of the parent element.

With these properties, you can add some breathing room around an element. For example, although you can place a border right against the bounding box of an element, we recommend that you always put some padding between the element and its border; otherwise, they look like they crowd each other.

The padding automatically takes on the same appearance as an element's background. (You set the background using the **background** property, which we discuss in Chapter 10, "Colors.") That is, if an element has a yellow background, the padding is also yellow.

Figure 8.7 shows an example of using padding to put space between an element and its margin.

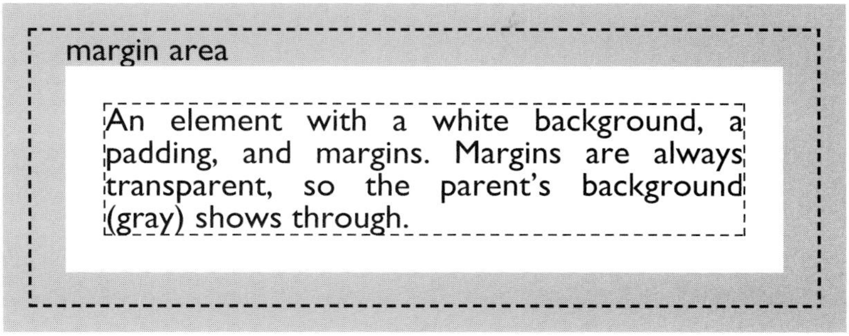

Figure 8.7 An element with padding around it (`padding: 1em`).

USING THE PADDING PROPERTY

By using the **padding** property, you can set all four padding lengths at once. Here's how it works:

- If only one value is set on this property, that value applies to all four sides.
- If two or three values are set, the missing value(s) are taken from the opposite side(s). For example, suppose the top is set to 3em, the right to 2em, and no values are assigned to the bottom and left. The bottom is the opposite of the top, so it takes the value of the top: 3em. The left padding is the opposite of the right padding, so it takes the value of the right side: 2em.
- If four values are set on this property, the order they are applied is top, right, bottom, and left.

The following are examples of code for using the **padding** property in these various ways:

```
/* All paddings will be 2em. */
BODY { padding: 2em }

/* The top and bottom padding will be 1em,
   and the right and left padding will be 2em. */
BODY { padding: 1em 2em }

/* The top padding will be 1em, the right and left
```

```
     will be 2 em, and the bottom padding will be 3em. */
BODY { padding: 1em 2em 3em }

/* All paddings will be set, and values will
   be applied in top/right/bottom/left order. */
BODY { padding: 1em 3em 5em 7em }
```

THE BORDER PROPERTIES GROUP

A *border* is a way to highlight an element. It is placed between an element's padding and its margin. Figure 8.8 shows an example of using a border around an element.

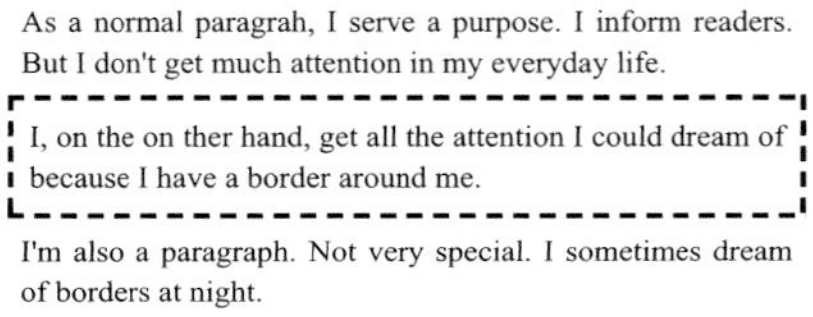

Figure 8.8 An element with padding and a border.

Twenty border properties form the border properties group, and you can set the width, color, and style of a border in various combinations. Five properties let you set the width, color, and style at the same time on one or more of the four borders of an element:

- **border-left**
- **border-right**
- **border-top**
- **border-bottom**
- **border**

We generally recommend that you use these five properties. The remaining 15 are useful if you need to set only one aspect of a border; that is, only the width, only the color, or only the style. You can set these on one or more borders in any combination:

- **border-left-color**
- **border-right-color**
- **border-top-color**
- **border-bottom-color**
- **border-color**
- **border-left-style**
- **border-right-style**

- **border-top-style**
- **border-bottom-style**
- **border-style**
- **border-left-width**
- **border-right-width**
- **border-top-width**
- **border-bottom-width**
- **border-width**

A border can be applied to any element. When applied to an inline element that contains text that spans more than line, the browser may render one border per line and possibly omit the edges. For example, the style sheet

```
EM { border: solid; padding: 1ex }
```

applied to this text

```
This line contains a <EM>long piece of emphasized
text, so long in fact that it is likely to be broken across
lines</EM> somewhere in the middle.
```

may produce this result:

This line contains a long piece of emphasized text, so long in fact that it is likely to be broken across lines somewhere in the middle.

The border is not closed at the end of the first line to indicate that it continues on the next line. This behavior is browser-specific; that is, the browser doesn't have to do this. With some borders, especially the 3D borders (groove, ridge, inset, and outset), closing the border may look better.

THE BORDER-COLOR PROPERTIES

The **border-color** property sets the color of a border. The color may be specified using any one of 16 predefined named colors or a numbered RGB color. (See Chapter 10 for more information about specifying colors.)

Cascading Style Sheets

FF	Op	Sa	IE	Pr	Name:	border-color
•	•	•	◐	•	Value:	$<color>\{1,4\}$
					Initial:	taken from the **color** property of the element
					Applies to:	all elements
					Inherited:	no
					Percentages:	N/A

FF	Op	Sa	IE	Pr	Name:	border-top-color, border-right-color,
•	•	•	◐	•		border-bottom-color, border-left-color
					Value:	$<color>$
					Initial:	taken from the **color** property of the element
					Applies to:	all elements
					Inherited:	no
					Percentages:	N/A

With the **border-color** property, you set all colors on all four borders at once, as follows:

- One value is set – That value applies to all four sides.
- Two values are set – The top and bottom borders are set to the first value, and the right and left borders are set to the second.
- Three values are set – The top border is set to the first value, the right and left borders are set to the second, and the bottom border is set to the third.
- Four values are set – The values are applied in top, right, bottom, and left order.

The following are examples of code for using the **border-color** property in these various ways:

```
/* All borders will be red */
BODY { border-color: red }

/* The top and bottom borders will be red,
   and the left and right borders will be black */
BODY { border-color: red black }

/* The top border will be red, the left and
   right borders will be black, and the bottom
   border will be yellow */
BODY { border-color: red black yellow }
```

```
/* All colors will be set, and values will be
   applied in top/right/bottom/left order */
BODY { border-color: red black yellow green }
```

If no color is specified for a border, it takes the color of the element itself. For example, in this case:

```
P {
  color: black;
  background: white;
  border: solid
}
```

the border does not have a color specified, so it is black, which is the same as the text of the **P** element.

THE BORDER-STYLE PROPERTIES

The **border-style** property sets the appearance of the border.

FF	Op	Sa	IE	Pr		
●	●	●	◐	◐	Name:	border-style
					Value:	*<border-style>* {1,4}
					Initial:	none
					Applies to:	all elements
					Inherited:	no
					Percentages:	N/A

FF	Op	Sa	IE	Pr		
●	●	●	◐	◐	Name:	border-top-style, border-right-style, border-bottom-style, border-left-style
					Value:	*<border-style>*
					Initial:	none
					Applies to:	all elements
					Inherited:	no
					Percentages:	N/A

These properties accept one of 10 keywords:

- none – No border is drawn, regardless of any border width that may be set (see later in this section). This is the default.

- dotted – A dotted line.
- dashed – A dashed line.
- solid – A solid line.
- double – A double line. The sum of the two lines and the space between them equals the **border-width** value.
- groove – A 3D groove. The shadow effect is the result of using colors that are a bit darker and a bit lighter than those given by **border-color** or **color**.
- ridge – A 3D ridge.
- inset – A 3D inset.
- outset – A 3D outset.
- hidden – Similar to none except for shared borders in tables where hidden will remove other borders.

Figure 8.9 shows an example of each type of border style.

Figure 8.9 Border styles.

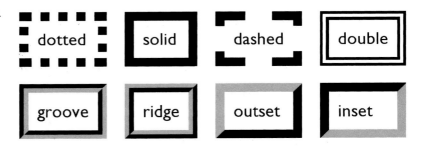

With the **border-style** property, you set the styles of all four borders at once, as follows:

- One value is set – That value applies to all four sides.
- Two values are set – The top and bottom borders are set to the first value, and the right and left borders are set to the second.
- Three values are set – The top border is set to the first value, the right and left borders are set to the second, and the bottom border is set to the third.
- Four values are set – The values are applied in top, right, bottom, and left order.

The following are examples of code for using the **border-style** property in these various ways:

```
/* All borders will be dotted. */
BODY { border-style: dotted }

/* The top and bottom borders will be dashed
   and the left and right borders will be solid. */
BODY { border-style: dashed solid }

/* The top border will be a 3d inset, the left and right
   solid, and the bottom border will be a double line. */
BODY { border-style: inset solid double }

/* Styles are applied in top/right/bottom/left order. */
BODY { border-style: ridge groove dashed dotted }
```

THE BORDER-WIDTH PROPERTIES

The border-width properties set the widths of the border individually or in any combination. There are five properties:

- Four properties let you set the border width for the left, right, top, and bottom of the element individually: **border-left-width**, **border-rightwidth**, **border-top-width**, and **border-bottom-width**.
- The fifth one – **border-width** – is a shortcut by which you can set all four border widths at once.

These properties can be described by the following definition. Four of the five properties accept only a single value, while **border-width** accepts up to four values.

FF	Op	Sa	IE	Pr		
•	•	•	•	•		
					Name:	border-width
					Value:	[thin | medium | thick | *<length>*] {1,4}
					Initial:	medium
					Applies to:	all elements
					Inherited:	no
					Percentages:	N/A

Name:	border-top-width, border-right-width, border-bottom-width, border-left-width
Value:	thin | medium | thick | *<length>*
Initial:	medium
Applies to:	all elements
Inherited:	no
Percentages:	N/A

These properties have keyword and length values:

- `thin`
- `medium` — This is the default.
- `thick`
- Length value — Either an absolute or relative unit.

When the keywords `thin`, `medium`, or `thick` are used, the actual width of the border depends on the browser. However, `medium` will be at least as thick as `thin`, and `thick` will not be thinner than `medium`. The thickness remains constant throughout a document. For example, a thick border will be the same thickness throughout the document regardless of any other properties you set. In the following code sample,

```
H1 {
    border-width: thick;
    font-size: 18pt }
P {
    border-width: thick;
    font-size: 12pt }
```

the borders will be the same width for both the **H1** and the **P** elements, even though the font sizes differ.

Figure 8.10 shows examples of the various border width values.

Figure 8.10 Examples of border-width values.

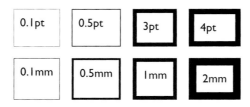

USING THE BORDER-WIDTH PROPERTY

Using the **border-width** property, you can set all four borders at once, as follows:

- One value is set – That value applies to all four sides.
- Two values are set – The top and bottom borders are set to the first value, and the right and left borders are set to the second.
- Three values are set – The top border is set to the first value, the right and left borders are set to the second, and the bottom border is set to the third.
- Four values are set – The values are applied in top, right, bottom, and left order.

The following are examples of code for using the **border-width** property in various ways:

```
/* All borders are set the same, to 2em. */
BODY { border-width: 2em }

/* Top and bottom = 1em; right and left = 2em. */
BODY { border-width: 1em 2em }

/* Top = 1em, right = 2em, bottom =  3em, left = 2em. */
BODY { border-width: 1em 2em 3em }

/* All borders are set and are applied in
   top/right/bottom/left order. */
BODY { border-width: 1em 3em 5em 7em }
```

THE BORDER PROPERTIES

The border properties let you set the border width, color, and style together on one or more borders. They build on the previously discussed properties and are the most commonly used properties to set border characteristics. Four of them let you set the border width, color, and style for each side of the element individually: **border-left**, **border-right**, **border-top**, and **border-bottom**. The fifth one is **border**; a shortcut by which you can set all four border properties at once.

FF	Op	Sa	IE	Pr		
●	●	●	●	●		

Name:	border-top, border-right, border-bottom, border-left, border
Value:	*<border-width>* || *<border-style>* || *<border-color>*
Initial:	see the individual properties
Applies to:	all elements
Inherited:	no
Percentages:	N/A

These properties accept all the legal values of **border-width**, **border-style**, and **border-color**. Omitted values are set to their initial values. For example, the rule

```
P { border: solid red }
```

sets all borders to solid red. Because **border-width** is not specified, its initial value — medium — is assumed. Also, the order in which you list the three values doesn't matter. All the following produces the same result:

```
border: thin solid red;
border: red thin solid;
border: solid red thin;
```

The following are example rules for using the **border-left**, **border-right**, **border-top**, and **border-bottom** properties. Figure 8.11 shows the results.

USING THE BORDER PROPERTY

Unlike the **margin** and **padding** properties, the **border** property cannot set different values on the four sides. With **border**, you can only set all four sides to the same style, color, and width. To set different values on the four sides, you must use one or more of the other border properties.

The following style sheet puts a thick red border around elements of type **DIV** with **CLASS** "warning." Between the text and the border is half an em vertically and one em horizontally:

Figure 8.11 Example uses of border properties.

As a normal paragrah, I serve a purpose. I inform readers. But I don't get much attention in my everyday life.

I, on the on ther hand, get all the attention I could dream of since I have a border around me.

I'm also a paragraph. Not very special. I sometimes dream of borders at night.

```
P.special {
    border-top: solid;
    border-right: solid;
    border-bottom: solid;
    border-left: solid
}
```

As a normal paragraph, I serve a purpose. I inform readers. But I don't get much attention in my everyday life.

I, on the on ther hand, get all the attention I could dream of since I have a border around me.

I'm also a paragraph. Not very special. I sometimes dream of borders at night.

```
P.special {
    border-right: solid;
    border-left: solid
}
```

As a normal paragraph, I serve a purpose. I inform readers. But I don't get much attention in my everyday life.

I, on the on ther hand, get all the attention I could dream of since I have a border around me.

I'm also a paragraph. Not very special. I sometimes dream of borders at night.

```
P.special {
    border-top: solid;
    border-right: solid thick;
    border-bottom: solid;
    border-left: solid thick
}
```
missing

As a normal paragraph, I serve a purpose. I inform readers. But I don't get much attention in my everyday life.

I, on the on ther hand, get all the attention I could dream of since I have a border around me.

I'm also a paragraph. Not very special. I sometimes dream of borders at night.

```
P.special {
    border-top: dashed;
    border-bottom: dashed;
}
```

As a normal paragraph, I serve a purpose. I inform readers. But I don't get much attention in my everyday life.

I, on the on ther hand, get all the attention I could dream of since I have a border around me.

I'm also a paragraph. Not very special. I sometimes dream of borders at night.

```
P.special {
    border-top: solid;
    border-right: solid thick;
    border-bottom: solid thick;
    border-left: thin;
}
```
missing

```
DIV.warning {
  border: solid red thick;
  padding: 0.5em 1em; }
```

WORKING WITH THE BORDER PROPERTIES

The properties in the border properties group have overlapping functionality to some extent. Hence, the order in which the rules are specified is important. For example, in this example,

```
BLOCKQUOTE {
  border-color: red;
  border-left: double;
  color: black }
```

the border's color will be red, except for the left border (**border-left**), which will be black. This is because the **border-left** property sets the width, style, and color at one time on the left border. Because the color is not explicitly set in that property, the value of the **color** property is automatically picked up; in this case, black.

OUTLINE BORDERS

FF	Op	Sa	IE	Pr		
○	●	●	○	○	Name:	outline
					Value:	*<outline-width>* || *<outline-style>* || *<outline-color>*
					Initial:	see the individual properties
					Applies to:	all elements
					Inherited:	no
					Percentages:	N/A

FF	Op	Sa	IE	Pr		
○	●	●	○	○	Name:	outline-color
					Value:	*<color>* | invert
					Initial:	invert
					Applies to:	all elements
					Inherited:	no
					Percentages:	N/A

FF	Op	Sa	IE	Pr
○	●	●	○	○

Name:	outline-style
Value:	<border-style>
Initial:	none
Applies to:	all elements
Inherited:	no
Percentages:	N/A

FF	Op	Sa	IE	Pr
○	●	●	○	○

Name:	outline-width
Value:	<border-width>
Initial:	medium
Applies to:	all elements
Inherited:	no
Percentages:	N/A

CSS has another kind of border, called an *outline*, which is like a normal border but doesn't take up any space. It is drawn around an element and may overlap the elements around it. Typically, this type of border is used for dynamic effects – borders that appear only for a short time; for example, while a new page is being fetched or while the mouse hovers over an element. For situations like that, it doesn't matter that the border overlaps something else, and you don't want to reserve any space for it anyway because, most of the time, there is no border.

Here is an example of an outline border added to a hyperlink while the mouse hovers over the link:

```
<STYLE TYPE="text/css">
  A:hover { outline: thick red }
</STYLE>
<BODY>
  <P>Here is a text with
    a <A HREF="other">link</A> in it.
</BODY>
```

You cannot set the four sides of the outline border to different styles, as with normal borders, but you can set the color, width, and style of the entire outline separately.

COLLAPSING MARGINS

The margins above and below elements are not simply added together to reach a total amount of space between the two elements. If they were, you'd often end up with a bit more space between elements than you want. Instead, the browser discards the smaller margin and uses the larger margin to space apart the two elements. This process is called *collapsing margins*. Collapsing margins affects only the top and bottom margins.

For example, suppose a **P** follows an **H1** – a common situation – and that the **P** has less space above it than the **H1** has below it – also common. To be more specific, assume the **P** has 1pc (1pica = 12pt) space above it and the **H1** has 2pc space below it. The browser discards the 1pc space and puts only 2pc space between the two elements; it does not add the two and use the total (3pc space).

Collapsing margins ensure that space is consistent between any pair of elements. In another example, a list (**UL** or **OL**) normally has more space above it than a **P** does, but when either follows an **H1**, designers usually want the same amount of space above both. By the browser's going with the larger **H1** margin, this can be accomplished.

The browser reacts similarly when two elements begin or end at the same time. For example, at the end of a list, usually three elements end at the same time: the last list item, the last paragraph within that item, and the list itself. There is one element, **P**, that begins at the same time as the other three are ending. Here is an example:

```
<UL>
  <LI><P>The first item in a list.
    <P>A paragraph below the first item of
    the list.
<UL>
  <LI><P>The second item in the list.
    <P>The last paragraph of the last item of
    the list.
</UL>
<P>Start of next paragraph. This paragraph is
not part of a list.
```

The space between the *last line of the list* and the *first line of the paragraph that follows it* will be the maximum of four margins:

1. The bottom margin of the last **P** in the **LI**
2. The bottom margin of the last **LI**
3. The bottom of the **UL**

4. The top margin of the **P** that follows the list

Normally, the **UL** is the largest, so that is the amount of margin that will be placed between the end of the list and the beginning of the next paragraph. Figure 8.12 illustrates this situation using these rules:

```
P { margin-bottom: 0em }
LI { margin-bottom: 0.6em }
UL { margin-bottom: 1.2em }
P { margin-top: 0em }
```

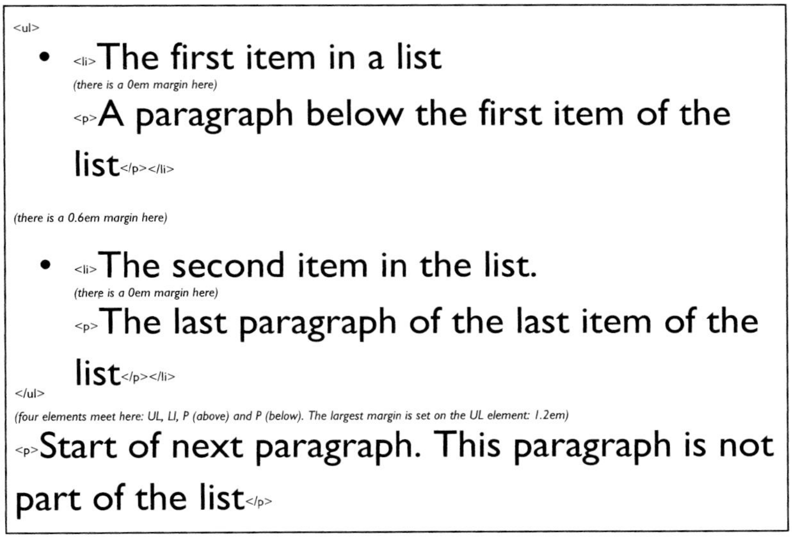

Figure 8.12 A demonstration of collapsing margins.

<ul>

• <li>The first item in a list
(there is a 0em margin here)
<p>A paragraph below the first item of the list</p></li>

(there is a 0.6em margin here)

• <li>The second item in the list.
(there is a 0em margin here)
<p>The last paragraph of the last item of the list</p></li>
</ul>
(four elements meet here: UL, LI, P (above) and P (below). The largest margin is set on the UL element: 1.2em)
<p>Start of next paragraph. This paragraph is not part of the list</p>

However, there's a twist to collapsing margins: Margins collapse only if they touch each other. In the previous example, we assumed that there was no padding or border. Hence, the margins touch. However, if either or both of the **UL** or the **LI** has a nonzero padding or a border, the margins no longer touch. Hence, they no longer collapse because something – padding or border – separates them.

For example, a style sheet like this:

```
P { padding-top: 5px; padding-bottom: 5px }
```

keeps any two paragraphs 10px apart (possibly more if there are other paddings and margins to consider).

THE WIDTH PROPERTY

The **width** property sets the width of the element. It is seldom used with block-level elements. In fact, its use with such elements may lead to some complications. This property is most useful with replaced elements (such as **IMG**) and floating text elements.

FF   Op   Sa   IE   Pr
●   ●   ●   ◑   ●

Name:	width
Value:	<length> | <percentage> | auto
Initial:	auto
Applies to:	block-level and replaced elements
Inherited:	no
Percentages:	refer to parent element's width

This property has three types of values:

*   Length – An absolute or relative value.
*   Percentage – A percentage of the width of the element in which this element is contained; for example, 80% means the element is 20% narrower than the containing block.
*   `auto` – This is the default.

By default, **width** has the value `auto`. Usually, you won't set the width of a block-level element explicitly; you set only the margins, padding, and border. Exceptions are possibly the **HTML** element and tables or table columns. The actual width of the element is what is left after you subtract the margin, padding, and border from the *available width*, also called the *inherited width*. We detail how to work with the **width** property in the section, "The whole story on width computation."

THE HEIGHT PROPERTY

The **height** property sets the height of the element. As with the **width** property, the **height** property is seldom used with block-level elements, and its use in those cases may lead to some complications. This property is used most often with images.

FF	Op	Sa	IE	Pr		
•	•	•	◑	•		

Name:	height
Value:	*<length>* | auto
Initial:	auto
Applies to:	block-level and replaced elements
Inherited:	no
Percentages:	N/A

This property has two values:

- Length – An absolute or relative value.
- auto – This is the default.

Usually, you won't set the height of a block element explicitly; you set only the margins and padding. By default, the height has the value auto. The height is determined simply by how much room is needed to display the number of lines in the element.

Explicitly setting the height is even rarer than specifying the width. If you do and the text needs more space to display than you have allotted, a scroll bar or similar device may be introduced into the element by the browser so that the user can get to the text that is out of sight. If the height is more than that needed by the text in the element, the extra space is treated as padding.

THE FLOAT PROPERTY

The **float** property allows you to place an element at the left or right edge of the parent element.

FF	Op	Sa	IE	Pr		
•	•	•	•	•		

Name:	float
Value:	left | right | none
Initial:	none
Applies to:	all elements
Inherited:	no
Percentages:	N/A

A value of left causes the element to be moved (to "float") to the left edge of its parent until it encounters any margin, padding, or border of another block-level element. A value of right causes the same action on the opposite side. A value of None causes the element to be displayed where it appears in the text.

The left and right values of the property, in effect, take an element out of the normal flow of elements. The element is then treated as a block-level element regardless of what **display** property setting it has. The text that followed the element either continues in the main flow or wraps around the floating element on the opposite side. If there is no room for the element to float at the specified edge, it moves down to the nearest spot in which it can fit.

This property is used most often for inline **IMG** elements, which are treated as a block-level element for purposes of this property. For example,

```
IMG.face {
   float: left;
   margin-left: 3px 3px 3px 0 }
```

places each **IMG** elements of the class face along the left side of the image's parent and flush against the parent's left edge with a little white space on the other sides. See Figure 8.13(a).

With this rule:

```
IMG.face {
   float: right;
   margin-right: 3px 0 3px 3px }
```

those same **IMG** elements are placed along the right of the parent flush against the parent's right edge. See Figure 8.13 (b).

Figure 8.13 Floating images.

Ad nulla nostrud nisl in illum in duis ea. Ut vulputate minim iusto. Consequat qui, diam feugiat facilisis suscipit ea velit. Lorem molestie wisi feugait. Lobortis molestie, exerci blandit nostrud, luptatum tincidunt vero et. Velit feugait ullamcorper erat euismod, minim wisi illum dolore qui, esse ullamcorper. Et magna, vel odio dolore ipsum ut enim dolore et eros nulla ex delenit illum luptatum ex feugiat in nostrud. Ut amet duis et volutpat qui iusto, consequat duis, vel feugiat, duis, duis at, adipiscing suscipit at. Esse feugait odio at delenit blandit eum lorem. Consequat enim eros in dignissim augue commodo in.

(a)

Ad nulla nostrud nisl in illum in duis ea. Ut vulputate minim iusto. Consequat qui, diam feugiat facilisis suscipit ea velit. Lorem molestie wisi feugait. Lobortis molestie, exerci blandit nostrud, luptatum tincidunt vero et. Velit feugait ullamcorper erat euismod, minim wisi illum dolore qui, esse ullamcorper. Et magna, vel odio dolore ipsum ut enim dolore et eros nulla ex delenit illum luptatum ex feugiat in nostrud. Ut amet duis et volutpat qui iusto, consequat duis, vel feugiat, duis, duis at, adipiscing suscipit at. Esse feugait odio at delenit blandit eum lorem. Consequat enim eros in dignissim augue commodo in.

(b)

Typically, all the floating element's margins, padding, and borders are honored; that is, margins are not collapsed with the margins of adjacent elements. There are cases in which a floating element can overlap with the margin, border, and padding of another element. For example:

1. When the floating element has a negative margin. Negative margins are honored as they are on other block-level elements (see Figure 8.14(a)).
2. When the floating element is wider or higher than its parent (see Figure 8.14 (b)).

Figure 8.14 Two cases when a floating element can overlap another element's margin, border, and padding: (a) the floating element has a negative margin; (b) the floating element is wider than its parent.

Ad nulla nostrud nisl in illum in duis ea. Ut vulputate minim iusto. Consequat qui, diam feugiat facilisis suscipit ea velit. Lorem molestie wisi feugait. Lobortis molestie, exerci blandit nostrud, luptatum tincidunt vero et. Velit feugait ullamcorper erat euismod, minim wisi illum dolore qui, esse ullamcorper. Et magna, vel odio dolore ipsum ut enim dolore et eros nulla ex delenit illum luptatum ex feugiat in nostrud. Ut amet duis et volutpat qui iusto, consequat duis, vel feugiat, duis, duis at, adipiscing suscipit at. Esse feugait odio at delenit blandit eum lorem. Consequat enim eros in dignissim augue commodo in.

(a)

Ad nulla nostrud nisl in illum in duis ea. Ut vulputate minim iusto. Consequat qui, diam feugiat facilisis suscipit ea velit. Lorem molestie wisi feugait. Lobortis molestie, exerci blandit nostrud, luptatum tincidunt vero et. Velit feugait ullamcorper erat euismod, minim wisi illum dolore qui, esse ullamcorper. Et magna, vel odio dolore ipsum ut enim dolore et eros nulla ex delenit illum luptatum ex feugiat in nostrud. Ut amet duis et volutpat qui iusto, consequat duis, vel feugiat, duis, duis at, adipiscing suscipit at. Esse feugait odio at delenit blandit eum lorem. Consequat enim eros in dignissim augue commodo in.

(b)

THE CLEAR PROPERTY

The **clear** property works with the **float** property. It specifies whether an element allows floating elements at its side; that is, more specifically, it lists the sides on which floating elements are *not* accepted.

FF Op Sa IE Pr
•   •   •   •   •

Name:	clear
Value:	none | left | right | both
Initial:	none
Applies to:	all elements
Inherited:	no
Percentages:	N/A

This property has four values:

- none – This is the default.
- left
- right
- both

None means the element allows floating elements on both of its sides. Left and right mean the element does not allow floating elements on its left side and right side, respectively. Both means the element will not have floating elements on either side.

This property enables you to control text wrapping as a result of setting the **float** property. Commonly, designers want text to wrap around a floating element. However, cases may arise when you don't want this to happen. For example, if your document is starting a new section, you may want to ensure that the heading of that section doesn't occur next to an image that belongs in the previous section. You can set the **clear** property on the heading so that it doesn't allow floating elements at its sides (value both). Instead, the heading moves down until it is free of the previous section's floating element. Figure 8.15(a) shows what would happen if you did not set **clear**, while Figure 8.15(b) shows the result when you do. Here is the code that you would write to achieve the latter effect:

```
/* Make all images float left: */
IMG { float: left }

/* H2 headings must not be next to images: */
H2 { clear: both }
```

Figure 8.15 (a) With **clear** not set (the default none is assumed), the heading of one section is next to an image in the previous section; (b) with **clear** set to both, the heading moves down until it is free of the image.

Ad nulla nostrud nisl in illum in duis ea. Ut vulputate minim usto.

THE NEXT SECTION

Lorem molestie wisi feugait.

(a)

Ad nulla nostrud nisl in illum in duis ea. Ut vulputate minim usto.

THE NEXT SECTION

Lorem molestie wisi feugait.

(b)

The **clear** property can also be used on floating elements. For example, this style sheet:

```
IMG {
    float: right;
    clear: right;
}
```

ensures that an image floats to the right edge of its parent *and* that it won't be placed next to another floating element that may already be on the right edge. It will instead move down until it finds a clear spot in which it can fit. Figure 8.16 shows how this works.

Figure 8.16 (a) If **clear** is not set the default value none is assumed and the images are placed beside each other; (b) With **clear** set to right, the second image moves below the first image.

Ad nulla nostrud nisl in illum in duis ea. Ut vulputate minim iusto. Consequat qui, diam feugiat facilisis suscipit ea velit. Lorem molestie wisi feugiat.   Lobortis molestie, exerci blandit nostrud, luptatum tincidunt vero et. Velit feugiat ullamcorper erat euismod, minim wisi illum dolore qui, esse ullamcorper. Et magna, vel odio dolore ipsum ut enim dolore et eros nulla ex delenit illum luptatum ex feugiat in nostrud. Ut amet duis et volutpat qui iusto, consequat duis, vel feugiat, duis, duis at, adipiscing suscipit at. Esse feugiat odio at delenit blandit eum lorem. Consequat enim eros in dignissim augue commodo in.

Ad nulla nostrud nisl in illum in duis ea. Ut vulputate minim iusto. Consequat qui, diam feugiat facilisis suscipit ea velit. Lorem molestie wisi feugiat. Lobortis molestie, exerci blandit nostrud, luptatum tincidunt vero et. Velit feugiat ullamcorper erat euismod, minim wisi illum dolore qui, esse ullamcorper. Et magna, vel odio dolore ipsum ut enim dolore et eros nulla ex delenit illum luptatum ex feugiat in nostrud. Ut amet duis et volutpat qui iusto, consequat duis, vel feugiat, duis, duis at, adipiscing suscipit at. Esse feugiat odio at delenit blandit eum lorem. Consequat enim eros in dignissim augue commodo in.

(a)   (b)

MINIMUM AND MAXIMUM WIDTHS AND HEIGHTS

In typical style sheets, block elements have margins, but their **width** property is not set (i.e., it is auto). That allows the user to resize the window and the element with it. But, you can protect the element from becoming too narrow or too wide by setting the properties **min-width** and **max-width**, respectively.

FF	Op	Sa	IE	Pr
●	●	●	○	○

Name:	min-width
Value:	*\<length>* | *\<percentage>* | inherit
Initial:	medium
Applies to:	all elements
Inherited:	yes
Percentages:	relative to parent's font size

FF	Op	Sa	IE	Pr
●	●	●	○	●

Name:	max-width
Value:	*<length>* | *<percentage>* | inherit | none
Initial:	none
Applies to:	replaced elements and block-level elements
Inherited:	no
Percentages:	refer to width of containing block

More rare is the use of **min-height** and **max-height**, but they exist in case you need them.

FF	Op	Sa	IE	Pr
●	●	●	●	○

Name:	min-height
Value:	*<length>* | *<percentage>* | inherit
Initial:	0
Applies to:	replaced elements and block-level elements
Inherited:	no
Percentages:	refer to width of containing block

FF	Op	Sa	IE	Pr
●	●	●	◐	○

Name:	max-height
Value:	*<length>* | *<percentage>* | inherit | none<
Initial:	none
Applies to:	replaced elements and block-level elements
Inherited:	no
Percentages:	refer to width of containing block

If the value is specified as a percentage, it is relative to the height of the block element in which this element is contained, but only if the height of that block is set explicitly; otherwise, the percentage (and the property with it) is ignored.

THE WHOLE STORY ON WIDTH COMPUTATION

We explained the normal uses of the various margin, padding, and border properties earlier in this chapter as they relate to block-level elements. In this section, we summarize all this information. We also explain some of the unusual cases you may run into.

The horizontal position and width of a nonfloating, block-level element is determined by seven properties:

- **margin-left**
- **border-left**
- **padding-left**
- **width**
- **padding-right**
- **border-right**
- **margin-right**

For any element, the values of these seven properties must always total the width of the block element in which the element is contained – the *inherited width*. This width is always known and cannot be changed from within. An element's width is computed according to the formula shown in Figure 8.17.

Figure 8.17 The relation between margin, padding, border, and width.

margin-left + **border-left** + **padding-left** + **width** + **padding-right** + **border-right** + **margin-right** = width of containing block

Figure 8.18 shows how the width is computed.

Figure 8.18 Diagram of the width computation.

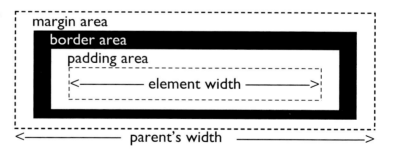

When specific values are used, adjustments may need to be made to one or more values to ensure that the total width does not exceed the inherited width. To simplify making these adjustments, CSS1 provides that the border and padding values are never adjusted. Only the **width**, **margin-left**, and **margin-right** values can be adjusted. That is, only they may be auto. However, the meaning of auto, as it relates to these properties, depends on the type of element.

	inline elements		block elements		floating elements	
	replaced	non-replaced	replaced	non-replaced	replaced	non-replaced
width	intrinsic width	N/A	intrinsic width	maximize (see description in text)	intrinsic width	0
margin-left, margin-right	0	0	maximize (see description in text)	maximize (see description in text)	0	0

Table 8.1 The meaning of auto on **width**, **margin-left**, and **margin-right**.

For replaced elements (such as images and objects), the **width** is automatically set to the *intrinsic width*. An image is assumed to have a preferred or built-in size as determined by its artist or designer. Although the image may be scaled larger or smaller, it still has this pre-ferred size. This is its *intrinsic size*. Any other value means the element is scaled.

For normal (non-replaced) elements, the meaning of auto depends on whether the element floats, and if not, on whether it is block or inline. For floating elements, a width of auto always means 0, so it is not very useful; for inline elements, the **width** property is ignored alto-gether; for block (and list-item) elements, the width will be what is left after subtracting the element's padding, border, and margin from the inherited width.

For inline elements and for floating elements, a value of auto on **margin-left** or **margin-right** means that margin is 0.

A margin with value auto in a block element, on the other hand, means that the margin should be as large as possible.

Table 8.1 summarizes the meaning of auto for **width**, **margin-left**, and **margin-right**.

What gets changed when depends on the interaction of auto and speci-fied values. These are the possibilities:

- None of the three values (**width**, **margin-left**, **margin-right**) is auto.
- Exactly one of the three values has the value auto.
- Two or three of the values has the value auto.

CASE 1: NO VALUE IS "AUTO"

When none of **width**, **margin-left**, or **margin-right** is set to auto, the right margin is ignored and treated as if it had been set to auto; that is, it is the value calculated automatically using the formula shown in Figure 8.17.

For example, if there is a **P** inside a **BODY**, and the style sheet reads

```
BODY {
  width: 30em }
P {
  width: 25em;
  margin-left: 3em;
  margin-right: 3em }
```

the **P** will be 25em wide and have a 3em margin on the left, but the right margin will be ignored and will be calculated as 30 − 25 − 3 = 2em (assuming no paddings and borders are set elsewhere).

CASE 2: ONE VALUE IS "AUTO"

When only one value is set to auto, that value is the one calculated automatically using the previous formula. That is, that value will be maximized − made as large as possible.

Here is the previous example, which is now slightly modified:

```
BODY {
  width: 30em }
P {
  width: 25em;
  margin-left: auto;
  margin-right: 3em }
```

Now, the right margin will indeed be 3em and the left margin will be calculated (2em).

CASE 3: TWO OR THREE OF THE THREE VALUES ARE "AUTO"

There are two possible cases: One case is where **width** is auto, and one where width has some other value. First, if **width** is auto, the **width** value is the one that is calculated using the formula in Figure 8.17. That is, the width will be maximized after consideration of the margin size. Any margins set to auto will become 0.

If **width** is not auto, but both **margin-left** and **margin-right** are, the two margins will be of equal size and as large as possible.

Here is an example with **width** set to auto:

```
<STYLE>
  DIV {
    width: 12cm }
  P {
    width: auto;
    margin-left: 7cm;
    margin-right: auto}
</STYLE>

<DIV>
<P>This paragraph is inside a DIV that is exactly 12cm wide.
The paragraph itself has a 7cm margin on its left and an auto
margin on its right. No padding or border has been specified,
so we assume there aren't any.
</DIV>
```

In this example, the parent of the **P** element, **DIV**, has a width of 12cm, so we use the formula as follows, filling in the blanks with the values of the various widths:

margin-left + **border-left** + **padding-left** + **width** + **padding-right** + **border-right** + **margin-right** = *width of parent*

7cm + *0 cm* + *0 cm* + auto + *0 cm* + *0 cm* + 0 cm = 12cm

The right margin is 0, and because 12 − 7 = 5, the resulting width of the **P** element is 5cm.

The second example shows both **margin-left** and **margin-right** set to auto. In this case, the two margins will each get half of the available space, thereby causing the element to be centered in its parent:

```
<STYLE>
  BODY { width: 10cm }
  P { width: 6cm; margin: auto }
</STYLE>
```

```
<BODY>
<P>This paragraph is 6 cm wide and will be centered inside
its parent (BODY, in this case).
</BODY>
```

Completing the width formula:

margin-left + **border-left** + **padding-left** + **width** + **padding-right** + **border-right** + **margin-right** = width of parent

auto + 0 cm + 0 cm + 6cm + 0 cm + 0 cm + auto = 10 cm

gives us 2cm of space each for the left and right margins; that is, $10 - 6 = 4$cm total to be divided equally between the two margins.

THE OVERFLOW PROPERTY

What happens when an element has a certain width, but one of its children is wider? From the formula in Figure 8.17, it follows that one of the margins must be negative. Margins can indeed be negative, so formally speaking, this is a perfectly valid situation. The result is that the child will stick out of its parent, usually at the right-hand side.

But, you may not want the child to stick out. If you don't want to change the width of the child either, a different solution has to be found. CSS offers two solutions, in addition to the default behavior:

- The part that sticks out is simply cut off and not displayed.
- A scroll bar (or something else with a similar function) is displayed so the user can move the child element sideways.
- The initial situation: The child element is allowed to stick out.

The same may happen in the vertical direction if the height of an element has been set to a fixed value. The property that determines the behavior is **overflow**.

FF	Op	Sa	IE	Pr		
●	●	●	●	○	Name:	overflow
					Value:	visible | hidden | scroll | auto
					Initial:	visible
					Applies to:	block level and replaced elements
					Inherited:	no
					Percentages:	N/A

Visible is the normal style: The children of this element may stick out. Hidden makes the parts that would stick out invisible. This is not useful if the child elements can contain text, but if there is only an image inside, this may be the right thing to do. Scroll and auto both make a scroll bar or some such mechanism appear. The difference is that, in the case of scroll, the scroll bar is always there, even if none of the children is too large, while in the case of auto, the scroll bar appears only when there is actually something to scroll.

Chapter 9

Relative and absolute positioning

The normal way a document is laid out is that the boxes for all elements are put one after the other or below the other (depending on whether they are inline or block), with their distances and alignments specified by properties such as margin, padding, and width. An occasional box is shifted to one side with the float property. In this way, the boxes fill the canvas, or the pages, starting from the top and continuing until all boxes are placed.

Relative positioning adds to this the ability to make corrections to the positions of individual boxes without affecting other boxes. For example, a box may be moved up or down to overlap another box. It is seldom needed in a style sheet. The place where the properties for relative positioning usually appear is in scripts. For example, a dynamic effect that cannot be achieved with CSS2 (although maybe with a future level of CSS) is to move text into place on opening a document: The text moves in from the side and the headers fall into place from the top, slowly reducing their relative offsets to zero. Scripts aren't very good at creating smooth motion effects, but so far, there is no other solution that works with HTML.

Absolute positioning is completely different. It takes an element out of the normal sequence (like `display: none` would do), but then it puts it somewhere else, without regard for what else might be there. Absolute positioning is good at creating displays with little pieces of text or images that are put seemingly independent of each other in fixed spots on the canvas. For an example, see Figure 9.1.

205

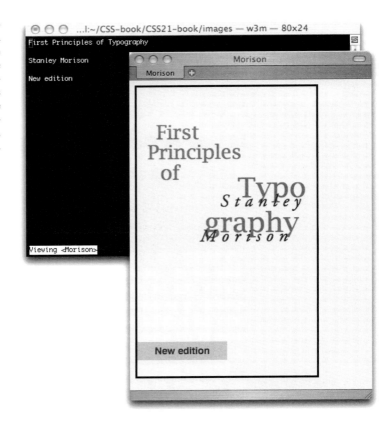

Figure 9.1 An example of absolute positioning: on the left in a non-CSS browser, on the right in a CSS2-capable browser. See the end of this chapter for the document source code. The example is an approximation in CSS of the cover of the 1996 edition (Academic Press, Leiden) of the essay, which first appeared in 1930.

A variation of absolute positioning also allows elements to be put at fixed positions not on the canvas, but in the viewport: If you view a page with such fixed elements on a browser, the elements appear to be glued to the glass of the monitor. While other elements scroll when you move the scroll bars, these fixed elements stay put. If you print such documents, you see that the fixed elements are glued to the page box: They appear in the same spot on every page that you print.

THE POSITION PROPERTY

The **position** property determines whether elements are "normal" elements, or whether they are subject to relative, absolute, or fixed positioning.

FF   Op   Sa   IE   Pr

●   ●   ●   ◖   ○

Name:	position
Value:	static | relative | absolute | fixed
Initial:	static
Applies to:	all elements
Inherited:	no
Percentages:	N/A

Elements that don't use any positioning methods are called *static*. This is the normal case. The values absolute and fixed imply that the element must be a block. The value of the **display** property is ignored in this case. Elements that are not static make use of the four positioning properties: **top**, **right**, **bottom**, and **left**.

FF   Op   Sa   IE   Pr

●   ●   ●   ●   ○

Name:	top, right, bottom, left
Value:	*<length>* | *<percentage>* | auto
Initial:	auto
Applies to:	elements with position other than static
Inherited:	no
Percentages:	width or height of "containing block"

These properties determine the position of a positioned element by setting the distance from the edge of a so-called containing block, which is explained in the next section. The meaning changes slightly with the type of positioning and will be explained in following sections.

THE CONTAINING BLOCK

Normal (static) elements are placed relative to their parent and to elements that precede them, as explained in Chapter 7. Positioned elements are placed relative to so-called *containing blocks,* which may be their parents, but are usually some ancestor higher up in the document tree.

The containing block for a fixed positioned element is always the viewport (in the case of scrolling media, such as most browsers) or the page box (in the case of paged media). The parent, or even any other positioned elements, has no influence on the position of an element with position: fixed.

Relatively positioned elements, like normal static elements, don't have a containing block. The positioning properties **bottom**, **left**, **top**, and **right** move the element up, right, down, or left from its normal position. However, relatively positioned elements can be the containing block for absolutely positioned elements.

The containing block for an absolutely positioned element is usually the viewport; i.e., the absolutely positioned element is placed somewhere inside the window or on the page with the help of the **top**, **right**, **bottom**, and **left** properties. However, if the element is inside some other positioned element (either absolute, relative, or fixed), that element will be its containing block.

Fixed elements stay fixed to the window. If the window has a scroll bar, the fixed elements do not move with the scroll bar. Absolutely positioned elements, even if they are initially placed relative to the window, move along with the scroll bar. The next sections describe each type of positioning in detail.

Here is an example: Consider the following HTML fragment. The two **DIV**s are each absolutely positioned. The first one will, therefore, be put at a certain distance from the edges of the viewport; the second, because it is inside the first, will be positioned relative to the first **DIV**:

```
<HTML>
  <STYLE>
    DIV.outer { position: absolute;
      top: 1cm; right: 2cm; width: 4cm }
    DIV.inner { position: absolute;
      top: 1cm; left: 1cm; width: 2cm }
  </STYLE>
  <BODY>
    <H1>Static header</H1>
    <P>Static paragraph.
    <DIV CLASS="outer">
      <P>Some text in outer...
      <DIV CLASS="inner">
        <P>Some text in inner...
      </DIV>
    </DIV>
    ...
```

The output may look like Figure 9.2.

Figure 9.2 Example of absolute positioning: one box is positioned relative to the top and right of the viewport, and the other to the top and left of the first box.

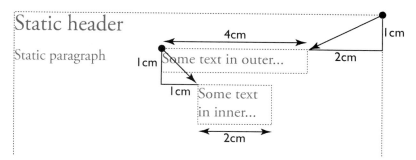

The edges that are used for positioning are the inside and outside of the border: the containing block is formed by the padding edges (the inside of the border) and the **top**, **right**, etc., are measured from there to the border edge (the outside of the border) of the absolutely positioned box. When an absolutely positioned element is inside some other absolutely positioned element, or inside a fixed positioned element, it is easy to establish the edges of the containing block. However, if the absolutely positioned element is inside a relatively positioned element, a complication may arise: If the relatively positioned element is inline, it may have been broken over several lines, and thus it has several boxes; which of them is the containing block for the absolutely positioned box inside?

What happens is that the top and left edges of the first of the inline boxes become the top and left edges of the containing block. The bottom and right edges of the last inline box become the bottom and right edges of the containing block. Figure 9.3 shows how this works. The image also shows that the right edge may easily end up to the left of the left edge! It may be difficult to predict where elements will be placed in such a case. So, be careful when putting absolutely positioned elements inside relatively positioned ones.

The code for this fragment is as follows. The **SPAN** element has been made relative, but without actually positioning it. It serves only as a containing block for the absolutely positioned image inside it.

```
<STYLE>
  SPAN.star { position: relative;
    font-weight: bold }
  IMG.star { position: absolute;
    top: -10px; left: -10px; z-index: -1 }
</STYLE>
```

```
... cleared for <SPAN CLASS="star"><IMG
CLASS="star" SRC="star.png"
ALT="">grazing and cultivation</SPAN>,
often by burning,...
```

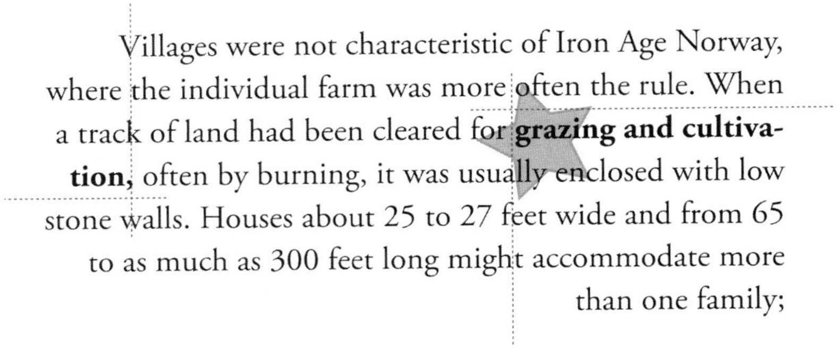

Figure 9.3 An image is placed near the upper-left corner of an inline element. The inline element consists of two boxes: The first one determines the upper-left corner of a containing block, the last one the bottom right (indicated by dotted lines).

Villages were not characteristic of Iron Age Norway, where the individual farm was more often the rule. When a track of land had been cleared for **grazing and cultivation,** often by burning, it was usually enclosed with low stone walls. Houses about 25 to 27 feet wide and from 65 to as much as 300 feet long might accommodate more than one family;

RELATIVE POSITIONING

As shown in the last example in the previous section, you can use relative positioning simply to create a containing block for some other absolutely positioned element. However, the typical use of relative positioning is to position elements away from their normal position without influencing the position of other elements. There aren't many reasons for doing that in a style sheet, and the main reason relative positioning exists at all is to provide a way for scripts to animate the text — to make it "explode" when a page is unloaded or make it slowly move into place when the page is loaded. These effects are well known in slide-show presentations, and with relative positioning and a clever script, you can do the same with HTML.

Unfortunately, scripting languages aren't good at animation. The way they do it is to enter a loop in which the value of the positioning properties slowly increases or decreases until they reach some preset value. With every change, part of the screen is redrawn. However, even on the fastest computers, the speed at which successive cycles of the loop are executed varies slightly, which causes a jerky motion — enough for the human eye to notice. Real animation programs don't rely on such loops, but calculate the path of the element in advance, and even create blurry images on purpose, based on the measured speed of the computer, to fool the human eye into believing the object is moving more than it actually is.

SMIL is an XML-based language specifically for multimedia, including animations. It is a W3C standard, like HTML and CSS. A better option for animations may thus be to create them in SMIL and link them to an HTML file the same way you include an image in HTML. However, the style sheet has no influence over the animation then.

For this reason, some of the most common animation effects may one day end up in CSS itself to allow browsers to use the sophisticated animation algorithms and to help designers, who don't have to write scripts anymore. But until that time, scripting and relative positioning will have to do.

By itself, relative positioning isn't difficult to use or to understand. You can think of a relatively positioned element as a normal element that is pushed away from its proper position after the page has been laid out. You use **top** to specify how far down the element goes from its normal top edge and **left** to give the distance to move it to the right of its left edge. Negative values move it up and left, respectively. (You can also use **right** or **bottom**; they work exactly the same, but with the direction reversed.)

Figure 9.4 shows an example. The word "high" has been moved up by 0.5em (top: -0.5em). Note that this causes the word to overlap with the line above. The **vertical-align** property can also raise text, but it would have caused the lines to be pushed apart to avoid overlap.

You can use percentages as the values of **left** or **right**, and they will be relative to the width of the element (if it is a block) or the width of the enclosing block-level element. Percentages on the **top** or **bottom** properties are only possible if the element (or the enclosing block, for inline elements) has a set **height** (i.e., the **height** is not auto). Otherwise, a percentage will be interpreted as 0.

Figure 9.4 The word "high" has been raised 0.5em by means of the **top** property.

Art is an indivua
The high point o

FIXED POSITIONING

Sometimes, it is desirable to keep an element onscreen at all times. For example, a short warning or a logo could be kept in the corner of the window at all times, no matter how the user scrolls the document. Similarly, when a document is printed, such an element may be printed in a fixed position on every page.

The containing block for a fixed element is thus always the viewport (i.e., the browser's window) or the page box (see Chapter 12, "Printing and other media"). The positioning properties set the distance between the edges of the containing block and the element. If the element is not an image or other "replaced element," you typically set the **width** property, and either the **left** or **right** property, and of course, **top** or **bottom**. The height can usually be left unspecified (auto). For replaced elements, you don't have to set the width unless you want to scale the image. Setting both **left** and **right**, and leaving **width** as **auto** is also possible: The width will then be calculated as the width of the viewport minus the **left** and **right** values.

The following document puts a small **DIV** along the left side of the window. Note that the left margin of the document has been made wide enough that the fixed element does not obscure any text:

```
<HTML>
  <STYLE>
  BODY { margin-left: 5em }
  DIV.status { position: fixed;
    top: 10%; left: 0; width: 4em }
  </STYLE>
  ...
  <DIV CLASS="status">
    <P><IMG SRC="logo" ALT="logo">
    <P>Draft!
  </DIV>
  ...
</HTML>
```

If this document is printed, the logo and the text "Draft!" will appear in the left margin, 10 percent from the top on every page. Of course, when you want it to appear somewhere else on paper than onscreen, or you don't want it to repeat on paper, you can use the @media rules (see Chapter 12).

Another way in which fixed positioning can be used is to divide a document into a small number of parts, each of which is displayed in one area of the viewport. For example, the following document with four **DIV**s can be displayed in such a way that each **DIV** takes up one quarter of the screen. If the contents of the **DIV**s is too large, scroll bars will appear (see Figure 9.5).

```
<HTML>
  <STYLE>
    DIV.one, DIV.two, DIV.three, DIV.four {
      position: fixed; width: 50%; height: 50% }
    DIV.one { top: 0; left: 0 }
    DIV.two { top: 0; left: 50% }
    DIV.three { top: 50%; left: 0 }
    DIV.four { top: 50%; left: 50% }
  </STYLE>
  <BODY>
    <DIV CLASS=one>... </DIV>
    <DIV CLASS=two>... </DIV>
```

Figure 9.5 A window divided into four areas by means of fixed positioning.

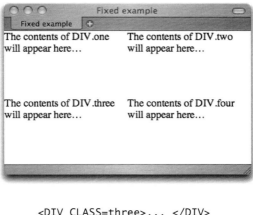

```
        <DIV CLASS=three>... </DIV>
        <DIV CLASS=four>... </DIV>
      </BODY>
    </HTML>
```

This is similar to what can be achieved with HTML frames, but the difference is that, in this case, the entire document is in one piece (which means a quicker display and avoids problems with the Back button) and the "frames" can be positioned more freely; they can even overlap.

ABSOLUTE POSITIONING

The simplest form of absolute positioning is when the elements to position are positioned relative to the initial containing block, i.e., the containing block of the root element. When absolutely positioned elements are descendants of other positioned elements, things become more complicated.

There are two major ways in which absolute positioning can be used. One is to have a few small absolutely positioned elements in an otherwise normal document; for example, to put a logo in a corner. The other way is to create "areas" for parts of the document, much like the last example for fixed positioning in the previous section. The difference is that the size of the window isn't taken into account. Although most browsers will use the width of the window for the width of the initial containing block, the height of the initial containing block is unspecified.

The method to position an absolutely positioned element is the same as for fixed elements: Use either **top** or **bottom** to determine the vertical position relative to the containing block, and either the **left** or **right** properties for the horizontal position. If the element is not a replaced element, you should normally also set the **width** property, although the value auto for **width** has a special meaning that may be useful in certain cases (see the following section). Instead of setting **width**, you can also set both the **left** and **right**. Here is an example:

```
IMG#stamp1 {
    position: absolute;
    top: 10px; right: 10px }
```

This puts the image with ID "stamp1" 10 pixels from the upper-right corner. Because it is an image, it has an intrinsic width, and you don't need to specify it (unless you want to resize it).

Here is another example. This creates a containing block out of a **DIV** and puts all the words inside it at random places. (You might want to use dice, or their electronic equivalent, to generate the percentages...) See Figure 9.6 for the result.

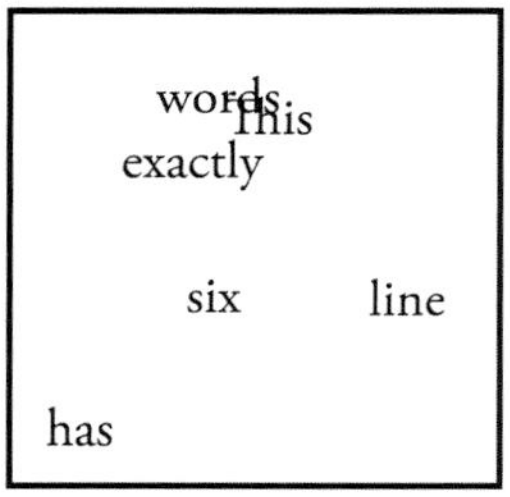

Figure 9.6 Six absolutely positioned words in a square.

```
<STYLE>
  #container { position: relative; border: solid;
    width: 4cm; height: 4cm }
  #w01 { position: absolute; top: 17%; left: 44% }
  #w02 { position: absolute; top: 56%; left: 74% }
  #w03 { position: absolute; top: 84%; left: 07% }
  #w04 { position: absolute; top: 26%; left: 23% }
  #w05 { position: absolute; top: 55%; left: 36% }
  #w06 { position: absolute; top: 12%; left: 30% }
</STYLE>
...
<DIV ID=container>
  <P><SPAN ID=w01>This</SPAN>
    <SPAN ID=w02>line</SPAN>
    <SPAN ID=w03>has</SPAN>
    <SPAN ID=w04>exactly</SPAN>
    <SPAN ID=w05>six</SPAN>
    <SPAN ID=w06>words</SPAN>
</DIV>
```

Using auto values

The value auto has some special functions when set on the **top** or **left** properties of an absolutely positioned element. When both **top** and **bottom** are auto, the browser makes a guess as to where the element would have been if it had been a static element and sets **top** to the value that puts the element there. Similarly for **left** and **right**, if both of them are auto, the browser tries to make the value **left** such that the element is put almost where it would have been as a static element.

The values are only approximations because it is difficult to compute the values precisely without actually doing the layout. But, computing the layout twice takes too much time. However, the approximations are usually accurate within a few pixels, especially if the positioned element would have been a block element. If it would have been a static inline element, the chance that the values are more than a few pixels wrong is higher.

Using auto values on **top** and **left** allows us to write the example of Figure 9.3 in a different way. The trick employed here is to use auto on top and left to put the image where it would have been (after the word "for"), and then use negative margins to move it up and left:

```
<STYLE>
  SPAN.star { font-weight: bold }
  IMG.star { position: absolute;
    top: auto; left: auto; z-index: -1;
    margin-top: -10px; margin-left: -10px }
</STYLE>

... cleared for <SPAN CLASS="star"><IMG
CLASS="star" SRC="star.png"
ALT="">grazing and cultivation</SPAN>,
often by burning,...
```

Whether this solution is "better" is a matter of taste.

Note that setting **left** and **right** to auto thus doesn't center an absolutely positioned element, like setting **margin-left** and **margin-right** to auto would do for a normal (static) block. But, there are various other ways to center an absolutely positioned block in its containing block. For example, you can calculate the correct value for **left** yourself, or you can set **left** and **right** to 0 and use the margins to center the element.

Let's also look at what happens when both **width** and **right** are auto. The situation is similar to what happens with static block elements when **width** and **margin-right** are auto: **right** is set to 0 and **width** takes the remaining space. This makes the absolutely positioned element extend from the position given by **left** all the way to the right edge of the containing block.

Everything we've said about left and right applies only in languages that are written left to right. If the absolutely (or fixed) positioned element is written right to left (the **direction** property is rtl), left and right switch roles: The magic auto value applies to **right** instead of **left**, and when both **left** and **width** are auto, **left** is set to 0.

THE Z-INDEX PROPERTY

Positioning elements frequently causes them to overlap and, in fact, the possibility of having elements overlap is an important reason for using positioning in the first place. The normal rule is that elements that come later in the source document are on top of earlier elements. But, as we saw in the example with the star (refer to Figure 9.2), that is not always what we want. That example therefore used the **z-index** property to explicitly put the image behind its containing block. Figure 9.7 shows an example.

```
<STYLE>
  DIV {position: absolute; border: solid;
    width: 5em; height: 5em; background: silver;
    text-align: right}
  .a1 {top: 1em; left: 1em; z-index: 3}
  .a2 {top: 2em; left: 3em; z-index: 2}
  .a3 {top: 3em; left: 2em; z-index: 4}
  .a4 {top: 4em; left: 4em; z-index: 1}
</STYLE>

<DIV CLASS="a1"><P>a1</DIV>
<DIV CLASS="a2"><P>a2</DIV>
<DIV CLASS="a3"><P>a3</DIV>
<DIV CLASS="a4"><P>a4</DIV>
```

FF	Op	Sa	IE	Pr
●	●	●	●	○

Name:	z-index
Value:	auto | <integer>
Initial:	auto
Applies to:	positioned elements
Inherited:	no
Percentages:	N/A

Figure 9.7 The effect of **z-index**: a3 has the highest z-index and is on top; a4 has the lowest z-index and is behind the others.

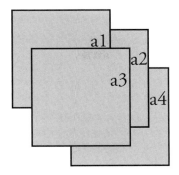

Figure 9.7 The effect of **z-index**: a3 has the highest z-index and is on top; a4 has the lowest z-index and is behind the others.

A negative value means that the element will be behind its containing block, and a value of zero or higher means it will be in front. auto is the same as zero (but see the following).

If two elements have the same containing block and the same **z-index**, the element that comes later in the source will be in front of the earlier element.

The value auto has an effect when containing blocks are nested. If an element that is a containing block for some other elements has a **z-index** of auto, it means that the z-index of the elements inside this block isn't relative to this containing block, but to the nearest enclosing containing block that doesn't have auto for its value. Thus, if you leave the z-index of all containing blocks as auto, all z-indexes will be relative to the root element, no matter how deeply nested the elements are.

MAKING ELEMENTS INVISIBLE

FF	Op	Sa	IE	Pr
●	●	●	◑	○

Name:	visibility
Value:	visible | hidden
Initial:	visible
Applies to:	all elements
Inherited:	yes
Percentages:	N/A

With **display**, you can remove elements from display (display: none), but there is another way to make elements invisible. The **visibility** property doesn't remove elements, but makes them completely transparent. In other words, if you set **visibility** to hidden, you see an empty space where the element is supposed to be.

This is most useful if you have multiple alternative style sheets for the same page, or if you have a script that changes the style. You can use it to selectively show the answers to a quiz (for example, while keeping everything else on the page the same).

The value visible makes elements visible, hidden makes them transparent. The property actually has a third value, collapse, which can make table columns disappear, but we won't discuss it here (refer to the CSS2 specification for an explanation).

CLIPPING ELEMENTS

It is possible to "clip" an element, so that only a small rectangle of it is visible instead of the entire element. This might be used to show only a part of an image, for example. Only absolutely positioned elements can be clipped.

FF	Op	Sa	IE	Pr
●	●	●	●	○

Name:	clip
Value:	*<shape>* | auto
Initial:	auto
Applies to:	absolutely positioned elements
Inherited:	no
Percentages:	N/A

The *<shape>* value describes a rectangle, for example:

```
#p1 { clip: rect(5px, 310px, 255px, 10px) }
```

The order of the values inside rect() is top, right, bottom, left. This rule therefore shows the part of the image that starts 5px from the top and 10px from the left, and is 300px wide (= 310 − 10) and 250px high (= 255 − 5).

AN EXAMPLE

Figure 9.1, the CSS version of the cover of Stanley Morison's book, was made by individually positioning each word. Here is the source code:

```
<body>
  <div id=co>
    <p>
      <span id=fi>First</span>
      <span id=pr>Principles</span>
      <span id=of>of</span>
      <span id=ty>Typo</span><span id=gr>graphy</span>
    <p>
      <span id=st>Stanley</span>
      <span id=mo>Morison</span>
    <p>
      <span id=ed>New edition</span>
  </div>
</body>
```

As Figure 9.1 shows, this HTML is "clean," in the sense that it is perfectly readable even without a style sheet.

The style sheet is as follows. It expresses the size of the cover (the **DIV** element) as a certain number of ems and the positions of all elements as percentages of the width and height of the **DIV**. Thus, the size only depends on the size of the body font and by changing only the body font, the result can be made larger or smaller at will:

```
BODY {
    font: 30px/1 "Lucida Bright", serif;
    background: #FEB;
    color: #874 }
#co {
    position: relative;
    width: 9em;
    height: 15em;
    border: solid 0.1em black }
#fi, #pr, #of, #ed {
    position: absolute;
    text-align: left }
#ty, #gr, #st, #mo {
    position: absolute;
    text-align: right }
#fi { top: 12%; left: 11% }
#pr { top: 19%; left: 6% }
#of { top: 26%; left: 13% }
#ty, #gr { font-size: 140% }
#st, #mo {
    font: italic 90%/1
      "Adobe Garamond Pro", "Garamond", serif;
    letter-spacing: 0.3em;
    color: #C00 }
```

```
#ty { top: 30%; right: 6% }
#gr { top: 42%; right: 10% }
#st { top: 37%; right: 6% }
#mo { top: 49%; right: 13% }
#ed {
    top: 88%;
    width: 45%;
    padding: 0.5em;
    background: #CCB;
    color: #C00;
    text-align: center;
    font: bold 50%/1 "Helvetica", sans-serif }
```

Absolute positioning is probably the most straightforward way to make this layout, but it isn't the only one. You can also use the **MARGIN** properties. In that case, to position the name of the author – which overlaps the title – you need negative margins. Here is another style sheet for the same layout:

```
BODY {
    font: 30px/1 "Lucida Bright", serif;
    background: #FEB; color: #874 }
#co {
    width: 9em;
    height: 15em;
    border: solid 0.1em black }
#fi, #pr, #of, #ed {
    display: block;
    text-align: left }
#ty, #gr, #st, #mo {
    display: block;
    text-align: right }
#fi { margin: 1.8em 0 0 11% }
#pr { margin: 0.1em 0 0 6% }
#of { margin: 0.1em 0 0 13% }
#ty, #gr { font-size: 140% }
#st, #mo {
    font: italic 90%/1
      "Adobe Garamond Pro", "Garamond", serif;
    letter-spacing: 0.3em;
    color: #C00 }
#ty { margin: -0.3em 6% 0 0 }
#gr { margin: 0.3em 10% 0 0 }
#st { margin: -3.5em 6% 0 0 }
#mo { margin: 1em 13% 0 0 }
#ed {
    margin: 10em 0 1em 0;
    width: 45%;
```

```
padding: 0.5em;
background: #CCB;
color: #C00;
text-align: center;
font: bold 50%/1 "Helvetica", sans-serif }
```

Chapter 10

Colors

Printing color is expensive. Hence, in books, color has always been used sparingly. On the Web, however, the use of color is virtually free. Most Web users have color monitors, so displaying color costs nothing, although printing it is still costly. So, there is no reason for Web designers not to incorporate color into their designs.

Of course, color can be overdone. As with all aspects of print, and Web, design – whether fonts, space, or images – color should be used to achieve a purpose with the design. Color thrown in at random doesn't work well. Remember, too much variety obscures instead of clarifies.

Some combinations of colors are difficult to read, such as red type on a blue background. A background that differs from the foreground text only in color and not in brightness also strains the eye. For some people, dark letters on a light background are easier to read, while for others, the opposite is true. People may also have associations with certain colors that may either help or hinder their understanding the text. For example, red seems to be almost universal in marking something that is important. But, the interpretations of other colors often depend on culture and even on the user's personal experiences. Colors and how we perceive them are both very technical and complex subjects, far beyond the scope of this book. We encourage interested readers to further explore the subject of color, particularly to learn how to effectively combine colors to achieve the desired effects.

The range of colors that can be reproduced by a computer monitor is called its *gamut*. The gamut depends not only on the color and brightness that a computer monitor can produce, but also on the brightness of the light that reflects off the screen. The effective gamut is reduced as the light in the room gets brighter; the largest gamut is available in a darkened room. Note that color printers work differently from computers, and their gamuts differ from that of computer monitors. Colors often appear one way on the monitor's screen and another when printed by a color printer or by a traditional printing process.

In this chapter, we show you how to use CSS to specify the color of text and borders. This is done with the **color** property. Also, we describe how to set backgrounds – either to a certain color or to an image. This is done with the various **background** properties. Before we describe the properties, we have to look at the different ways color values can be set in CSS.

SPECIFYING COLORS

Color can be specified in may ways. The English language – and all other languages – has words for the most common colors; for example, "red," "blue," and "brown." If you tell someone that your house is red, your listener gets a general idea about the color of your house, but many different shades of red can be described as "red."

Another way to describe a certain color is to use numbers. Paint manufacturers often provide sets of numbered color swatches so that you can ask for paint that is "blue number 216," for example. On computer screens, the most common way to specify a color is to give an RGB value, which specifies the mixture of red, green, and blue. However, this, too, is an imprecise way to select colors because the result depends on the type of screen you have and how much light is in the room in which the monitor is located.

A third way to specify a color is to refer to the color of something else. For example, you may want the color of your curtains to be the same as the color of your sofa. A more relevant example for a style sheet is to set the text color of a document to be the same as a system color (for example, the foreground color of the user's window system).

CSS allows you to specify colors using all these methods. A small number of color names and system colors are defined, and other colors can be specified as RGB values.

Color names

CSS 2.1 predefines 16 color names: aqua (a light greenish blue, sometimes called cyan), black, blue, fuchsia (light purple/pink), gray, green, lime (light green), maroon (dark red), navy (dark blue), olive, purple, red, silver (light gray), teal (blue-green), yellow, white, and orange (which was added in CSS 2.1).

Figure 10.1 shows samples of all the predefined colors. The exact same colors are also used in HTML. Note that colors onscreen look different on paper; keep this in mind when selecting your colors. If you plan to print your page on paper, some of the colors you choose for screen display may surprise you once they're printed. If this book was specifically about color, we would have tried for a better match – and the book would have been more expensive....

Here is a simple example of a style sheet that sets the color and background using the color names:

```
BODY {
    color: black;
    background: yellow;
}
```

The predefined color names are easy to use for those who write style sheets in a simple text editor. More advanced tools allow designers to graphically select colors that are then turned into RGB colors.

maroon #800000	red #ff0000
orange #ffA500	yellow #ffff00
olive #808000	purple #800080
fuchsia #ff00ff	white #ffffff
lime #00ff00	green #008000
navy #000080	blue #0000ff
aqua #00ffff	teal #008080
black #000000	silver #c0c0c0
gray #808080	

Figure 10.1 Samples of the 17 predefined colors in CSS 2.1.

RGB colors

Computer monitors commonly use the RGB *color model* to display color. In addition to RGB, a few other color models could have been used. One of them is the HSB (Hue Saturation Brightness) model, which is often used by artists because it is similar to how artists mix colors. Another is CMYK (Cyan Magenta Yellow Black), which is a color model commonly used by professional printers. We chose the RGB model because it represents how color is displayed on a color video monitor. Red, green, and blue light is mixed in specified proportions to represent colors on the monitor.

In the RGB color model, each of the three colors is represented by a value between 0 and 100%, where 100% represents the maximum brightness of a color. The values are arranged as a triplet, where the first number represents red, the second green, and the last blue. Black is represented as the triplet (0, 0, 0) – zero amounts of all three colors

— and white by (100%, 100%, 100%) — 100% of all three colors. Every triplet with equal amounts of each color is a shade of gray. For example, (90%, 90%, 90%) is a light gray, while (40%, 40%, 40%) is a dark gray. When the values are not equal, it is often difficult to predict what the color looks like. That (100%, 0, 0) is red is not too hard to see. But, that a color with the values (65%, 16%, 16%) is a shade of brown is not so obvious.

As you know, computers work best with bytes. A byte can contain a number from 0 to 255, so when working onscreen, it is usual to remap the RGB percentage values to values within the range of 0, inclusive, to 255, inclusive. Thus, 100% remaps to 255. White, then, remaps as (255, 255, 255), red remaps to (255, 0, 0), and the brown we mentioned in the previous paragraph remaps to (165, 42, 42).

Because each color is represented by 3 bytes, each a value between 0 and 255, the number of potential available colors is 16,777,216; that is, 256 x 256 x 256. These are usually enough colors for most applications. Unfortunately, many monitors don't have enough memory to store 3 bytes for every pixel, particularly when it is not uncommon for a million pixels to be on a screen. So, monitors play tricks (which we won't go into) in their efforts to display as many colors as possible. This usually means that, although potentially you can use all 16,777,216 colors, you cannot use them all at the same time. Many monitors have a limit of 256 colors that can be displayed at any given time, although a 65,536-color limit is becoming more common.

This limit may not seem important when you work with a style sheet because you usually will specify only a handful of colors. However, a typical HTML document also contains images, which may use up colors quickly. There is actually little you can do to ensure the desired color is available on the user's monitor. You can only hope that the browser takes care that if the exact color is not available (which it often isn't), at least one that is close is available.

* M. Stokes, M. Anderson, S. Chandrasekar, and R. Motta: A Standard Default Color Space for the Internet – sRGB. Available from http://www.w3.org/ Graphics/Color/sRGB

The RGB values of CSS1 are called sRGB (standard-RGB). sRGB is a "color space" that ensures that all colors specified in CSS are exactly defined. This means that the computer that displays the document knows exactly what colors are specified in the style sheet and all Web devices should be able to display the exact color. As previously noted, however, limitations in computer hardware make this a difficult promise to fulfill. An article* describes the technical details of the sRGB system.

To specify an RGB color in CSS, three values – a triplet – must be provided. That can be done by using any of three methods. We've already discussed the first two. The one you use is a matter of taste because they all produce the same result:

1. *Percentages* – For example, a color specification such as rgb(100%, 35.5%, 10%) specifies a maximum amount (100%) of red light, 35.5% of green light, and 10% of the blue light. The result is a deep orange red: ▮

2. *Numbers in the range of 0 to 255* – Thus rgb(255, 91, 26) should be the same color as rgb(100%, 35.5%, 10%) in the percentage example.

3. *Hexadecimal numbers* – For example, #FF5B1A, which produces the same shade of red as in (1) and (2).

In either the first or second method, if you enter a value that is outside the acceptable range (for example, 125% in method one or 300 in method two), the value will be "clipped." That is, the errant value is reduced to the maximum value allowed by the Web device. Because different devices have different ranges (for example, a color printer is different from a computer screen), you need to avoid values outside the acceptable range.

The third method for specifying a color needs more explanation. You use the same numbers as with the second method, 0 to 255, but you write them as a single hexadecimal number preceded by a hash mark (#); for example, #FF5B1A, which produces the same color red as rgb(100%, 35.5%, 10%) and rgb(255, 91, 26). This notation is not very intuitive, but is included because it is also used in HTML. The hexadecimal notation can be written in two variations that use either three or six hexadecimal digits. The three-digit form defines the same color as the six-digit form does but with all digits doubled; that is, #A84 is the same color as #AA8844.

System colors

CSS2 introduced the concept of *system colors*. System colors aren't real colors; instead, they are pointers to colors defined elsewhere in the computer that displays the document. For example, the system color Background refers to the background color of the user's desktop.

System colors are not widely used on the Web and there is a proposal to remove them from future version of CSS. We therefore do not recommend using them in your style sheets. For reference purposes, the system colors are listed in Appendix C, "System colors."

HEXADECIMAL NUMBERS

The relation between hexadecimal and normal decimal numbers is as follows: the digits 0 to 9 stand for themselves, the letters A to F mean A=10, B=11, C=12, D=13, E=14 and F=15. In a group of two hexadecimal digits, the first one is multiplied by 16 and added to the second. For example: 11 (= 1 × 16 + 1) = 17. Some more examples:

- A7 = 10 × 16 + 7 = 167
- FF = 15 × 16 + 15 = 255
- 22 = 2 × 16 + 2 = 34
- 5B = 5 × 16 + 11 = 91
- 1A = 1 × 16 + 10 = 26

We can apply this to color values:

- #FF5B1A = rgb(255, 91, 26), since FF=255, 5B=91 and 1A=26
- #CEAA13 = rgb(206, 176, 19)

THE PROPERTIES

We have already seen some examples of the **color** property and the background properties in use. This section defines them more formally and gives more examples.

The color property

The **color** property sets the color of the text of an element. It is the foreground color. It can also set the color of text decorations, which was discussed in Chapter 5, "Fonts," such as underline, as well as borders that have been created with the border properties discussed in Chapter 8, "Space around boxes."

FF	Op	Sa	IE	Pr
●	●	●	●	●

Name:	color
Value:	*<color>*
Initial:	UA specific
Applies to:	all elements
Inherited:	yes
Percentages:	N/A

The property takes one value – a color – which is specified by one of the methods discussed in the previous section. The following are examples of rules to specify a color for text or a text decoration:

```
EM { color: red }
P { color: rgb(255, 0, 0) }    /* red */
H1 { color: #f00 }             /* also red */
H1 { color: #ff000 }           /* again, red */
```

A color is inherited by child elements. The default color is set in the user's default style sheet, if one exists. Otherwise, the default color depends on the browser.

SETTING THE COLOR OF A BORDER

Setting the color of a border can be done in two ways. One way is to set it directly by including the color via the border properties, as done here:

```
P { border: 5pt solid red }
```

Figure 10.2(a) shows the result. We discussed this method in Chapter 8.
Another way is to set the color of the text that is the content of the element, as done here:

```
P {
   border: 5pt solid;
   color: blue;
}
```

In this case, no color has been set on the border, so it assumes the color of the text, which is blue. This is shown in Figure 10.2(b).

Figure 10.2 Different ways to set the color of a border using the **color** property: (a) setting the border using the **border** properties; (b) setting the border to the text color.

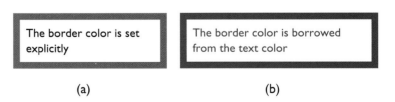

(a)   (b)

SETTING THE COLOR OF HYPERLINKS

Until CSS, the most common use of color in Web browsers (other than in images) was to draw attention to hyperlinks. Some browsers use two colors: one for links that the user has traversed before and another for links that he hasn't tried yet. Others use a third color for an "active" link; that is, for the short duration while the user keeps the mouse button pressed over the text. In CSS, rules for these can be written through a pseudo-class on an **A** element, as follows:

```
A:link { color: blue }      /* unvisited links */
A:visited { color: red }    /* visited links */
A:active { color: yellow }  /* active links */
```

For more information on pseudo-classes, see Chapter 4, "CSS selectors."

THE BACKGROUND PROPERTIES

The **background** properties set aspects of the background of an element, that is, the surface onto which text is displayed. That background can be either transparent, a color, or an image. You can also set the position of an image, if and how often the image should be repeated on the screen, and whether it should be fixed or scrolled relative to the canvas. Five of the properties set specific aspects of the background, while the sixth, the background property, is a shorthand method that lets you set all the first five properties at one time. The properties do not inherit. The following are the background properties:

- **background-color**
- **background-image**
- **background-repeat**
- **background-attachment**
- **background-position**
- **background**

We discuss each of these in the following sections.

THE BACKGROUND-COLOR PROPERTY

The **background-color** property sets the background color of an element.

FF	Op	Sa	IE	Pr	Name:	background-color
•	•	•	•	•	Value:	*<color>* │ transparent
					Initial:	transparent
					Applies to:	all elements
					Inherited:	no
					Percentages:	N/A

This property has two values:

- A color
- The keyword transparent – This is the default.

When a color value is provided, the specified color is visible behind the text of the element. How much of the surface actually gets that color depends on the type of element and on the amount of padding. We discussed the effect of padding on color in Chapter 8. It also depends on whether there is a background image in addition to the color, as specified with the **background-image** property.

Background color in inline elements

For an inline element, color is only visible behind the text itself and behind the padding around an element. Hence, if an element is broken across lines, the background color is visible behind the words and spaces at the end of the first line and behind the words and spaces on the second line. For example, in Figure 10.3, the words in the middle of the sentence are displayed in white on black by putting them in an **EM** element with color: white and background-color: black. Here is the code to produce this result:

```
<STYLE TYPE="text/css">
  EM {
    background-color: yellow;
    color: black
  }
</STYLE>
<BODY>
  <P>This paragraph has <EM>a few emphasized
  words</EM> in the middle.
</BODY>
```

Figure 10.3 Use of the **background-color** property with an inline element.

This paragraph has *a few emphasized words* in the middle.

Background color in block elements

For block-level elements, the color occupies a rectangular region that includes the indent of the first line (if any) of the paragraph and any empty space at the end of each line. It also occupies the padding around the block, if any. In such cases, it is a good idea to add some padding to leave room between the letters and the edge of the background, as has been done in the example shown in Figure 10.4. This figure was generated with the following style sheet set on the middle paragraph:

Readers don't pay much attention to plain-looking paragraphs like this one. However, paragraphs of the "standout" class are are noteworthy!

Figure 10.4 Use of the **color** and **background** properties on a block-level element.

```
P.standout {
    background: black;
    color: white;
}
```

Background color in list items

For list item elements, the background is not applied to the label if the label is outside the text box. If the label is inside the text box, the background will be behind the label as well.

The transparent value

If no color or image is specified, the background is transparent. In this case, the background of the parent element is visible behind the text (or if that is transparent, the background of the parent's parent is visible, and so on). If all elements have a transparent background, the browser's default background is used (this is often white).

For example, the following code sets the background of certain paragraphs to red and the background of **EM** elements to yellow. Other elements keep their default transparent background. Figure 10.5 shows how a document with this style sheet may look.

Many readers prefer black text on a white background, even for *emphasized text.*

However, special paragraphs can ask for other colors. Even inline elements — like this *emphasized text* — can be highlighted.

Figure 10.5 Example of transparent and colored backgrounds.

FF	Op	Sa	IE	Pr
●	●	●	●	●

```
P.special { background-color: red }
EM { background-color: yellow }
```

A background is not inherited; if it is not set explicitly, it is transparent, so you often can omit this value. You only need to set it to `transparent` explicitly if you need to override an earlier rule — whether in your style sheet or another's — for the **background-color** or **background** properties.

THE BACKGROUND-IMAGE PROPERTY

The **background-image** property lets you set an image as the background for an element.

Name:	background-image
Value:	[*<url>* | none]
Initial:	none
Applies to:	all elements
Inherited:	no
Percentages:	N/A

This property has two values:

- A URL
- The keyword none — This is the default.

To specify an image as a background, enter the URL of the image as the *<url>* value. When specifying an image as the background, you should also specify a color (by using the **background-color** property). When the document is displayed, the image overlays the color. You should do this for several reasons:

- The color can be used to fill transparent regions of the image; otherwise, these areas remain transparent.
- It can be used to fill in the screen while the image is loading; for example, if loading takes too long.
- It can be used in place of the image if the image cannot be loaded; for example, if the browser cannot locate it.

The following rule specifies both an image and a color for the background. Figure 10.6 shows the result.

```
P {
    background-image: url(ball.gif);
    background-color: #FFAA00;
}
```

Figure 10.6 Setting both an image and a color as the background of an element.

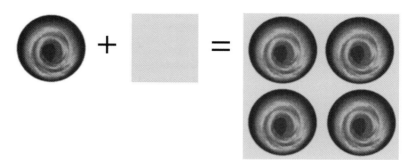

THE BACKGROUND-REPEAT PROPERTY

The **background-repeat** property determines whether and how an image is repeated in the element. By default, an image is initially placed in the upper-left corner of the element (or of the window if the image has the **background-attachment** value of fixed; we discuss this property shortly). Repetition of an element begins from either this default position or from a new position that you set with the **background-position** property, which we discuss shortly.

FF	Op	Sa	IE	Pr
•	•	•	•	•

Name:	background-repeat
Value:	repeat | repeat-x | repeat-y | no-repeat
Initial:	repeat
Applies to:	all elements
Inherited:	no
Percentages:	N/A

This property has four possible values:

- repeat — The image is repeated both horizontally and vertically as often as needed to fill the entire element. This process is called *tiling*. This is the default.

- repeat-x – The image is repeated horizontally (along the x-axis) across the element in a single row, both left and right from the initial position.
- repeat-y – The image is repeated vertically (along the y-axis) down the element in a single column, above and below the initial position.
- no-repeat – The image is not repeated. It appears only once, in the upper-left corner of the element, or wherever it is placed with the **background-position** property.

A repeated image is most often a picture of a repeat pattern, such as a dot or wave pattern. But, you can repeat an image of anything you want. Note that repeating images may cause part of the images to be cut off at one or more edges of the screen, as Figure 10.7(a) and 10.7(c) show.

The following are examples of rules for each value of **background-repeat**. Figure 10.7(a)–(d) show the result of each.

Figure 10.7 The four values of background-repeat in action: (a) repeat; (b) repeat-x; (c) repeat-y; (d) no-repeat.

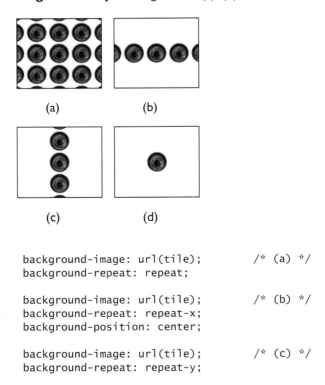

(a) (b)

(c) (d)

```
background-image: url(tile);        /* (a) */
background-repeat: repeat;

background-image: url(tile);        /* (b) */
background-repeat: repeat-x;
background-position: center;

background-image: url(tile);        /* (c) */
background-repeat: repeat-y;
```

```
background-position: right;

background-image: url(tile);          /* (d) */
background-repeat: no-repeat;
```

THE BACKGROUND-ATTACHMENT PROPERTY

The **background-attachment** property determines whether the image should be fixed or moveable on the canvas.

FF Op Sa IE Pr

•   •   •   •   •

Name:	background-attachment
Value:	scroll | fixed
Initial:	scroll
Applies to:	all elements
Inherited:	no
Percentages:	N/A

This property has two values:

- `scroll` – The image scrolls along with the content. This is the default.
- `fixed` – The image is fixed in regard to the canvas.

A background image is visible only behind the element to which it belongs. When the element scrolls, you usually want its background to move along. The `scroll` value causes the background to be attached to its element so that where the element goes, so goes its background. That is, as the user scrolls the document up or down or left or right, the background stays behind its element. This is the default. The value `fixed`, however, means the background is not attached to the element. As the user scrolls the document, the element moves, but the background doesn't.

Unfortunately, we cannot show the effect in this book...

The `fixed` value is most useful with **BODY**, where you would set **BODY**'s background and you don't want it to move as the document is scrolled.

You can use `fixed` to establish a "watermark" that stays where you place it independent of the movement of any other element. A watermark is a translucent design that is impressed on paper during the (tra-

235

ditional) printing process and that can be seen faintly when the paper is held up to the light. They are often corporate logos or other designs and are often used for stationery. Obviously, we can't produce a true watermark on a Web page. But it is possible to create the general effect: an image (usually faint so that text and images can be placed over it and still be read) that remains fixed on the window. A good place for a watermark would be the **HTML** or **BODY** element. Here's an example rule that establishes a watermark:

```
HTML {
    background: white url(watermark) no-repeat center fixed
}
```

(It uses the compound **background** property, which is explained later in this chapter.)

You can use `fixed` further to form a horizontal or vertical band that remains in place even as the document is scrolled over it. The following is an example code that shows how you could do this. It specifies a wave pattern image (back/waves.png) across the top of the **BODY** element that repeats in a horizontal band (using the `repeat-x` value). Figure 10.8 shows the result.

```
BODY { background: url(backs/waves.png) repeat-x fixed }
```

Figure 10.8 Using "fixed" to place a permanent horizontal band across the top of the body element: when the scrollbar is scrolled up or down, the pattern across the top will stay where it is.

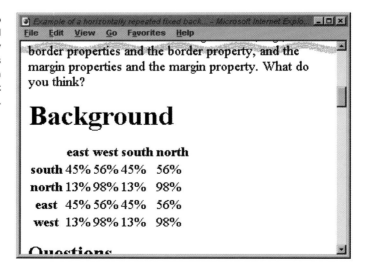

THE BACKGROUND-POSITION PROPERTY

The **background-position** property lets you override the default position of an image and specify the image's *initial* position, whether it's a single image or an image that is repeated.

FF Op Sa IE Pr

•   •   •   •   •

Name:	background-position
Value:	*\<percentage>* | *\<length>*]{1,2} | [top | center | bottom] | | [left | center | right]
Initial:	0 0
Applies to:	all elements
Inherited:	no
Percentages:	refer to the size of the element itself

Essentially, you can set the position of a background image in one of three ways:

- Percentages
- Absolute positions
- Keywords

Placing images using percentages

When you place an image using percentages, you tell the browser where the background image is relative to the size of the element.

Here's an example of how this works. Suppose you have an element, and you want to place an image in that element. Assume the element is **BODY** and your percentage values are 20% and 60%, written as a rule like this:

```
BODY {
   background-position: 20% 60%;
   background-image: url(tile.png)
}
```

First, you locate the upper-left corner of the element and the upper-left corner of the image. From there, find the point in **BODY** that is 20% across and 60% down. Next, find the point in the image that is 20% across the image and 60% down the image. Finally, you put the image in the element and match the points.

Positioning images using percentages makes it easy to specify some common positions. For example, to center an image in an element, you would write simply 50% and to place an image against the right edge of the element requires simply 100%. (See also Figure 10.10.)

If the background image is fixed (see the **background-attach-ment** property), the position is not calculated relative to the element, but relative to the window.

there is no figure 10.10

Placing images using absolute positions

When you give two length values instead of two percentages, the upper-left corner of the image will be that far away from the upper-left corner of the element. For example:

```
BLOCKQUOTE {
    background-image: url(shape.png);
    background-position: 1cm 5mm
}
```

puts the background image shape.png at 1cm from the left and 5mm from the top of the element.

As with percentages, if you give only one value, the image is centered vertically. That is, a value of 1cm is equivalent to 1cm 50%.

Negative values are possible, if you want to put the image partially outside the element. Only the part that is inside the element will be visible, however.

Placing images using keywords

When placing an image using keywords, you use any combination of two keywords. One of three keywords – top, center, and bottom – represents the horizontal (x-axis) dimension. One of three keywords – left, center, and right – represents the vertical (y-axis) dimension.

You cannot combine keywords with percentage values or absolute values.

Figure 10.9 shows the nine positions you can indicate with the keywords, and in parentheses the equivalent percentage values. The order in which you list the keywords in your code doesn't matter. For example, top left produces the same result as left top. This is not the case, however, when using percentages. The order in which you give the percentages makes a big difference in the result. For example, in the previous example in which we explained how to use percentages, we chose 20% and 60% as our values. Reversing the values – to 60% and 20% – in our code produces a different effect than that shown in Figure 10.9.

If you specify only one dimension, say, top, the unspecified dimension is assumed to be center. Hence, the rule

```
BODY { background: url(banner.jpeg) top }
```

produces the same effect as

```
BODY { background: url(banner.jpeg) top center }
```

Figure 10.9 The most common combinations of **background-position** keywords and their percentage equivalents and effects obtained.

top left left top (0% 0%)	top center center top top (50% 0%)	top right right top (100% 0%)
left center center left left (0% 50%)	center center center (50% 50%)	right center center right right (100% 50%)
left bottom bottom left (0% 100%)	bottom center center bottom bottom (50% 100%)	right bottom bottom right (100% 100%)

THE BACKGROUND PROPERTY

The **background** property is a shortcut means to set all the first five properties at the same time. Its values are all the possible values of those five properties. You may set from one to five of the properties in any order. However, this property always sets all five of the properties regardless of whether you explicitly set values for all five. If you don't explicitly set a value for a specific property, the **background** property uses that property's initial value as the property's value. For example:

```
BODY { background: red }
```

only the value of the **background-color** property has been set. The **background** property assumes the initial values for all the other properties. In contrast:

```
P { background: url(chess.png) gray 50% repeat }
```

sets values for four of the properties, but not that for the **background-attachment** property; hence, that property's value is the initial value (which is scroll). In other words, the previous rule is exactly equivalent to

```
P {
  background-image: url(chess.png);
  background-color: gray;
  background-position: 50%;        /* = 50% 50% */
  background-repeat: repeat;
  background-attachment: scroll; /* implicit */
}
```

You can separately set the five aspects of a background – color, image, repeat, scrolling and position – but we don't recommend this as a rule. The different aspects of a background are so tightly linked in how they work to produce effects that you could end up with some unexpected, even weird, results. For example, setting a **background-repeat** value without setting the image at the same time may produce a strange-looking background. The same is true with specifying an image without also setting the color behind it. In both cases, problems could arise when style sheets are cascaded. Cascading involves using more than one style sheet for your document; for example, yours (that is, the designer's), the browser's default style sheet, and possibly one attached by the user. If you were to specify an image without also setting a color behind it, the background might be composed of any combination of background from these three style sheets.

Although the user might be able to adjust his style sheet to compensate for such an effect, you as the designer should be careful to set all pertinent aspects at the same time so that all aspects work together to produce pleasing results. The **background** property is the shortest way to set all five aspects of the background, and using it ensures that you don't forget one of them.

SETTING THE BACKGROUND OF THE CANVAS

Sometimes, you need to specify the background color of the window; for example, if the document is so short that it doesn't fill the entire window.

The window (or *viewport*, as the CSS2 specification calls it since it could also refer to paper if the document is printed) does not correspond to any element in the document. Hence, its color has to come from somewhere else. The background of the window will be the same as the background of the root element. In HTML, the **HTML** element is always the root element, but XML-based documents will have other root elements. Because it's common to set backgrounds on the **BODY** element in HTML, the **BODY** element serves the role of the root element if the background of the **HTML** element is transparent.

It is as if the background of the root element is stretched to the edges of the window. Even if there is a margin set on the root element, the background will stretch into the margin as well. Some people have described this rule as the canvas "stealing" the background of the root element.

Chapter 11

From HTML extensions to CSS

If you produce material for the Web, chances are you use tables and other HTML-based tricks to achieve some of the stylistic effects that CSS offers. This chapter presents several case studies on how to convert current designs that use HTML extensions into a CSS-based design. Switching to CSS results in a more compact document that downloads faster and prints better. We chose these case studies because we like their design. We do not improve the end result, but describe ways to enhance the underlying code.

The last section, "Case 6: CSS Zen Garden," is a showcase for CSS-based designs. Designers start out with exactly the same HTML markup and combine it with their own CSS style sheets. The results are visually stunning, while the underlying markup remains structural.

CASE 1: MAGNET

The original page design is done as one single image that contains all the text (see Figure 11.1). The background color of the document has been set (through an attribute on the **BODY** tag) to be the same as the background color of the image. Although the page looks good onscreen, the image has the undesirable effects of being slow to download and difficult to print (although few users would want to print short pages like what's shown in Figure 11.1; printing is more important for longer documents).

When converting an existing design into CSS, start by collecting design features that are used throughout the page. These design features will be turned into declarations on the **BODY** element and thereby affect all elements through inheritance. Let's start with the colors. The background color throughout the page is brownish (with an RGB value of #c96 – see Chapter 10, "Colors," for a description) and the dominating text color is very dark (#424). This is easily expressed in CSS:

```
BODY {
    background: #c96;    /* brownish */
    color: #424;         /* very dark */
}
```

Not all the text on the page is dark, and we later express the exceptions. For now, we are still collecting declarations on the **BODY** element.

The dominant font family in the original design is a *serif* (see Chapter 5, "Fonts," for a description), but unless you are a typespotter, it's not immediately clear which one is being used. Studies reveal that the font in use is Bodoni.

Typespotting is the fine art of detecting font families when seeing them. Becoming a true connoisseur in the field requires years of training and an appreciation of details.

Not all computers have the Bodoni font installed, so it's important to specify a generic font family as a fallback option:

```
BODY { font-family: Bodoni, serif }
```

Giambattista Bodoni: Italian printer and type engraver, 1740–1813. The Bodoni fonts are typically used in advertising and newspaper headlines.

The dominant font size should also be set on the **BODY** element, and the two declarations can be easily combined with the font family on one line by using the **font** property:

```
BODY { font: 30px Bodoni, serif }
```

By using the **font** property, you also set the other font properties to their initial values (see Chapter 5).

The last declaration to be added to the **BODY** element is a value on **text-align** to center the text:

```
BODY { text-align: center }
```

In the original design, the lines are centered relative to each other, but are still on the left side of the window. With a center value on **text-align**, the lines will be centered in the window as well, which is arguably a better design.

The off-white text in the original design is clickable links, but because they are embedded in an image, their appearance does not change when clicked. To set colors on links, we use the anchor pseudo-classes

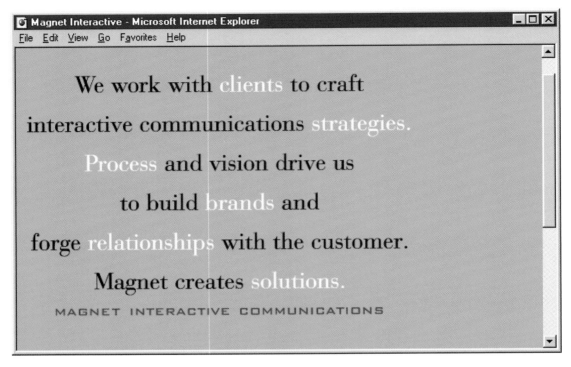

Figure 11.1 Original design: Magnet Interactive Communications.

described in Chapter 4, "CSS selectors." The following rules (there are three rules, although it may look like one because the selectors are grouped) express the same design in CSS by assigning the same color to all three pseudo-classes:

```
A:link, A:visited, A:active { color: white }
```

The only stylistic aspect that has not been described yet is the signature at the bottom of the window. It shows the name of the company that produced the page and is embedded in the same image as the main text. When you convert the image to HTML and CSS, it's natural to place this text inside an **ADDRESS** element. This gives us a selector for the element, and we can easily set the color:

```
ADDRESS { color: #c11 }          /* reddish */
```

Also, we need to set the font for the **ADDRESS** element. The font family is clearly `sans-serif`, but it's not the common Helvetica or Arial. Instead, we're probably looking at a bold variant of Eurostyle. The font size is roughly half that of the dominant text, and by using the **font** property, we can set all the font values on one line:

```
ADDRESS { font: bold 50% Eurostyle, sans-serif }
```

Often, companies feel strongly about the presentation of their name and logo, and because Eurostyle isn't generally available, you may want to let the company name remain an image.

CASE 2: CYBERSPAZIO

The original design uses some common HTML extensions to create this simple, balanced page seen in Figure 11.2. First, the background and text colors are set as attributes on the **BODY** tag. Second, the image (there is only one image on the page) has text wrapping around by way of an attribute on the **IMG** element. Third, to give the page more white space (actually, it's "black space" on this page), the entire page except the headline and horizontal rule has been put inside a table to set margins on the sides. A chain of **BR** elements has also been used to set more space around the headline. Fourth, **TT** elements have been used to set a monospace font.

Still, compared to most pages on the Web, this is a good page with a distinct design. No text has been put inside images, so the page downloads quickly and prints well. The main purpose of using CSS on a page like this is to simplify the HTML markup.

We follow the same strategy as in the first example: find design features that are used throughout the page and list the exceptions. Let's start by converting the attributes in the **BODY** element.

Colors

The **BODY** element of the Cyberspazio page looks like this:

```
<BODY bgcolor="#000000" text="#999999"
  link="#006666" vlink="#993300">
```

Figure 11.2 Original design:
Construct Internet Design.

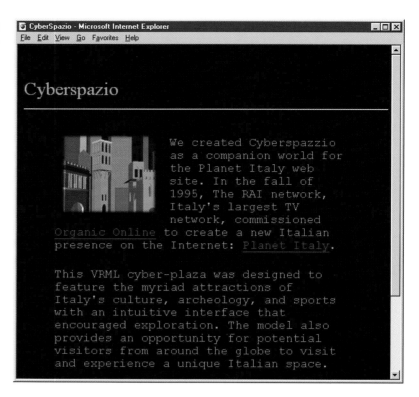

In Chapter 15, "Other approaches," you find the full set of guidelines on how to convert these attributes into CSS rules. Here is the resulting style sheet:

```
BODY { background: #000000; color: #999999 }
A:link { color: #006666 }
A:visited { color: #993300 }
```

Because CSS allows color to be specified in only three digits, you can shorten the previous style sheet:

```
BODY { background: #000; color: #999 }
A:link { color: #066 }
A:visited { color: #930 }
```

Images

The only image on this page is found in the first paragraph. Text floats around it because of the **ALIGN** attribute on the **IMG** element:

```
<IMG ALIGN=LEFT SRC="..">
```

It's easy to express the same in CSS:

```
IMG { float: left }
```

To set some space around the image, the original design uses the **VSPACE** and **HSPACE** attributes on **IMG**. In CSS, the **margin** property allows you to express the same:

```
IMG { margin: 5px 10px 10px 10px }
```

Fonts

The dominant font family on the page is monospace. In the original design, this is expressed with a **TT** (see Chapter 1, "The Web and HTML," for a description) element, but because each element has a font family value in CSS, there is no need for an extra element. By setting it on the **BODY** element, it inherits to all other elements:

```
BODY { font-family: monospace }
```

The font size of the two paragraphs has been increased using the **FONT** element with a **SIZE** attribute. Chapter 15 describes the **FONT** element as defined in HTML 3.2 and gives examples of how it can be used. We would, however, recommend not using it at all and instead set CSS properties on existing elements. For example, to increase the document's default font size, you could say the following:

```
BODY { font-size: x-large }
```

If you hand-craft your style sheets (i.e., write them in a text editor), you will appreciate the **font** property, which allows you to combine the two declarations into one:

```
BODY { font: x-large monospace }
```

The headline ("Cyberspazio") uses another font family. The original design does not specify a font family, so the browser default will be used. This is fine, but most designers would probably set a font as follows:

```
H1 { font: 20pt serif }
```

(The original design does not use the **HI** element, but the presentational **FONT** element. Because the role of "Cyberspazio" is to be the main headline, the use of **HI** is recommended.)

White space

The original design uses empty columns in a table to create margins on the side of the text. In CSS, margins are more easily expressed as the following:

```
BODY {
  margin-left: 10%;
  margin-right: 10%;
}
```

Because the margin properties are set on the **BODY** element, they establish document-wide margins that also apply to the **HI** element. In the original design, the headline (and the horizontal rule) has only a small left margin. You can accomplish the same by setting a negative margin on the headline:

```
H1, HR {
  margin-left: -8%;
  margin-right: -8%;
}
```

Alternatively, we could have set only a small document-wide margin and then added extra margins on the **P** element:

```
BODY {
  margin-left: 2%;
  margin-right: 2%;
}

P {
  margin-left: 8%;
  margin-right: 8%;
}
```

This solution assumes that the paragraphs have been marked as **P** elements.

To set some extra white space around the headline, the original design uses chains of **BR** elements to add blank lines. CSS offers a better solution by allowing you to declare exactly how much white space you want above and below the element. To replicate the effect shown in Cyberspazio, you could write the following:

```
H1 {
    margin-top: 3em;
    margin-below: 0.5em;
}
```

Recall from Chapter 5 that *em* units refer to the font size in use in the element itself. The previous example therefore gives you three blank lines above the element and half a line below it.

Similarly, you would want to set extra space below the horizontal rule:

```
HR { margin-below: 1em }
```

It may seem weird to use the em unit on the **HR** element. The em unit refers to the font size of the element, but the **HR** element has no text – it simply draws a horizontal line. For CSS, however, this is natural. All elements have a value for the **font-size** property even if the element never results in text being displayed.

CASE 3: "THE FORM OF THE BOOK"

Figure 11.3 shows a recreation in CSS of the cover of a bundle of essays by one of the great typographers of this century, Jan Tschichold (1902–1974). He didn't design this particular cover, but in one of the essays, he describes some similar ones. Great reading! Just for fun, we created an alternative cover for our own book in the same style.

Jan Tschichold. *The Form of the Book*. Hartley & Marks Publishers Inc., Point Roberts, Washington, USA (1991).

Here is the HTML source that we will work with. Nearly every word will be positioned individually, so we need many **SPAN** elements:

```
<html>
  <title>Jan Tschichold cover</title>
  <body>
  <p class=title>
    <span id=th>The</span>
```

```
      <span id=fo>form</span>
      <span id=of>of the</span>
      <span id=bo>book</span>
    <p class=subtitle>
      <span id=es><span id=es2>Essays</span></span>
      <span id=on><span id=on2>on the</span></span>
      <span id=mo><span id=mo2>morality of</span></span>
      <span id=go><span id=go2>good design</span></span>
    <p class=author>
      <span id=ja>Jan Tschichold</span>
    </body>
  </html>
```

Figure 11.3 "The form of the book." in a non-CSS browser.

Let's start with the basic fonts and colors. The background of the **BODY** will be black, and the text color will be white. We use a serif font and center all text:

```
BODY {
  background: black;
  color: white;
  font-family: serif;
  text-align: center;
  line-height: 1.0;
  margin: 1em 4em
}
```

The reason the line height is set to 1 is to make the following computations easier. One line of text will be 1em high.

Next, we set the font size and text attributes of the three paragraphs: title, subtitle, and author. The title's font is four times the size of the subtitle's font, and the author's font is twice the size. The title and subtitle are also converted to uppercase:

```
.title {
  font-size: 400%;
  text-transform: uppercase
}
.subtitle {
  text-transform: uppercase;
  letter-spacing: 0.2em
}
.author {
  font-size: 200%
}
```

Now, we are ready to attack the vertical positioning. The trick is to make all the **SPAN** elements into blocks, give the four parts of the title plenty of padding (and a bottom border), and then use a negative margin to move back to the top of the page, before doing the same to the four parts of the subtitle:

```
#th, #fo, #of, #bo, #es, #on, #mo, #go, #ja {
   display: block
}
```

All **SPAN**s are now blocks. (We use **SPAN**, not **DIV** because in a non-CSS browser, we want the words to be on one line, not below each other; see Figure 11.4.) Next, add padding and a border to the parts of the title:

```
#th, #fo, #of, #bo {
   padding: .6em 0 .4em 0;
   border-bottom: .025em solid white
}
```

Figure 11.4 "The form of the book."

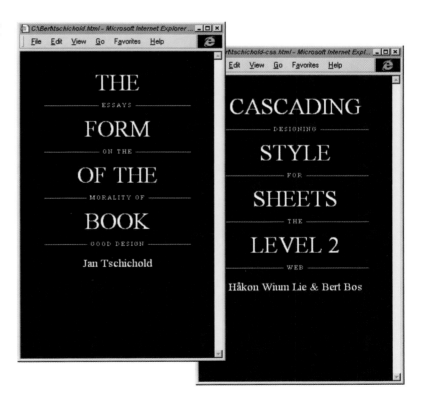

A negative margin at the bottom of the last part of the title brings us back to the top of the page. The sum of the text, padding, and border so far is 8.1em (8.1 times the font size of the title):

```
#bo {margin-bottom: -8.1em}   /* back to top */
```

Between the four parts of the subtitle, there is just a little over 7 times the font size. Remember that this is the base font size, or one quarter the size of the main title. We have backed up all the way to the top, so now there is nearly 8em above the first part of the subtitle. The subtitle is printed right on top of the border of the title:

```
#es {margin-top: 7.9em}
#on, #mo, #go {margin-top: 7.1em}
#ja {margin: 0.8em 0}
```

You're nearly done. If you wonder why we needed two **SPAN** elements around the parts of the subtitle, here is the answer: The horizontal rules should not be visible behind the words of the subtitle, so we give them a black background:

```
#es2, #on2, #mo2, #go2 {
  background: black;
  padding: .3em
}
```

CASE 4: "THE NEW TYPOGRAPHY"

Jan Tschichold. *The New Typography*. University of California Press, Berkeley, CA, USA (1995).

Figure 11.5 shows the jacket of another famous book: Jan Tschichold's *Die neue Typographie* of 1928, in a 1995 English translation. The design is by Steve Renick and, of course, the version shown is again only an interpretation. We haven't asked the designer how the layout should change if the window becomes wider or the font larger.

This example is much simpler than the previous one. There is no need for negative margins. The interesting parts are the red rectangle behind the letters "typo" and the first line of the subtitle, which is uppercase. For the red rectangle, we need a **SPAN** around the four letters. The uppercase first line can be handled with a :first-line pseudo-element. For the rest, the design relies on a large line height and wide margins. Here is the complete document with its style sheet:

Figure 11.5 "The new
typography."

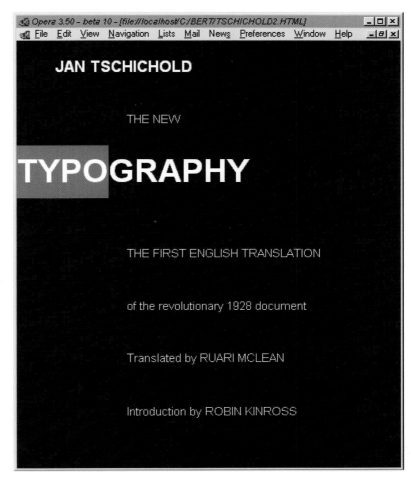

```
<style>
  BODY {background: black; color: white;
    font-family: "Helvetica", sans-serif;
    margin: 0; padding: 0; line-height: 4.5em}
  P {margin: 0 6em 0 9em}
  .author {font-weight: 800;
    font-size: 133%; margin-left: 2.5em;
    text-transform: uppercase}
  .title {margin: 0 0 2em 0;
    text-transform: uppercase}
  #th {display: block; margin-left: 9em}
  #ty, #gr {font-weight: 800; font-size: 280%}
  #ty {background: red; padding: 0.3em 0}
```

```
    .desc:first-line {text-transform: uppercase}
    .name {text-transform: uppercase}
</style>
<body>
<p class=author>
  Jan Tschichold
<p class=title>
  <span id=th>The new</span>
  <span id=ty>typo</span><span id=gr>graphy</span>
<p class=desc>
  The first English translation of the
  revolutionary 1928 document
<p>
  Translated by
  <span class=name>Ruari McLean</span>
<p>
  Introduction by
  <span class=name>Robin Kinross</span>
</body>
```

CASE 5: TSDESIGN

This elegant and seemingly simple page (see Figure 11.6) is the first case study that uses HTML tables for layout. It also includes an interesting text effect (the "what we do" is blurred), and the spatial layout poses some extra challenges. Still, the design is within the scope of CSS, and the rewritten code, when converted into CSS, is considerably simpler and more compact than the original design.

To follow the discussion in this case study, you need to understand the concepts described in Chapter 7, "Space inside boxes," and Chapter 8, "Space around boxes."

When converting a page like this into CSS, you should follow the same process as described in the previous case studies. To not repeat ourselves unnecessarily, we skip the full description of that process and concentrate on the design features that make this page more difficult than the others.

First, notice that one of the lines on the left is blurred, as if it is out of focus. Manipulating focus is a common cinematographic technique that is also often used in contemporary graphic design. CSS2 has a property called **text-shadow** that can do this, among other things. However, because of poor support in browsers, this feature was removed from CSS 2.1. Remember, CSS 2.1 only includes features that are supported by two or more browsers. In the hope that **text-shadow** will one day return to the Web, we show the code to achieve the effects:

```
text-shadow: 0 0 0.2em
```

Figure 11.6 Original design: TSDesign.

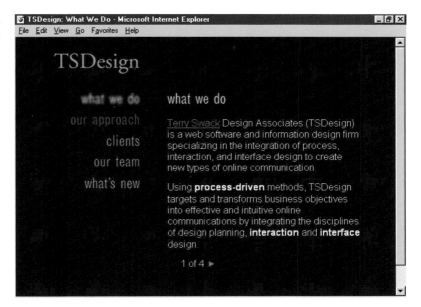

Second, the layout of the page is more complex than in the previous case studies. We can split the page into three distinct areas (see Figure 11.7):

1. Top-level headline ("TSDesign")
2. Vertical menu on the left side below the headline
3. Right side, which includes a second-level headline and some paragraphs

Figure 11.7 Three areas of the
page.

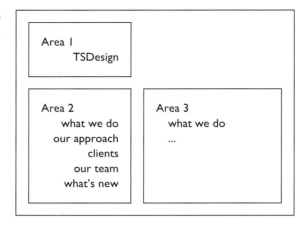

In the original design, a table was used to place the various elements on the page. CSS can work alongside tables, but offers layout features of its own that have several advantages: The markup is simpler and the pages work in browsers that do not support tables.

Another design feature you will notice on this page is that the text in area 2 is right aligned (see Chapter 7 for a description of text alignment). Also, the headline in area 1 is right aligned with area 2. Area 3 is more traditional; all text is left aligned.

To express this layout in CSS, start by finding one HTML element that corresponds to each area. Area 1 is the simplest because it contains only one element:

```
<H1>TSDesign</H1>
```

We need to set two properties to make the **H1** element correspond to area 1. First, the width of the element must be limited; by default, an element will stretch out as wide as possible. Second, the text within the element must be set to be right aligned. The style sheet becomes

```
H1 { width: 30%; text-align: right }
```

Area 2 is slightly more complex because it has multiple elements in it. The elements form a list, and it's therefore natural to put them inside a **UL** element, although the original design doesn't do this. The added benefit of using a **UL** is that we get an element that corresponds to area 2:

```
<UL CLASS=main-menu>
  <LI CLASS="what"> what we do
  <LI CLASS="approach"> our approach
  <LI CLASS="clients"> clients
  <LI CLASS="team"> our team
  <LI CLASS="new"> what's new
</UL>
```

Because there may be other **UL** elements in the document, we added a **CLASS** attribute on **UL**. Because each list item has a different style, we also gave them a **CLASS**.

Normally, **LI** elements within **UL** have a list marker. This is not the case in the original design, so we turn it off with the following:

```
UL.main-menu { list-style: none }
```

We must also set the width and the text alignment as we did for area 1:

```
UL.main-menu { width: 30%; text-align: right }
```

Area 3 is the last and the most complex among the three areas. It contains multiple elements of various types and the area has no natural enclosing element that corresponds to it. Thus, we have to add one of our own, and the **DIV** element serves this purpose:

```
<DIV CLASS=main-text>
  <H2>what we do</H2>
  <P>...
</DIV>
```

Recall from Chapter 4 that the **DIV** element, in combination with a **CLASS** attribute, allows you to create your own elements. Now that we have an element, we attach style sheet rules to it:

```
DIV.main-text {
  width: 60%;
  text-align: left
}
```

Setting the text alignment is probably not necessary because this is how Western languages are normally presented. Setting the width, however, is necessary unless you want the content of the area to use all the available space.

We have now found three elements that each represent an area shown in Figure 11.7. Also, we have assigned values to the **width** and

text-align properties so that they resemble the original design. What remains is there to position the elements. The original design uses tables to accomplish the spatial layout, but we will – no surprise – use CSS.

The key property to achieving table-like behavior in CSS is the **float** property. Earlier in this chapter, we used **float** to have text wrap around an image, thus placing the image and the text next to each other horizontally. When using HTML extensions, you can only make images float, but CSS has no such restriction – any element can float.

By making area 2 (or, more correctly, the **UL** element that represents area 2) float, we allow area 3 to be placed next to it:

```
UL.main-menu { float: left }
```

If you have trouble understanding why this will work, think of area 2 as an image for a moment: Surely, images can have text float around them. The only difference is that area 2 is not an image, but a textual element (namely **UL**).

Actually, there is one more difference. The text in area 3 is placed on the side of area 2, but it doesn't wrap around it as text wraps around the image of Case 2. Instead, it continues downward along the same left margin. This is achieved by setting the left margin:

```
DIV.main-text { margin-left: 40% }
```

Recall that the width of the **DIV** element has been set to 60% of the available width. Therefore, a left margin of 40% makes sure the element moves over to the right.

Because not all aspects of recreating this example in CSS were discussed, the complete style sheet is included as a reference:

```
<HTML>
  <TITLE>TSDesign: What We do</TITLE>
  <STYLE TYPE="text/css">
    BODY {
      background: #003;
      color: #fff;
      font: 16px sans-serif;
      margin-left: 5%;
      margin-right: 5%;
    }
    A:link { color: #969 }
    A:visited { color: #666 }
    H1 {                                    /* area 1 */
```

```
      font: 35px Garamond, serif;
      font-weight: 200;
      width: 30%;
      text-align: right;
      margin-top: 0.8em;
      margin-below: 0.8em;
    }
    UL.main-menu {                          /* area 2 */
      width: 30%;
      float: left;
      text-align: right;
      font-size: 20px;
      list-style: none;
    }
    LI.what { text-shadow: 0 0 0.2em }
    LI.what { color: #669 }
    LI.approach { color: #c33 }
    LI.clients { color: #996 }
    LI.team { color: #699 }
    LI.new { color: #f93 }
    DIV.main-text {                         /* area 3 */
      width: 60%;
      margin-left: 40%;
    }
    H2 { font: 20px sans-serif }
  </STYLE>
  <BODY>
    <H1 STYLE="color: #999">TSDesign</H1>
    <UL>
      <LI CLASS="what">what we do
      <LI CLASS="approach">our approach
      <LI CLASS="clients">clients
      <LI CLASS="team">our team
      <LI CLASS="new">what's new
    </UL>
    <DIV CLASS=main-text>
      <H2 STYLE="color: #ff9">what we do</H2>
      <P><A HREF="http://www.tsdesign.com">Terry
         Swack</A> Design Associates (TSDesign)
         is a web software... and information design
    </DIV>
  </BODY>
</HTML>
```

CASE 6: CSS ZEN GARDEN

You can find the CSS Zen Garden at http://www.csszen-garden.com

In May 2003, when the number of CSS-aware browsers reached a critical mass, Dave Shea launched a Web site that challenged graphic artists to start taking CSS seriously. Dave, a Web designer from Vancouver, Canada, provided entrants with an HTML file as a starting point and asked people to write style sheets that would turn the text into visually stunning presentations. At the time of writing this (October 2004), he has received well over 500 sumbissions and has selected 100 or so that he showcases on the site. Figures 11.8–11.13 shows some of the designs.

There isn't room in this book to describe how all the designs are achived technically. (Reading this book, however, gives you the insights to understand what is going on in the various Zen style sheets.) We limit ourselves to explaining one of the tricks that is commonly used in the Zen style sheets. To understand how it works, we must first study the underlying HTML code. Here is a fragment:

```
<div id="pageHeader">
  <h1><span>css Zen Garden</span></h1>
  <h2><span>The Beauty of <acronym
    title="Cascading Style Sheets">CSS</acronym>
    Design</span></h2>
</div>
```

As you can see in this code, the two lines of text are wrapped in several levels of elements, both block-level (**DIV**, **H1**, **H2**) and inline (**SPAN**, **ACRONYM**). Most elements are structural and we easily understand – at least after having read Chapter 1 – what they mean. However, the **SPAN** elements look slightly out of place. Why are they there?

To understand why the **SPAN** elements are there, we need to look at the accompanying style sheet. Here is an excerpt from Dave Shea's sample style sheet, which describes the **H1** element:

```
#pageHeader h1 {
  background: transparent url(h1.gif) no-repeat top left;
  width: 219px;
  height: 87px;
}
#pageHeader h1 span {
  display:none
}
```

The first declaration block sets properties on the **H1** element itself. The element is given a background image and a size. The second declaration block, which describes **SPAN**, has an element of surprise in it: display: none! This means that the element is not displayed. Why would you not want to display the **SPAN** element? The answer is that the designer wants you to see the background image of the **H1** element, but not the textual content of the element. The **SPAN** element is there so that the text can be safely removed. If display: none had been put on the **H1** element, the background image would not have been visible at all. Background images are an important part of the Zen garden.

The next question becomes if most of what we see in the Zen garden is images, why doesn't the designer use the **IMG** element instead of the **background** property? This question is important and has two answers. First, by using elements such as **H1** and **H2**, the document retains information about the *meaning* of the text, not only its presentation. Second, by attaching the images to the style sheets, the browser can safely assume that the document can be displayed without the images. For example, a mobile device with scarce bandwith may ignore the style sheet altogether, but the document can still be shown to the user. Figure 11.14 shows what the HTML document looks like without any styling from author style sheets.

You can find more information about the license from http://creativecommons.org

All the style sheets on display in the CSS Zen Garden are released under the Creative Commons license. This means that you can study them and reuse the code as long as you give credit to the original author, do not use it for commercial purposes, and release any derivative works under the same license.

Figure 11.8 "Brushwood" by Katrin Zieger.

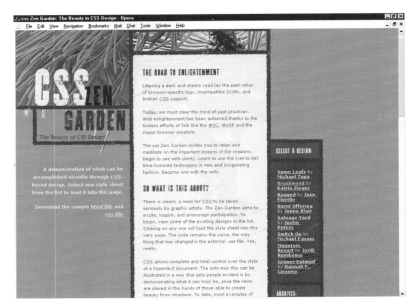

Figure 11.9 "Invitation" by Brad Daily.

Figure 11.10 "Mediterranean" by John Whittet.

Figure 11.11 "Pleasant Day" by Kyle Jones.

Figure 11.12 "Skyroots" by Axel Hebenstreit.

Figure 11.13 "Switchon" by Michael Fasani.

Figure 11.14 The Zen HTML document shown without any author style sheet. The presentation is plain, but the document's structure remains.

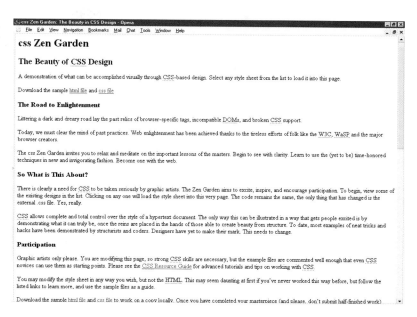

Figure 11.14 The Zen HTML document shown without any author style sheet. The presentation is plain, but the document's structure remains.

Chapter 12

Printing and other media

Most users see the Web through a looking glass, also known as a computer screen. One of the characteristics of the computer screen is that it's a highly dynamic device: It refreshes itself 60 times per second. This allows video clips, animations, and other dynamic behavior to be incorporated into Web documents.

The printed page, on the other hand, is static: Once printed, a page never changes (except when the ink smears or the paper fades) and the hyperlinks on the page become inactive. Still, many people prefer to read from paper rather than from a computer screen. The paper provides higher resolution and higher legibility. You can make notes on paper and fold it into a plane and send it off. Try doing that with a computer screen!

Printouts from the Web are often of poor quality. CSS2 adds functionality to improve printing, and this chapter describes the new features:

- Page breaks – You can say where you want page breaks to occur or where they should be avoided.
- Page margins and page orientation.

Also, CSS2 introduces a way to say that a style sheet (or a section of a style sheet) only takes effect on certain output media (for example, on a printer or a handheld Web device). This feature is known as media-specific style sheets, and it is described at the end of this chapter.

PAGE BREAKS

The term *page* has two meanings on the Web: It's an informal term for a document (a "Web page"), and it refers to sheets of paper that come out of the printer when you print a document. In this chapter, "page" always refers to the latter of the two.

One of the most common complaints people have when printing from the Web is that page breaks appear in the wrong places and don't appear in the right places! For example, a page break should not normally occur immediately after a heading. Instead, the page should be broken before the heading so that the heading occurs on the top of the next page. This way, the heading and the first paragraph, which logically belong together, remain together visually as well.

Similarly, a single line of a paragraph should never be left alone at the bottom or top of a page. Typographers refer to these as "orphans" and "widows," respectively, and avoid them like the plague. The traditional remedy is to make sure that at least two lines always remain together on the same page. Figure 12.1 shows these common page-break mistakes.

Printing

Most users see the Web through a looking glass, also known as a computer screen. One of the characteristics of the computer screen is that it's a highly dynamic device: it refreshes itself 60 times per second. This allows dynamic

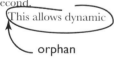

orphan

widow

behavior in documents. The printed page, on the other hand, is static: once printed a page never changes (except when the ink smears) and the hyperlinks on the page become inactive. Still, many people prefer paper.

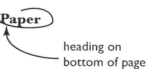

Paper

heading on bottom of page

You can make notes on paper, fold it into a plane and send it off. Try that with a computer screen!

CSS 2 introduces a way to say that a style sheet only take effect on certain output media, for example on a printer.

This chapter describes the new features:

list on top of page

- page breaks
- page margins
- page orientation

Figure 12.1 Some of the most common page-break mistakes.

CSS2 has five properties for controlling page breaks: **page-break-before**, **page-break-after**, **page-break-inside**, **widows**, and **orphans**.

FF	Op	Sa	IE	Pr
●	●	●	○	●

Name:	page-break-before
Value:	auto | always | avoid | left | right
Initial:	auto
Applies to:	all elements
Inherited:	no
Percentages:	N/A

This property indicates if there should or should not be a page break before the element. For example, if each **HI** element in a document is a chapter heading, you might want to force a page break before the element. This is easily done with the **page-break-before** property:

```
H1 { page-break-before: always }
```

The left and right values indicate that there should be a page break before the element, and that the element should end up on the left or right page, respectively. (A "left" page is a page that ends up on the left side of the fold when the pages are bound to a book; vice versa for "right" pages.) For example, it's common for all chapters to start on the right page, which can be achieved with this rule:

```
H1 { page-break-before: right }
```

Lists, on the other hand, should never start at the top of a page. This can be avoided with this rule:

```
UL, OL, DL { page-break-before: avoid }
```

Because cases can arise when the browser isn't able to fulfill this request, the keyword is "avoid" rather than "never." This is true for all properties related to page breaks: They indicate preferences, but there is no guarantee that the wish can be granted. The reason is that the problem is "overconstrained" – the style sheet specifies too many wishes and not all of them can be granted. For example, consider this document, which only contains lists with one list item each (unlikely, but possible):

```
<UL>
  <LI>item</LI>
</UL>
<UL>
  <LI>item</LI>
```

```
</UL>
<UL>
  <LI>item</LI>
</UL>
...
```

Given enough lists like this one, the browser will have to break the page at some point, and because the document contains only lists, one of them will end up on top of the page.

The auto value on **page-break-before** indicates that browsers should behave as they always have: breaking pages when they have to because no more space is left on the page.

FF	Op	Sa	IE	Pr		
●	●	●	◐	●	Name:	page-break-after
					Value:	auto | always | avoid | left | right
					Initial:	auto
					Applies to:	block-level elements
					Inherited:	no
					Percentages:	N/A

The **page-break-after** property takes the same values as **page-break-before**. In fact, the two properties are almost identical with the important exception that one of them indicates page breaks *before* an element and the other indicates page breaks *after* the element. So, a value of left means that the *next* element will end up as the first element on the next left page.

A typical use of this property is to declare that page breaks should not occur after heading elements:

```
H1, H2, H3, H4 { page-break-after: avoid }
```

This rule is part of the default style sheet for HTML documents and authors should, therefore, not have to set it in their own style sheets.

FF	Op	Sa	IE	Pr		
○	●	○	○	●	Name:	page-break-inside
					Value:	avoid | auto
					Initial:	auto
					Applies to:	block-level elements
					Inherited:	no
					Percentages:	N/A

The **page-break-inside** property indicates if a page break can or can't occur within an element. For example, this rule tells all items of a list to remain on the same page:

```
UL, OL, DL { page-break-inside: avoid }
```

A problem arises when a list has too many items to fit on a single page. In these cases, the avoid value cannot be honored and the list has to be broken when the page is filled. Conceivably, the browser could honor the avoid value by reducing the font size. Because this would quickly make documents illegible, CSS chooses to honor **font-size** instead of **page-break-inside** when a conflict occurs.

FF	Op	Sa	IE	Pr
○	●	○	○	●

Name:	widows
Value:	*<integer>*
Initial:	2
Applies to:	block-level elements
Inherited:	yes
Percentages:	N/A

Widows is a typographical term for isolated lines at the top of the page. For example, if a page break occurs within a paragraph, the lines which end up on top of the second page are called widow lines (refer to Figure 12.1). The value on this property specifies the minimum number of widow lines that can appear together. The value 2 is a common value on this property – common enough to be the initial value.

FF	Op	Sa	IE	Pr
○	●	○	○	●

Name:	orphans
Value:	*<integer>*
Initial:	2
Applies to:	block-level elements
Inherited:	yes
Percentages:	N/A

Orphans is a typographical term for isolated lines at the bottom of a page. When a page break occurs within a paragraph, the lines which end up on the bottom of the page (the first lines of the paragraph) are called orphan lines (refer Figure 12.1). The value on this property sets the minimum number of orphan lines that must appear together. As with **widows**, 2 is a common value, as well as the initial value, and authors seldom have to change it.

Use of page break properties

As a designer, you seldom have to set values on the properties previously described. For **orphans** and **widows**, the initial value is two lines and this works well for most documents; they rarely have to be changed. The other three properties (**page-break-before**, **page-break-after**, and **page-break-inside**) don't have equally universal initial values, but the HTML default style sheet contains the most common settings. For example, this is what it says about headings:

```
H1, H2, H3, H4, H5, H6 {
    page-break-after: avoid;
    page-break-inside: avoid;
}
```

So, browsers will try to avoid page breaks after heading elements, thus eliminating some of the problems in Figure 12.1. To eliminate the page break before the list, this rule is also found in the default style sheet:

```
UL, OL, DL { page-break-before: avoid }
```

So, after eliminating page breaks after headings, page breaks before lists, widows and orphans, the sample page now looks like what's shown in Figure 12.2.

Printing

Most users see the Web through a looking glass, also known as a computer screen. One of the characteristics of the computer screen is that it's a highly dynamic device: it refreshes itself 60 times per second.

This allows dynamic behavior in documents.

The printed page, on the other hand, is static: once printed a page never changes (except when the ink smears) and the hyperlinks on the page become inactive. Still, many people prefer paper.

Paper

You can make notes on paper, fold it into a plane and send it off. Try that with a computer screen!

CSS 2 introduces a way to say that a style sheet only take effect on certain output media, for example on a printer.

This chapter describes the new features:

• page breaks
• page margins
• page orientation

Figure 12.2 The most common mistakes have been corrected. (Compare with Figure 12.1.)

PAGE AREAS

Before the browser can put content on paper, it needs to know the dimensions of the area that can be printed on. This area depends on the size of the paper that is being used and the width of the margins around the edges of the paper. Also, the browser needs to know if the page should be printed in "portrait" or "landscape" mode (see Figure 12.3). After all this is established, the *page area* has been defined and printing can start.

Figure 12.3 Portrait and landscape pages.

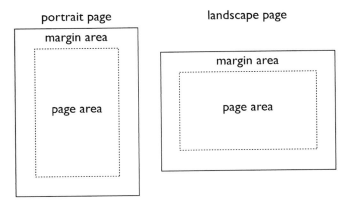

Page selectors and margins

CSS provides designers with a special selector and a set of properties to define the page area. No element in HTML represents a page (because HTML has no concept of pages) and, therefore, we have no selector to attach the properties and values to. Therefore, a special selector has been introduced in CSS2:

```
@page { margin: 1in }
```

The @page selector selects pages. Declarations inside the curly braces apply to pages on which the document is printed. This example sets the margins on all four sides to 1 inch.

Only a limited set of the CSS properties can be used in combination with the page selectors. The list includes all **margin** properties and the **size** property (which is described later). This means that, for example, the **color** property is not valid so you can't make all text on a certain page have a certain color.

Margins that are set on the page will be in addition to margins specified on elements. Consider this example:

```
<HTML>
  <STYLE TYPE="text/css">
    @page { margin: 1cm }
    BODY { margin: 1cm }
    H1 { margin: 0 }
  </STYLE>
  <BODY>
    <H1>J'accuse</H1>
  </BODY>
</HTML>
```

First, the page has a 1cm margin on each side. Second, the **BODY** element also has a 1cm margin on each side. The result is a 2cm margin on the left and right side of the page, and a 1cm margin on the top (see Figure 12.4).

Figure 12.4 How page margins and element margins add up on top of a page. The horizontal margins are simply added, while adjacent vertical margins are collapsed.

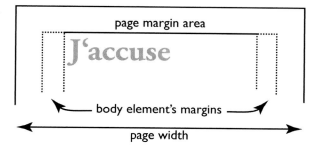

The top margin is smaller than the left and right margins because of the collapsing of vertical margins, which we discussed in Chapter 8, "Space around boxes." The fact that one of the margins is a page margin and not an element margin does not stop the margins from collapsing.

Left and right pages

When printing double-sided documents, it's common for "left" and "right" pages to have different margins. This can be expressed in CSS with left and right pseudo-classes:

```
@page { margin: 1in }
@page :left { margin-left: 2in }
@page :right { margin-right: 2in }
```

This style sheet results in left pages having a 2 inch margin on the left side of the page and a 1 inch margin on the right side of the content. For right pages, the numbers are switched so that left and right pages are symmetrical (see Figure 12.5).

Figure 12.5 Left and right pages often use a symmetrical layout.

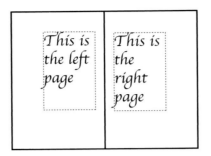

Just as there can be conflicts between normal selectors in CSS, there can be conflicts between @page selectors. In the previous example, there is a conflict between the first rule, which sets all page margins on all pages, and the other two rules, which specifically set the margins for left and right pages. Just as with normal selectors, conflicts between page selectors are resolved through specificity: Page selectors with pseudo-classes on them are more specific than page selectors without them. Therefore, the last two rules win over the first rule.

The :left and :right pseudo-classes work even if the document is printed on a single-sided printer. There are two reasons for this. First, it is often impossible for the browser to know if a printer is single- or double-sided. Second, a set of sheets printed on a single-sided printer may later be transferred into a double-sided publication (for example, using a double-sided copying machine).

First pages

Often, the first page of a document uses a different page box from the rest of the pages. A third pseudo-class addresses only the first page:

```
@page :first { margin-top: 4in }
```

Just as the @page :left and @page :right pseudo-classes are more specific than the plain @page selector, the @page :first selector is more specific than :left and :right. Intuitively, this makes sense: Even if the first page of a document also is a "right" page (which is true in most

Western books), the fact that it's the first page is more significant than it being a right page.

Units for page margins

The examples in the previous section used inches and centimeters to describe the width of the page margins. These are absolute length units that precisely describe how wide the margins should be. Absolute units work well when you know the exact dimensions of the sheets that are being printed. On the Web, this is generally not the case. If your documents are universally accessible, people from different parts of the globe will print the documents, and paper sizes vary depending on where you are.

In the U.S., the "letter" size (8.5in. by 11in.) is the most common, while "A4" (21.0cm by 29.7cm) is widely used in the rest of the world. One inch is equal to 2.54 centimeters, so the A4 page is slightly higher and narrower than its American cousin.

To make sure that documents print well on all paper sizes, we recommend using percentage units over absolute units when describing margins:

```
@page { margin: 10% }
```

Percentage value calculations are based on the size of the paper. So, if the document is printed "portrait mode" in Europe, the margins will be 21mm on each side horizontally and 29.7mm vertically. On U.S. letter, the margins will be 0.85in. horizontally and 1.1in. vertically. Figure 12.6 shows the page boxes of A4 and U.S. letter page sizes with 10% margins.

The amazing "em" unit, which was given extensive coverage in Chapter 3, "The amazing em unit and other best practices," doesn't work when setting length values in the page box. The reason is that the page doesn't know anything about fonts – only elements do – and therefore has no font size to relate to. (This will change in CSS level 3, which has provisions for adding page numbers and other text to a page box.)

MEDIA-SPECIFIC STYLE SHEETS

The bulk of this chapter is about writing style sheets for print. Besides computer screens, printers are the most common Web devices. How-

Figure 12.6 A4 and U.S. letter
page sizes. The stippled boxes
indicate the page box of a 10%
margin.

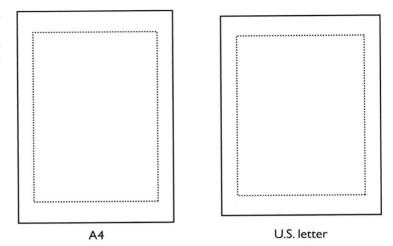

A4 U.S. letter

ever, there are many other types of Web devices, and part of the moti-
vation for creating style sheets is to ensure that content remains in a
form that can be displayed on all devices. For example, by storing text
as characters — and not as, say, images — speech synthesizers can read
documents aloud, and your cell-phone screen can show Web pages.

CSS2 groups the different devices into *media types* and allows you to
write different style sheets for each type. For example, here is a style
sheet that only has an effect on computer screens:

```
@media screen {
   BODY { font-size: 12pt }
   H1 { font-size: 2em }
}
```

The @media keyword is followed by the name of a media type. (CSS2
defines nine different media types; see the next section.) Inside the curly
brackets that follow is a perfectly normal style sheet. Because it applies
only to a certain media type, it is said to be a *media-specific* style sheet.
Note that media-specific style sheets come complete with selectors that
have their own curly brackets. Always make sure that the left and right
curly brackets are balanced. The left curly bracket should come after
the media type name, and the right curly bracket should come after the
style rules.

The **font-size** property is an example of a property that is useful
for many different media types, but which may require different values
depending on the media type. For example, because legibility is higher

on paper, the same text can be read comfortably with a smaller font size:

```
@media print {
  BODY { font-size: 10pt } /* slightly smaller */
  H1 { font-size: 2em }
}
```

You can have many @media sections in a style sheet, so the two previous examples can be combined:

```
@media screen {
  BODY { font-size: 12pt }
}
@media print {
  BODY { font-size: 10pt }
}
H1 { font-size: 2em }
```

Because the **H1** rule is the same for both media types, it has been taken out of the media-specific parts and it now applies to all media types.

The **font-size** property used in the previous examples applies to several media types. Other properties are only defined for a certain media type. For example, the **speech-volume** property only makes sense in an aural style sheet:

```
@media speech {
  BODY { volume: soft }
}
```

(Properties for speech synthesizers will be in CSS level 3, which was not yet ready when this book was written.)

Media types

Screen, print, and speech are three media types defined by CSS2. Here is the complete list:

screen

Scrollable color computer screens.

print

Printers, when printing on paper (as opposed to transparencies). This media type should also be used when the browser does a "print preview."

speech

Speech synthesizers, which read Web documents aloud.

braille

Electronic Braille readers, which "display" characters by making tactile patterns.

embossed

Braille printers, which emboss Braille on paper.

handheld

Handheld devices, which typically have small screens and limited bandwidth.

The following example does not display images on handheld devices. If the style sheet is evaluated in a proxy server, this can save much bandwidth:

```
@media handheld {
    IMG { display: none }
}
```

projection

Projected presentations (for example, transparencies or a computer hooked up to a projector). Typically, these presentations have few lines per page and need large font sizes.

The following style sheet sets the font size to be extra large and ensures a page break before every **H1** element:

```
@media projection {
    BODY { font-size: x-large }
    H1 { page-break-before: always }
}
```

tty

Text-based terminals and other devices using a fixed-pitch character grid:

```
@media tty {
  H1 { margin-below: 1em }
}
```

Because these devices are based on characters and not pixels, they are not able to display rich styles. Even the otherwise trusted em unit will have difficulties when used horizontally.

tv

Television-based presentations, typically on screens with colors, low resolution, long viewing distance, and limited capabilities for scrolling.

The following example sets colors to be white on black for TV screens:

```
@media tv {
  BODY {
    color: white;
    background: black;
  }
}
```

all

This media type is suitable for all devices:

```
@media all {
  BODY {
    line-height: 1.4;
  }
}
```

Media types were not part of CSS1. Therefore, this media type can be used to hide style sheets from older browsers. For example, some early CSS browsers have problems handling declarations on the **line-height** property. In the previous example, only newer browsers that are aware of media-specific style sheets see the style sheet inside.

Some people would like to have more detailed information about the device. For example, they want to write one style sheet for computer screens with resolutions of 800 × 600, and another for 640 × 480 screens. In general, it is better to design style sheets so that they work on any size screen – which means they have a good chance to work on future devices as well — but it is indeed possible to add such details to the @media rule. For example:

```
@media screen and (max-width: 1023px) {
   BODY { margin: 5% }
}
```

But, this is part of CSS level 3, which, as we said, is still in development at the time of writing, and, therefore, we won't describe these so-called "media queries" in more detail.

Chapter 13

Cascading and inheritance

CSS is sometimes referred to as a style sheet *language* because the most visible part of CSS is the language in which one expresses style sheets. However, a major part of CSS is the mechanism that interprets style sheets and resolves conflicts between rules. All browsers that support CSS are required to use the same mechanism for this. The mechanism has two main parts: cascading and inheritance.

Inheritance was introduced in Chapter 2, "CSS," where we briefly described cascading. However, we left out the technical details of how inheritance and cascading work. We present those in this chapter. You do not need to understand this chapter in detail to use CSS productively, but if you ever wonder why one rule wins over others, you will find the answer in this chapter.

Cascading refers to the cascade of style sheets from different sources that may influence the presentation of a document. Style sheets come from the browser and the designer and may come from the user. The cascading *mechanism* is designed to resolve conflicts between these style sheets. Compared to other style sheet proposals, CSS is traditional in the stylistic properties it supports. However, as far as we know, cascading is unique to CSS.

The mechanism used now is not the first devised for CSS. The first published CSS proposal described a cascading mechanism that tried to combine conflicting rules to reach a median result in a process called *interpolation*. If a designer wanted, for example, headlines in sans-serif fonts while a user preferred serif fonts, the result would be something in between (fonts like this do exist). Interpolation didn't always work, however. For example, if a designer wanted fully justified text

(text-align: justify) while a user wanted left-aligned text (text-align: left), there was no acceptable median alternative. So, the interpolation of values was dropped at an early stage while the concept of cascading remained.

The current cascading mechanism always chooses only one value. That is, when more than one style sheet rule tries to set a certain property value on a certain element, the cascading mechanism picks one of the rules. The selected rule is given full control of the value in question. The challenge is to pick the right rule. This is not always easy, because conflicts can appear in several areas:

- *Designer style sheets versus user style sheets* – The most articulated conflict, and certainly the most political one, is the one between users and authors. Designers that come from a paper-based environment are used to having full control over the presentation of information. However, on the Web, users expect to have a say in how documents are presented. CSS supports the users' position by allowing user style sheets.
- *User style sheets versus browser style sheets* – Each browser has a built-in style sheet that is also part of the cascade. The default style sheet ensures that there is always a description of how documents are to be presented.
- *Conflicting rules set on the same element* – Different rules in the same style sheet may set conflicting values on the same element/property combination.
- *Added weight given to certain rules* – Designers and users can increase the weight of certain rules. These then escape the normal cascading order.

The inheritance mechanism is used only when no rules in any of the style sheets in the cascade try to set a certain property value. The property value will then be inherited from the parent element. The initial value will be used instead if the property does not inherit, (Most properties do inherit.)

The difference between cascading and inheritance can be illustrated graphically using a variation of the now familiar tree structure. In Figure 13.1, inheritance works vertically. That is, values are inherited from parent elements to child elements as described in Chapter 2. Cascading, in contrast, works horizontally. All rules that apply to an element, no matter what style sheet they come from, are collected and subsequently sorted. In the cascading order, rules coming from the browser default style sheet have the lowest priority, followed by user style sheets and designer style sheets (see Figure 13.1).

Figure 13.1 Cascading is horizontal; inheritance is vertical. Inheritance moves values from parent elements to child elements. Cascading collects rules that apply to the same elements. The "cascade" moves from left to right: The right-most style sheet has the highest weight.

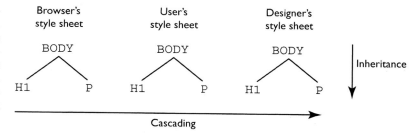

If you don't fully grasp the differences yet, don't worry. The following examples demonstrate how cascading and inheritance work.

EXAMPLE 1: THE BASICS

Here's a simple example of cascading and inheritance in action. We begin with a simple HTML document:

```
<HTML>
  <TITLE>A sample document</TITLE>
  <BODY>
    <H1>The headline</H1>
    <P>The text</P>
  </BODY>
</HTML>
```

Then, we add two style sheets:

Browser's style sheet

```
BODY {
  font-family: serif
}
```

Designer's style sheet

```
H1 {
  font-family: sans-serif
}
```

Graphically, the document structure with style sheets attached looks like what's shown in Figure 13.2.

Cascading Style Sheets

Figure 13.2 Style properties attached to elements.

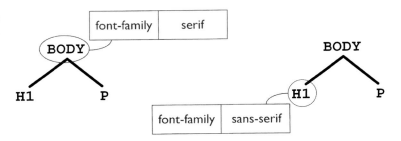

CSS now must resolve differences between these style sheets. First, the cascading mechanism gets to work. For each element in the tree, rules are collected. In this example, no element has more than one rule for the same property, so no conflicts need to be resolved. After cascading, the document structure looks like what's shown in Figure 13.3.

Figure 13.3 Style properties attached to elements after cascading.

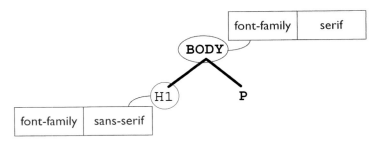

Next, the inheritance mechanism kicks in. The **P** element has no rule attached to it, so it inherits its parent's value. The document structure now looks like what's shown in Figure 13.4.

Figure 13.4 Style properties attached to elements after cascading and inheritance.

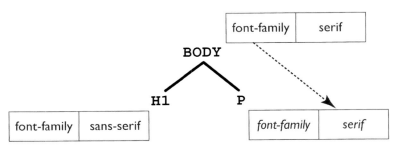

Because there are no conflicting rules in this example, combining the two style sheets only used the inheritance mechanism. In the next example, conflicts are introduced.

EXAMPLE 2: CONFLICTS APPEAR

The following example demonstrates how CSS resolves conflicts between designers and users:

```
<HTML>
  <TITLE>A sample document</TITLE>
  <BODY>
    <H1>The headline</H1>
    <P>The text</P>
  </BODY>
</HTML>
```

Two style sheets try to influence the presentation of the document:

User's style sheet	Designer's style sheet
`BODY {`	`BODY {`
` color: black;`	`   color: white;`
` background: white`	`   background: black`
`}`	`}`

(Although the browser's default style sheet will always be there as well, we omitted it to simplify the example.)

Graphically, the document structure with the style sheets attached looks like what's shown in Figure 13.5.

Figure 13.5 Style properties attached to elements before cascading.

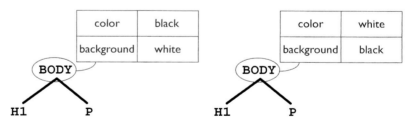

As you can see, both the user and the designer are trying to set the color and background for **BODY**, so the rules conflict. CSS first applies the cascading mechanism. The following principle resolves the conflict: *Designer style rules override user style rules.*

(Some people think that this rule is unfair. Read on. We offer two alternatives in the next example.) Hence, after cascading, the document looks like this (see Figure 13.6).

Figure 13.6 Style properties attached to elements after cascading.

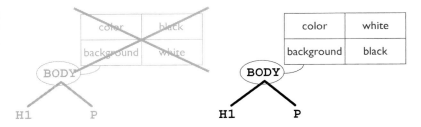

Next, CSS applies the inheritance mechanism. The color property inherits, but the background property is among those that don't. So, the background's initial value `transparent` will be used (see Figure 13.7).

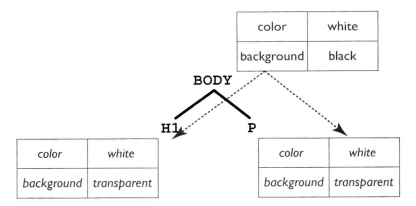

The background of the parent element shows through the transparent background, thereby producing, in effect, the same result as would inheritance. In this example, both the **H1** and **P** elements appear to have black backgrounds.

EXAMPLE 3: ACCOMMODATING USER STYLES

In the previous example, we showed how the cascading mechanism gives designer style sheets more weight than user style sheets. Some people consider this unfair, so in CSS, we include two alternatives for letting the user's rules prevail:

- The user can turn off style sheets. The CSS specification recommends that browsers allow the user to selectively turn style sheets on and off. Typically, the opportunity to do this would be offered via a pull-down menu that displays all the available style sheets, thereby allowing the user to pick the one desired.

- Users can mark rules in their style sheets as "important," thus overriding the designer's rule for the same element.

In the previous example, the designer's style rules were given more weight than the user's. To do the opposite, we change the user's style sheet as follows:

User's style sheet
```
BODY {
  color: black !important;
  background: white !important
}
```

Designer's style sheet
```
BODY {
  color: white;
  background: black
}
```

Adding the keyword !important gives a rule added weight. That rule thereafter overrides the designer's rule for the same property and element. After cascading, the document structure looks like what's shown in Figure 13.8.

Figure 13.8 Style properties attached to elements, after cascading and inheritance. This time, the user's rules win.

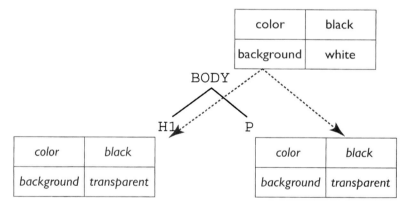

To keep CSS symmetric, we also allow the designer to mark rules as important. However, the designer's !important does not override the user's !important.

This is a change from CSS level 1. In CSS1, the designer's ! important had more weight than the user's, but in CSS2, the weights were reversed to give users with special devices or with disabilities a better chance.

A word of caution: Overriding another style sheet is often much harder than this example indicates. For example, if the designer's style sheet includes color and background rules for the **H1** element, the user must also override these rules. To fully override the effect of another style sheet, one must override each and every rule in it. This is difficult to do if you don't know what the incoming style sheet contains.

EXAMPLE 4: A MORE COMPLEX EXAMPLE

In this example, we follow the steps a browser goes through to find the value of a certain property for a certain element. The numbered steps correspond to the definition of cascading in the CSS1 specification.

We will use a slightly more complicated sample HTML document:

```
<HTML>
  <TITLE>A sample document</TITLE>
  <BODY>
    <H1 CLASS=first ID=x45y>The headline</H1>
    <P>The text
  </BODY>
</HTML>
```

Also, the involved style sheets are more elaborate than the earlier ones. They are written to demonstrate the specifics of the cascading and inheritance mechanisms.

Designer's style sheet:

```
1  H1 { letter-spacing: 1em }
2  H1.initial { letter-spacing: 2em }
3  #x45y { letter-spacing: 3em }
4  #x45y { letter-spacing: 4em }
```

User's style sheet:

```
5  BODY H1 { letter-spacing: 3em }
6  H1 { letter-spacing: 1em }
7  BODY { letter-spacing: 1em }
8  H1 { word-spacing: 1em }
```

The goal is to find the value of the **letter-spacing** property for the **H1** element. This involves several steps. The search ends when the one specific rule is found that will set the value.

Step 1: Find all rules that apply

We begin by going through the rules in the style sheet examples and identifying the ones that apply:

- Rule 1 – A simple selector that matches all **H1** elements. We are looking for the value of letter-spacing on an **H1** element, so the rule applies.
- Rule 2 – The selector is more complex. It matches **H1** elements, but only those that are of class "initial." The element in question is of class "first," so the selector does not match and the rule does not apply. Note that class matching is based on a comparison of the class names. The fact that "first" and "initial" are synonyms isn't important.
- Rule 3 – The selector looks for an element with a certain **ID** attribute. The element in question has an **ID** attribute with a matching value, so the rule applies.
- Rule 4 – Same as rule 3: The **ID** selector matches the element in question, so the rule applies.
- Rule 5 – The selector is contextual. It matches only if the element in question has a **BODY** element as an ancestor. This will always be the case in HTML, so the rule applies.
- Rule 6 – This rule is similar to rule 1 except it comes from the user's style sheet, not the designer's. The selector matches for the same reason rule 1's selector matches.
- Rule 7 – This rule tries to influence the property in question, but the selector is **BODY**, so the rule does not apply.
- Rule 8 – This rule has the same selector as rules 1 and 4, so it applies to the element in question. However, it sets a value for another property (**word-spacing**), so we ignore it.

Here's the situation after the first step. If a rule is marked ~~like this~~, it means that it doesn't apply.

Designer's style sheet:

```
1   H1 { letter-spacing: 1em }
2   H1.initial { letter-spacing: 2em }
3   #x45y { letter-spacing: 3em }
4   #x45y { letter-spacing: 4em }
```

User's style sheet:

```
5  BODY H1 { letter-spacing: 3em }
6  H1 { letter-spacing: 1em }
7  BODY { letter-spacing: 1em }
8  H1 { word-spacing: 1em }
```

If no rules had applied, the inherited value would have been used. That is, the inheritance mechanism is only used if there is no applicable rule. This demonstrates that the cascading mechanism is stronger than inheritance.

Step 2: Sort the rules by explicit weight

Rules can be given extra importance by labeling them !important. None of the remaining sets of rules in the example are labeled, so this step has no effect on the cascading order. If a rule did have this label, it would have won the competition, and the rule we seek would have been found.

Step 3: Sort by origin

Although CSS allows both designers and users to submit style sheets, users are usually happy to accept the designer's style sheet. This assumption is reflected in this step: Designer style sheets are given a greater weight than user style sheets. (As described in Example 3, however, users have ways to circumvent this.) Accordingly, because there is a rule from the designer that applies, the remaining user's rules can be dismissed. Here is the result:

Designer's style sheet:

```
1  H1 { letter-spacing: 1em }
2  H1.initial { letter-spacing: 2em }
3  #x45y { letter-spacing: 3em }
4  #x45y { letter-spacing: 4em }
```

User's style sheet:

```
5  BODY H1 { letter-spacing: 3em }
6  H1 { letter-spacing: 1em }
7  BODY { letter-spacing: 1em }
8  H1 { word-spacing: 1em }
```

Step 4: Sort by specificity

We now try to find the most *specific* rule among those remaining. The principle is that a specific rule (for example, one that targets a specific element) should win over a more general rule that applies to a large number of elements.

CSS computes the specificity of a rule based on the rule's selectors. A selector that addresses all elements of a certain type (for example, all **H1** elements) is considered general. This is the case with rule 1. Rules 3 and 4, however, apply only to one element (because the **ID** attribute is guaranteed to be unique across the document), so their specificity is higher.

In general, the rule of specificity says that any selector with an **ID** is more specific than any selector without; and any selector with a class selector, attribute selector, or pseudo-class is more specific than a selector with only type selectors (see Chapter 4, "CSS Selectors").

Furthermore, a selector with two class selectors (for example, P.sum EM.name) is more specific than a selector with only one class selector (for example, EM.name); and two type selectors (for example, P EM) is more specific than only one (for example, EM).

(For the exact formula for computing the specificity of a selector, see the CSS specification.)

We now have two rules left.

Designer's style sheet:

```
1   H1 { letter-spacing: 1em }
2   H1.initial { letter-spacing: 2em }
3   #x45y { letter-spacing: 3em }
4   #x45y { letter-spacing: 4em }
```

User's style sheet:

```
5   BODY H1 { letter-spacing: 3em }
6   H1 { letter-spacing: 1em }
7   BODY { letter-spacing: 1em }
8   H1 { word-spacing: 1em }
```

Step 5: Sort by order specified

Finally, we sort rules by the order in which they are specified. The later a rule is specified, the more weight it is given. Rule 4, therefore, has a higher weight than rule 3 and can be declared the winner: The **H1** element will have a letter-spacing of 2em.

THE "INHERIT" KEYWORD

We have seen that inheritance only comes into play after cascading, when there are no rules that apply to an element directly. But, just as the cascading order can be influenced with the !important flag, the importance of inheritance can also be increased. That is done with the keyword inherit.

Whenever you want to make sure that an element inherits a property value from its parent, you can make an explicit rule for that element, and specify inherit as the value of the property. For example:

```
H1 { font-family: inherit }
```

This rule takes part in the cascade as previously described, and if it wins, it causes the **font-family** value of **H1** elements to be inherited from the elements' parent.

To make absolutely sure that a value is inherited, you can even combine inherit with !important. For example, a user could put in his style sheet that the shape of the mouse pointer should never change when the mouse moves into an **A** element, with this rule:

```
A { cursor: inherit !important }
```

The inherit keyword can be used on *all* properties, even those that normally don't inherit. It won't happen often that you want to make a non-inherited property into an inherited one, but if needed, it can be done. For example, to make sure that **P**s have the same borders as their parents (and no borders if their parents have no borders), you can write the following:

```
P { border: inherit }
```

Chapter 14

External style sheets

For a style sheet to influence the presentation of a document, the two have to be linked together. In the HTML examples we have seen so far, the style sheets have been inserted into the document using the **STYLE** element (see Chapter 2, "CSS") and the **STYLE** attribute (see Chapter 4, "CSS selectors"). Chapter 16, "XML documents," shows a way to *link* to an external style sheet from a document. This chapter details how to use external style sheets, both from HTML and XML documents. The quickest way to start using external style sheets is to point to one that already exists on the Web. W3C has published a suite of core style sheets that are also described in this chapter.

WHY EXTERNAL STYLE SHEETS?

Before going into the technicalities, we should review the arguments, which show that separating style and content is a good idea. Some document formats do not separate the two (for example, PostScript and PDF) so it's fair to ask what the benefits of making the separation are. Here are the most important reasons:

- *Reusability* – By putting all the style information in one place, it can be pointed to by many documents and maintaining a consistent Web site becomes easier. For example, you can design an organization-wide style sheet that applies to all documents so that they are all given the same background color.
- *Performance* – After a style sheet is downloaded, the browser can cache it. This means that the next document that uses the same

style sheet can be displayed faster because the style sheet doesn't have to be fetched from the Web.

- *User selection* – A document can link to several external style sheets from which the user can make a selection. Unfortunately, at the time of writing, browsers don't let users make the choice.

EXTERNAL HTML STYLE SHEETS

In HTML, there are four ways to "glue" style and content together:

- **STYLE** element
- **STYLE** attribute
- **LINK** element
- @import declaration

The first two of these are described in Chapter 2 and Chapter 4, respectively. The last two are described in the next section.

LINKING TO STYLE SHEETS

The easiest way to apply a style sheet to multiple documents is via the **LINK** element. For **LINK** to work, the style sheet being linked to must exist as a separate file. Then, the following line must be added at the head of each document that is to link to the style sheet:

```
<LINK REL="stylesheet" TYPE="text/css" HREF="mystyle">
```

The value of the **HREF** attribute, mystyle, is the URL of the requested style sheet. The attribute **REL="STYLESHEET"** tells the browser that the link is to a style sheet and not to something else. Without this attribute, the browser will not attempt to load the style sheet designated by the URL. Here is a more complete example:

```
<HTML>
  <TITLE>Bach's home page</TITLE>
  <LINK REL="stylesheet" TYPE="text/css"
    HREF="http://www.w3.org/StyleSheets/Core/Steely">
  <BODY>
    <H1>Bach's home page</H1>
    <P>Johann Sebastian Bach was a prolific
       composer. Among his works are:
    <UL>
```

```
      <LI>the Goldberg Variations
      <LI>the Brandenburg Concertos
      <LI>the Christmas Oratorio
    </UL>
  </BODY>
</HTML>
```

This example links to the Steely style sheet, which is one of several in the suite of W3C Core Styles (described later). Figure 14.1 shows the result of linking Steely to the sample document used in Chapter 2. Feel free to put the same link into your own documents.

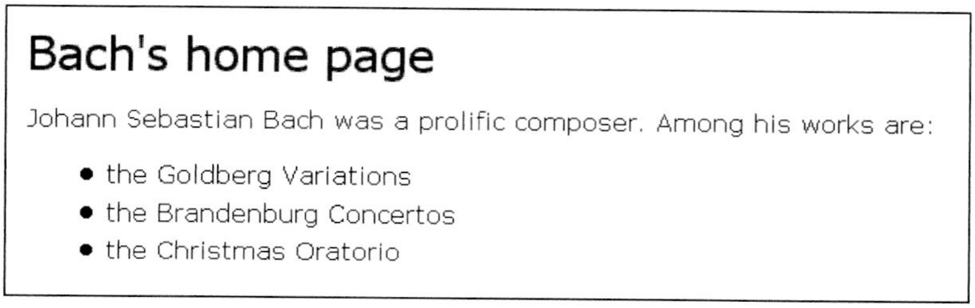

Figure 14.1 The sample page from Chapter 2, styled with one of the W3C Core Styles.

Bach's home page

Johann Sebastian Bach was a prolific composer. Among his works are:

- the Goldberg Variations
- the Brandenburg Concertos
- the Christmas Oratorio

In this example, the external style sheet has replaced the **STYLE** element and Steely is fully in charge of the presentation. Often, it's convenient to base the presentation on an external style sheet, but it's equally convenient to be able to make small adjustments that are specific to the document. This can be easily achieved by reintroducing the **STYLE** element:

```
<HTML>
  <TITLE>Bach's home page</TITLE>
  <LINK REL="stylesheet" TYPE="text/css"
    HREF="http://www.w3.org/StyleSheets/Core/Steely">
  <STYLE TYPE="text/css">
    H1, H2, H3 { font-family: serif }
  </STYLE>
  <BODY>
    <H1>Bach's home page</H1>
    <P>Johann Sebastian Bach was a prolific
       composer. Among his works are:
    <UL>
      <LI>the Goldberg Variations
      <LI>the Brandenburg Concertos
      <LI>the Christmas Oratorio
    </UL>
  </BODY>
</HTML>
```

The external style sheet and the rules in the **STYLE** element are now *cascaded* together – i.e., they are combined when displaying the document. The result is a page where headlines use serif fonts and all other stylistic settings come from Steely (see Figure 14.2).

Bach's home page

Johann Sebastian Bach was a prolific composer. Among his works are:

- the Goldberg Variations
- the Brandenburg Concertos
- the Christmas Oratorio

Persistent, preferred, and alternate author style sheets

At the time of writing, Microsoft's Internet Explorer does not allow users to turn style sheets on/off. Therefore, the features described on this page has only seen limited use on the Web although they are supported by Opera and Mozilla.

As used in the previous example, both the external style sheet and the one inside the **STYLE** element are examples of what HTML calls *persistent style sheets*. Persistent style sheets are always applied to the document. That is, unless the user has turned off author style sheets in the browser setting, the persistent style sheets will always be applied to the document.

In addition to persistent style sheets, the HTML specification defines two other categories of author style sheets: *preferred* and *alternate*. *Preferred style sheets*, like persistent style sheets, are applied to the document by default. The difference between preferred and persistent style sheets is that preferred style sheets can be turned on and off individually by the user. For this reason, preferred style sheets are given a name (through the **TITLE** attribute) that can be used in a dialog box with the user.

Alternate style sheets are not applied by default. For them to have any effect, the user must actively select the alternate style sheet. CSS doesn't describe *how* this user interaction should be performed, but having a pull-down menu that lists alternate style sheets seems like a natural way. Table 14.1 summarizes the differences between the three categories.

Category	Applied by default?	Has a name?	Syntax
Persistent	Yes	No	`<STYLE TYPE="text/css">...</STYLE>` `<LINK REL="stylesheet" ...`
Preferred	Yes	Yes	`<LINK REL="stylesheet" TITLE=".." ...`
Alternate	No	Yes	`<LINK REL="alternate stylesheet" TITLE=".."` `...`

Table 14.1 The differences and similarities between persistent, preferred, and alternative style sheets.

Here is a document that uses all three types of author style sheets:

```
<HTML>
  <TITLE>Bach's home page</TITLE>
  <LINK REL="stylesheet" TITLE="Steely" TYPE="text/css"
    HREF="http://www.w3.org/StyleSheets/Core/Steely">
  <LINK REL="alternate stylesheet" TYPE="text/css"
    HREF="http://www.w3.org/StyleSheets/Core/Midnight">
  <LINK REL="alternate stylesheet" TYPE="text/css"
    HREF="http://www.w3.org/StyleSheets/Core/Swiss">
  <STYLE TYPE="text/css">
    H1, H2, H3 { font-family: serif }
  </STYLE>
  <BODY>
    <H1>Bach's home page</H1>
    <P>Johann Sebastian Bach was a prolific
        composer. Among his works are:
    <UL>
      <LI>the Goldberg Variations
      <LI>the Brandenburg Concertos
      <LI>the Christmas Oratorio
    </UL>
  </BODY>
</HTML>
```

In this document, the Steely style sheet and the rules inside the **STYLE** element are initially applied to the document. User interaction might lead to Steely being turned off and Midnight or Swiss (two of the other W3C Core Styles) being turned on. The **STYLE** element is always persistent and is only turned off if the browser provides a switch to turn off all author style sheets.

A word of warning: When providing a combination of persistent, preferred, and alternate style sheets, it's important that you test all combinations to make sure that they work well together. For example, the Midnight style sheet (one of the alternate style sheets in the previous example) displays light text on a dark background, while Swiss and Steely do the opposite. Therefore, the **STYLE** element, which is applied after the external style sheets, shouldn't say anything about colors because it doesn't know if the text is light on dark or dark on light.

The MEDIA attribute

CSS2 allows you to write different style sheets for different kinds of Web devices. These are known as media-specific style sheets and in Chapter 12, "Printing and other media," we showed how you could label a style sheet — or part of a style sheet — using an at-rule:

```
@media screen {
  BODY { font-size: 12pt }
  H1 { font-size: 2em }
}
```

This method is good if only part of the style sheet is media-specific. In cases where the entire style sheet applies to one media type, there is a better way. By using the **MEDIA** attribute of the **LINK** element, browsers can find out what media types a style sheet applies to without downloading it. Here is an example:

```
<LINK REL="stylesheet" TITLE="Steely" TYPE="text/css"
    MEDIA="screen"
    HREF="http://www.w3.org/StyleSheets/Core/Steely">
```

The value of the **MEDIA** attribute is one of the media type keywords described in Chapter 12: *screen*, *print*, *aural*, *braille*, *embossed*, *handheld*, *projection*, *tty*, *tv*, and *all*. The previous example makes the external style sheet (the by-now famous Steely) apply only to computer screens.

The **MEDIA** attribute can take a list of different media types to indicate that the external style sheet applies to more than one media type:

```
<LINK REL="stylesheet" TITLE="Steely" TYPE="text/css"
    MEDIA="screen, print"
    HREF="http://www.w3.org/StyleSheets/Core/Steely">
```

In this example, Steely would be applied to both screen presentation and printouts.

@IMPORT

The **LINK** element is HTML's way of linking to external style sheets. CSS also has a way of importing external style sheets that offer some of the same functionality:

```
<STYLE TYPE="text/css">
  @import url("http://www.w3.org/StyleSheets/Core/Steely");
</STYLE>
```

Because there always comes a URL after @import, you can safely drop the url( ) notation. The following example therefore has the same effect as the previous one:

```
<STYLE TYPE="text/css">
  @import "http://www.w3.org/StyleSheets/Core/Steely";
</STYLE>
```

As used in the previous examples, @import doesn't offer any benefits over using the **LINK** element. One example from W3C illustrates how using @import can make your life easier. Along the way, you learn more about how W3C produces specifications for the Web.

Using @import: a case study

W3C publishes technical specifications. A specification normally starts out as a *Working Draft* in one of several *Working Groups* inside W3C. Working Drafts are available to W3C Members and, most often, to the public. When the Working Group considers it ready, the specification becomes a *Proposed Recommendation*. If the W3C Members consider the specification worthwhile, it is thereafter turned into a *Recommendation*.

For W3C, it's important to convey at what stage a specification is in. A Working Draft is often immature and is mostly made available for discussion purposes. A Recommendation, on the other hand, is an industrial-strength specification that W3C actively promotes. Style sheets are a good way to visually communicate at what stage a specification is at. For example, by using an informal font for Working Drafts, the style sheet communicates that the draft is subject to change:

```
@import "W3C-specifications.css";
BODY { font-family: cursive }
```

In this example, most of the style settings are found in the imported style sheet. However, the rule on the second line overrides any **font-family** setting on the **BODY** element inside the external style sheet. The more mature documents can be given a more formal font. For example, the style sheet for Proposed Recommendations might say:

```
@import "W3C-specifications.css";
BODY { font-family: sans-serif }
```

While W3C Recommendations, which are the ultimate rubberstamp W3C will use, may have this code:

```
@import "W3C-specifications.css";
BODY { font-family: serif }
```

The benefit of organizing your style sheets into hierarchies like this one is that you can easily make changes to large sets of documents. For example, by changing the base style sheet (W3C-specifications.css), you can change the color and background for all three types of specifications.

The examples in this case study are fictional – the style sheets in use by W3C are slightly more complex.

@import: the details

You always write the @import declaration as the first declaration in the **STYLE** element. The local rules follow, as the following example shows, and override any conflicting rules in the imported style sheet:

```
<STYLE TYPE="text/css">
  @import "mystyle";
  H1 { font-style: palatino, sans-serif }
  P { color: blue; background: white }
</STYLE>
```

You can import any number of external style sheets using @import by inserting multiple @import declarations, each with the URL of a style sheet.

Importing multiple style sheets can result in a tier of style sheets. This is because an imported style can have its own @import declarations, which point to style sheets that may also have @import, and so on. The order of the declarations is significant. Each additional level of @import has a lower priority in case of conflicting rules; that is, style sheets that are imported later override those imported earlier. So, you should place your primary style sheet(s) first and follow with supplementary style sheets included for specialized purposes.

You can use @import declarations in a modular fashion to customize your documents. For example, you may have style sheets as separate files that define different background images, methods for handling tables, default fonts, and special kinds of paragraphs and lists. Then, in any particular document, you can use @import to pull in the appropriate style sheets to create the desired effect. For example:

```
<STYLE TYPE="text/css">
  @import "basics";
  @import "list-styles";
  @import "headings";
  @import "smaller-headings" print;
</STYLE>
```

Notice the word "print" after the last @import statement in this example. Remember how the **MEDIA** attribute on the **LINK** element was used to declare media-specific style sheets? You can do the same on @import by adding the media types after the URL. If more than one media type exists, there should be commas between the keywords:

```
<STYLE TYPE="text/css">
  @import "bigger-headings" screen, projection;
  @import "smaller-headings" print, handheld;
</STYLE>
```

If no media types are specified, imported style sheets apply to all media types.

EXTERNAL XML STYLE SHEETS

The first part of this chapter shows how to link to style sheets from HTML documents. Most documents on the Web are HTML documents, and we expect this to be the case in the future. We also expect some new document formats to be developed for the Web. These are likely to be based on XML. Unlike HTML, XML-based documents will come with no conventions on how to display them and a style sheet will always be required. Therefore, work has been started to find a common way for all XML-based document formats to link to style sheets. So far, only the XML equivalent of HTML's **LINK** element has been defined. For example, in HTML, you could use the **LINK** element like this:

```
<LINK HREF="/style/mystyle" REL="stylesheet" TYPE="text/css">
```

The XML equivalent would be as follows:

```
<?xml:stylesheet href="/styles/mystyle" type="text/css"?>
```

Note the question marks that appear inside the angle brackets — one at the beginning and one at the end. The question marks turn what would otherwise be a normal element into a *processing instruction*. Processing instructions are not used in HTML documents. In XML-based documents, they are used to do various tasks and linking to style sheets is one of them.

In Chapter 16, we see that XML documents are case-sensitive. So, although you could write `<LINK...>` or `<link...>` in HTML, you must always use the lowercase `<?xml:stylesheet href...type...>` in XML.

We expect that XML-based formats will also offer the equivalence of the **STYLE** element and the **STYLE** attribute as found in HTML, but at this point, this is only a proposal.

W3C CORE STYLES

The quickest way to start using style sheets is to link to one that already exists. W3C has published a suite of style sheets called W3C Core Styles. Designed by Todd Fahrner of Studio Verso, these style sheets offer you professional designs without the need to learn how to write your own style sheets. If you decide to write your own style sheets — because you're reading this book, this has probably crossed your mind — you can combine the Core Styles with those of your own.

The W3C Core Styles are built up from a set of modules that can be combined in infinite ways, much like LEGO bricks can. Eight of the combinations have proved to be particularly pleasing and have been given names for easy reference. The names are Chocolate, Midnight, Modernist, Oldstyle, Steely, Swiss, Traditional, and Ultramarine. You can see screenshots of them over the following pages.

To refer to one of them, put this in your HTML document:

```
<LINK REL="stylesheet" TYPE="text/css"
  HREF="http://www.w3.org/StyleSheets/Core/Steely">
```

Then, exchange Steely with the name of your favorite style.

One benefit of using the W3C Core Styles is that the W3C server "sniffs" what kind of browser you are using and witholds modules that are known to cause problems in old browsers. In the past, not all CSS browsers have handled all style sheets correctly. The problem is disappearing as new CSS implementations replace older ones, and W3C expects to remove the need for "browser sniffing" in the future. Figures 14.3–14.8 shows the results of using different W3C Core Styles.

Figure 14.3 The sample document without any style applied.

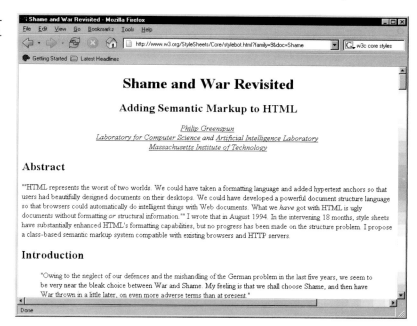

Cascading Style Sheets

Figure 14.4 The "Steely" style sheet.

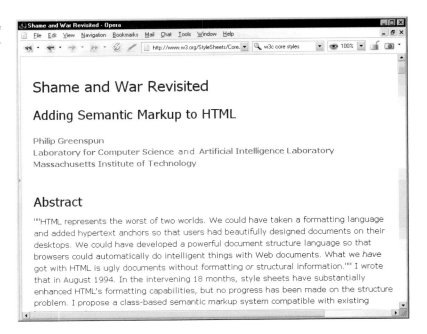

Figure 14.5 "Modernist."

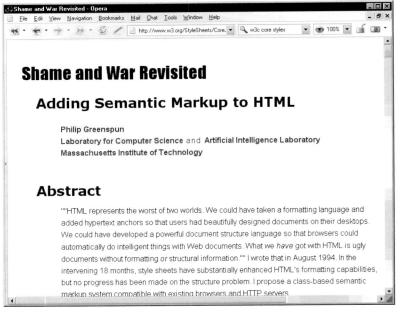

Figure 14.6 "Oldstyle."

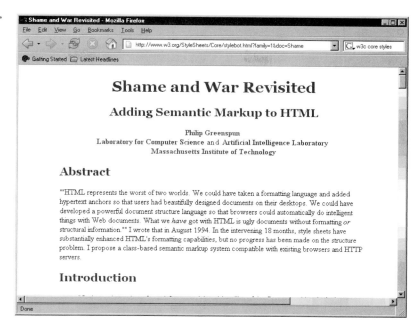

Figure 14.7 "Chocolate."

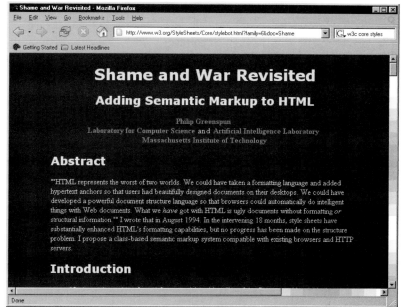

Figure 14.8 "Midnight."

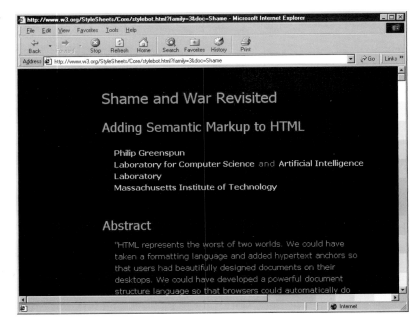

When using W3C Core Styles, be aware that most HTML documents are not valid according to the HTML specification. Invalid documents, in combination with the Core Styles, may lead to unexpected results. W3C operates a validator service that checks your documents and helps fix problems.

The W3C validator can be found from http://validator.w3.org/

For best results, the HTML markup should be non-presentational (avoid, e.g., **FONT** tags, tables for layout, overuse of **BR**, and so on) and structural (e.g., use **H1**, **H2** for headlines).

Chapter 15

Other approaches

We based this book on the premise that both the HTML text and the style sheet should be reusable as much as possible. The text must stay "clean" so that it can be shown with different style sheets or on different media, and the style sheet should be general enough to be applicable to other HTML documents.

In this chapter, we show what happens if we change some of those parameters, such as

- Using a different style language from CSS
- Creating a document without using a style sheet
- Using a different format from HTML

This chapter assumes that you have a little more knowledge of Web-related technology than the preceding chapters. It is included for those who want to compare CSS to other systems. You can skip it if you only want to know how to use CSS.

CREATING A DOCUMENT WITHOUT USING A STYLE SHEET

HTML 3.2 has some attributes and elements – commonly called *extensions* – that allow you to specify the layout to some degree. However, this is done at the cost of making the document less portable and more difficult to maintain.

These extensions were added by various browser vendors before it was clear that style sheets would provide a better alternative. Most of these stem from the Netscape browser.

In HTML 4.0, most of these extensions are no longer available, although there is a companion version of HTML 4.0, called HTML 4.0 Transitional, in which they still exist. In the new, XML-based version of HTML, XHTML, they have disappeared completely. When it is still necessary to use these elements and attributes (because the document is to be displayed on old, pre-HTML 4.0 browsers, for example), you have to write your document in HTML 4.0 Transitional or in HTML 3.2.

Using elements for layout

Some elements have little or no meaning apart from indicating a certain style, while some others are structural elements that have often been misused for the effect they usually have on the layout. The first category contains the following elements. Note that many of these are not part of HTML, but are browser-specific extensions:

- **B**
- **HR**
- **BASEFONT**
- **I**
- **BLINK** (in Netscape Navigator)
- **MARQUEE** (in Microsoft Internet Explorer)
- **BIG**
- **SMALL**
- **BR**
- **SPACER** (in Netscape Navigator)
- **CENTER**
- **SUB**
- **FONT**
- **SUP**
- **FRAME**
- **TT**

Structural elements that are often abused for their visual effect include **BLOCKQUOTE**, **DL** (to indent paragraphs), and the heading elements **H1** to **H6** (to enlarge the text).

SUB and **SUP** are borderline cases: It is arguable whether they carry semantics or not. Their role is to indicate subscripts and superscripts,

MathML is a specialized markup language for mathematical expressions. If you need more than just a superscript or subscript, but need to include any formulas – for physics, statistics, etc. – you should probably look at that.

You can create a formula in MathML, and include it in HTML with the help of the **OBJECT** element, the same way you can include an image or other external content. However, browsers are increasingly supporting MathML directly inside the HTML document.

but they don't tell anything beyond that. They don't tell how the subscript or superscript is used (for example, as an index item, an exponent, an atom number, and so on). However, inventing more meaningful names than **SUB** and **SUP** would be almost impossible because so many different functions exist. In mathematics, many of the roles subscripts and superscripts play don't even have agreed-upon names.

Also borderline is **BR**. Recall that it is an empty element that represents a hard line break; a line break will be placed where it is used, no matter how the text of the paragraph around it is aligned or justified. Like **SUB** and **SUP**, **BR** doesn't tell *why* there is a line break at that point: Is it because a line in a poem ended? Does it separate lines of an address? It really should have been a character instead of an element, but the intended character is not part of the Latin-1 character set. This character set contains only about 200 characters and was the only one allowed in early versions of HTML. With the advent of support for the Unicode character set of more than 30,000 characters, **BR** could have been replaced by, for example, the line separator character. But, people were used to **BR**, so it stuck.

Here is an example that exclusively uses the extension elements:

```
<font size="+2"><b>How to write
HTML</b></font><br><br>
For headings, the FONT element is ideal, since
it can enlarge the font. The BR breaks lines,
so two BR's in a row make for a perfect
paragraph separator. When a word needs
emphasis, the I tag will <i>italicize</i> it.
For even more emphasis, the B element puts the
text in <b>bold</b>...
```

Because extensions are inserted purely to force a particular style, their meanings can be expressed completely in CSS, as given in Table 15.1.

Element	CSS equivalent
`<tt>`	`font-family: monospace`
`<i>`	`font-style: italic`
`<b>`	`font-weight: bold`
`<u>`	`text-decoration: underline`
`<big>`	`font-size: bigger`
`<small>`	`font-size: smaller`

Element	CSS equivalent
`<sub>`	`vertical-align: sub`
`<sup>`	`vertical-align: sup`
`<hr>`	`border-top: solid` On some browsers, the border style is groove rather than solid.
`<center>`	`text-align: center`
`<font size=...>`	`font-size: ...` Where the value depends on the value of the **SIZE** attribute: **SIZE**=1 corresponds to `xx-small` and **SIZE**=7 to `xx-large`.
`<font color=...>`	`color: ...`
`<base-font size=...>`	`BODY {font-size: ...}` Where the value is determined as for `<font size=...>`.
`<spacer>`	A shortcut for the "single-pixel GIF trick," see the next section.
`<blink>`	`text-decoration: blink`

Table 15.1 HTML extension elements and their CSS equivalent.

MARQUEE is not translatable to CSS2. Its effect is to make the text scroll horizontally. It would be a text decoration, much like `blink`.

FRAME divides the window into a number of rectangles, each containing a different document. In CSS2, the same effect can be achieved with absolute positioning (in particular, using `position: fixed`). That has the added benefit that the entire document is in a single file. See Chapter 9, "Relative and absolute positioning," for examples of fixed positioning.

Frames are often used to keep part of the user's screen the same while he navigates related pages. With fixed positioning, that requires that the shared part of the screen is repeated in every page. If the shared part is large, that may result in slightly longer download time, but in view of the frustration that frames cause users (cannot bookmark, hard to get rid of unwanted frames, and hard to navigate without a mouse), that is well worth it.

Using attributes for layout

You can also use these extension attributes on a number of elements to set layout:

- **ALIGN** (various elements)
- **LINK** (on **BODY**)
- **ALINK** (on **BODY**)
- **BACKGROUND** (on **BODY**)
- **TEXT** (on **BODY**)
- **VLINK** (on **BODY**)
- **BGCOLOR** (on **BODY**)
- **VSPACE** (on **IMG**)
- **HEIGHT** (on **IMG**)
- **WIDTH** (on **IMG** and **TABLE**)
- **HSPACE** (on **IMG**)
- **BORDER** (on **IMG** and **TABLE**)

ALIGN combines a number of functions, depending on the element to which it is attached and on the value. On headings and paragraphs, it sets the alignment of the text. For example, to center a title, you would write the following:

```
<H1 ALIGN=CENTER>Centered title</H1>
```

On **IMG**, it makes the image float to the left or right or align vertically with the text around it. For example, the following two lines have the same effect:

```
<IMG SRC="image" ALIGN=left>
<IMG SRC="image" STYLE="float: left">
```

as have these:

```
<IMG SRC="image" ALIGN=top>
<IMG SRC="image" STYLE="vertical-align: top">
```

WIDTH and **HEIGHT** on **IMG** allow an image to be scaled. **HSPACE** and **VSPACE** add padding around an image. **BORDER** sets the thickness of a border around an image, in case it is part of a hyperlink. All these attributes accept only numbers as values, which are interpreted as lengths in pixels.

Setting the width and height attributes of an image may also help the browser reserve the space on the page and lay out the rest of the page after the image without waiting for the image to be downloaded. For that reason, many authors add these attributes, not to scale the image, but to speed up the display of the text on the page.

WIDTH on table cells allow the cells to be rendered with a fixed size in pixels or as a percentage of the screen width. A fixed-size table is often misused to add fixed margins to a text or to align the text to a background image. On a browser that supports tables but not CSS, this is the only way to get something that looks like margins or side heads, but it is also one of the worst offences against accessibility. We would like to urge authors not to do this, even if that means the text looks less attractive on certain browsers. Consider also that the number of such browsers will diminish, while the number of browsers that cannot show tables in this way is increasing: handheld devices, TV-based browsers, and speech browsers. Some of those will even support CSS and @media. (See Chapter 12, "Printing and other media.")

ALINK, **BACKGROUND**, **BGCOLOR**, **LINK**, **TEXT**, and **VLINK**, set on **BODY**, are means to add a background image and color to the document and set colors for link anchors.

The single-pixel GIF trick for controlling space

Siegel, D. *Creating Killer Web Sites,* First Edition. Hayden Books (1996).

One trick to control the spacing outside of a style sheet comes from David Siegel, who is the author of *Creating Killer Web Sites.* He calls it the "single-pixel GIF trick." The trick is to create a transparent GIF image of 1x1 pixel. Although the image is essentially invisible, it still takes up space. Everywhere you need to add some space, you insert such an image. For example, here's how to indent paragraphs using this trick:

```
<P><IMG SRC="1pixel.gif" WIDTH=20 HEIGHT=1> text text text...
```

Don't look at a document like this with image loading turned off!

You can even use this trick to affect line spacing. Here's how you would insert a few extra pixels between lines:

```
... some text<IMG SRC="1pixel.gif" WIDTH=1 HEIGHT=20
ALIGN=MIDDLE> with a narrow, tall<IMG
SRC="1pixel.gif" WIDTH=1 HEIGHT=20 ALIGN=MIDDLE>
image every four words<IMG SRC="1pixel.gif" WIDTH=1
HEIGHT=20 ALIGN=MIDDLE> or so...
```

Doing this is a bit of a gamble because you don't know the size of the user's font. Assuming that, in many cases, the font will be around 14 pixels high, creating a 20-pixel image should therefore ensure about 6 pixels between lines.

The single-pixel GIF trick also can do word spacing and letter spacing. The nice part of doing this is that it doesn't add much to the download time. The downside is that pages containing these images are a nightmare to maintain: You have to make sure that there is an image between every two words or every two letters, and that they are all the same. If you change one, you'll have to change all of them. Also, robots will have a difficult time finding the keywords among the images.

USING A DIFFERENT FORMAT FROM HTML

You can avoid using HTML altogether by using a different format from HTML, such as Portable Document Format (PDF) or an image.

Portable Document Format

Portable Document Format (PDF), often called the Acrobat format after the program most commonly used to display it, is a format for storing formatted documents in a device-independent manner. Created by Adobe Systems, it inherits much from PostScript, which is another page-description language by Adobe.

PDF is like "digital paper." It can store one or more pages of text and images, ready to be printed or viewed onscreen. Compared to image formats such as PNG, GIF, and JPEG, it has a number of advantages. First, it can contain actual text, not just images of text (bitmaps). As a result, it can scale the pages and print at any resolution: The text looks as good as the printer allows. Second, it can replace fonts by generated approximations (multiple master fonts) in case the document uses uncommon fonts and the document's creator didn't embed the font, either for copyright reasons or just to save space. Third, because the text in the document is stored as text and not as bitmaps, you can search the document for keywords. Fourth, PDF can even contain hyperlinks, not only within the document but also as URLs that point to documents on the Web.

The disadvantage is that the text is already formatted as you get it. Resizing the window won't change the number of words per line, as it normally does in HTML. The structure of the text is also lost: You cannot save the document and edit it. Even if you manage to save the text and load it into some other program, no tags tell you that a certain piece of text is a heading or a list item. Because spaces are often not stored explicitly, and letters don't necessarily appear in the file in the order they appear onscreen, the PDF software has to use heuristics to even recognize words.

PDF is a good solution for old documents that cannot be converted to HTML or would need a lot of work to allow conversion. Usually, when you can print a document, you can also convert it to PDF. Many documents created with old word processors were never meant for use on the Web and printing them is pretty much the only thing you can do with them.

Images

You can also use images that are stored in PNG, GIF, or JPEG format. We briefly discussed using images in place of text in Chapter 1, "The Web and HTML." A Web page consisting of just an image gives the page's designer control over every pixel, especially when the PNG format is used. PNG is the most accurate when it comes to defining the color of pixels. But, that level of control comes at a price.

First, robots cannot read the page. Second, the page is much larger in terms of bytes than a page that consists of text with a style sheet and thus takes longer to download.

Third, the page has a fixed size. As a result, users may have trouble reading the image for several reasons. On large screens, the image may be too small. On small screens, the image may be too large. On monochrome screens, too many colors may be shown as almost the same shade of gray. On text-only browsers, users won't see anything.

Fourth, printing the page also gives less than satisfactory results. Not all printers can print in color. The result may either be small or look grainy (see Figure 15.1).

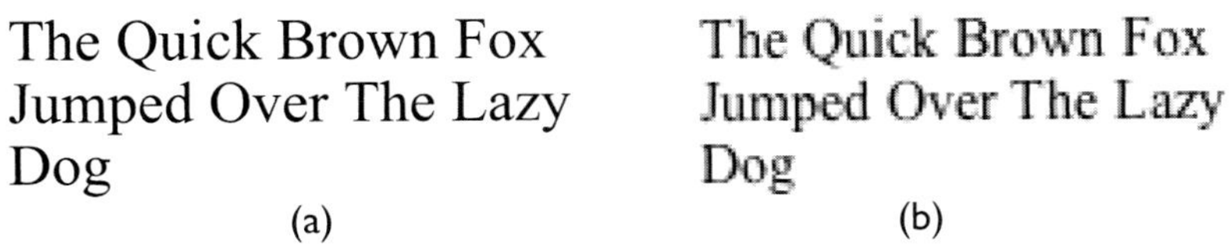

Figure 15.1 Normal text (a) and an image (b). On the screen, the two look the same, but on paper, the text was printed with all the quality the printer could offer, while the image was just copied pixel for pixel.

The Quick Brown Fox Jumped Over The Lazy Dog

(a)

The Quick Brown Fox Jumped Over The Lazy Dog

(b)

Fifth, as with any format that doesn't rely on style sheets for the layout, it will not be readable by someone who is blind (images can be converted neither to speech nor to Braille) and will be difficult to read for someone with limited eyesight. (Although the images can be enlarged, it is difficult to change the colors as you can with text.)

Finally, when you want to modify the document, it is more difficult to change an image than a text or a style sheet.

For these reasons, it is advisable to use images only for effects that cannot be achieved with a style sheet. And then, only if the look is so important that it outweighs the disadvantages. Of course, you should also include the text in the *alt* attribute of the **IMG** element for people who cannot see the image.

USING XSL

XSL, the "eXtensible Style sheet Language," is so called because it is designed specifically for XML, the "eXtensible Markup Language."

The XSL language is itself based on XML, which means it looks very different from CSS. Ease of reading and writing isn't as important for XSL as it is for CSS. Writing XSL requires more training than writing CSS.

XSL has two parts: transformation and formatting. The transformation can be used on its own to translate XML documents to other XML documents, or – to a limited extent – to other types of text-based formats. It can also be combined with formatting to transform an XML document to a document with "formatting objects," which is just another XML document, but one in which all elements have a full set of CSS properties. You can think of the formatting process performed by XSL as a transformation of an XML document to an HTML document in which all elements have a **STYLE** attribute with the properties that apply to that element.

An XSL script contains a series of template rules, each of which contains a pattern similar to a CSS selector and a piece of text, representing how to rewrite a matching piece of the input document. An XSL interpreter tries to match all patterns and thereby replaces parts of the XML document with new text until no more templates match.

XSL is meant to be used for tasks such as sorting parts of a document, generating a table of content, generating a report for an XML-based database, and other tasks related to formatting documents. The focus is on printed output. Much of XSL processing is expected to be invisible to users: A server might use an XSL script to create an HTML document dynamically from a large database of XML documents.

But, XSL could also be used in browsers as an alternative to CSS for documents that need to be re-ordered before they can be displayed to a reader.

XSL is currently mostly used to transform documents before sending them to a browser, but it is possible that more browsers will support XSL in the future, and it becomes possible to send XSL to the browser the same way you can send a CSS.

In many cases, XSL will be used to condense a large document or set of documents into one or more small Web pages. In that case, the logical place is near the server because it would be wasteful (and time-consuming) to send the large document plus XSL script to a browser, when the user eventually only sees a small part of it. But, if XSL is used to expand a compact piece of machine data into a human-readable description of the data, sending the compact document and the XSL script to a browser for processing makes sense.

Although XSL looks different from CSS – no semicolons (;), no curly braces ({...}), no colons (:), etc. – when XSL is used for formatting, it won't be difficult to recognize the CSS properties. Nearly all CSS properties are available with the same names and values as in CSS.

Chapter 16

XML documents

XML is one of the most widely used acronyms of the Web and any Web designer should be aware of it. Not that you necessarily will use it that much – so far, people seem to talk about XML more than they actually use it – but XML is an ingredient in many of the Web languages that are being developed for the Web. Also, knowing XML helps put other languages, such as HTML and CSS, in perspective. Before we describe how CSS and XML work together, XML will be introduced through a small essay Bert Bos wrote for W3C: *XML in 10 points*.

XML IN 10 POINTS

1. XML is for structuring data

Structured data includes things like spreadsheets, address books, configuration parameters, financial transactions, and technical drawings. XML is a set of rules (you may also think of them as guidelines or conventions) for designing text formats that let you structure your data. XML is not a programming language, and you don't have to be a programmer to use it or learn it. XML makes it easy for a computer to generate data, read data, and ensure that the data structure is unambiguous. XML avoids common pitfalls in language design: It is extensible, platform-independent, and it supports internationalization and localization. XML is fully Unicode-compliant.

2. XML looks a bit like HTML

Like HTML, XML makes use of *tags* (words bracketed by "<" and ">") and *attributes* (of the form name="value"). While HTML specifies what each tag and attribute means, and often how the text between them will look in a browser, XML uses the tags only to delimit pieces of data, and leaves the interpretation of the data completely to the application that reads it. In other words, if you see "<p>" in an XML file, do not assume it is a paragraph. Depending on the context, it may be a price, a parameter, a person, a p... (and who says it has to be a word with a "p"?).

3. XML is text, but isn't meant to be read

Programs that produce spreadsheets, address books, and other structured data often store that data on disk, using either a binary or text format. One advantage of a text format is that it allows people, if necessary, to look at the data without the program that produced it; in a pinch, you can read a text format with your favorite text editor. Text formats also allow developers to more easily debug applications. Like HTML, XML files are text files that people shouldn't have to read, but may when the need arises. Compared to HTML, the rules for XML files allow fewer variations. A forgotten tag, or an attribute without quotes makes an XML file unusable, while in HTML such practice is often explicitly allowed. The official XML specification forbids applications from trying to second-guess the creator of a broken XML file; if the file is broken, an application has to stop right there and report an error.

4. XML is verbose by design

Since XML is a text format and it uses tags to delimit the data, XML files are nearly always larger than comparable binary formats. That was a conscious decision by the designers of XML. The advantages of a text format are evident (see point 3), and the disadvantages can usually be compensated at a different level. Disk space is less expensive than it used to be, and compression programs like zip and gzip can compress files very well and very fast. In addition, communication protocols such as modem protocols and HTTP/1.1, the core protocol of the Web, can compress data on the fly, saving bandwidth as effectively as a binary format.

5. XML is a family of technologies

XML 1.0 is the specification that defines what "tags" and "attributes" are. Beyond XML 1.0, "the XML family" is a growing set of modules that offer useful services to accomplish important and frequently demanded tasks. *XLink* describes a standard way to add hyperlinks to an XML file. *XPointer* is a syntax in development for pointing to parts of an XML document. An XPointer is a bit like a URL, but instead of pointing to documents on the Web, it points to pieces of data inside an XML file. *CSS*, the style sheet language, is applicable to XML as it is to HTML. *XSL* is the advanced language for expressing style sheets. It is based on *XSLT*, a transformation language used for rearranging, adding and deleting tags and attributes. The *DOM* is a standard set of function calls for manipulating XML (and HTML) files from a programming language. *XML Schemas 1* and 2 help developers to precisely define the structures of their own XML-based formats. There are several more modules and tools available or under development. Keep an eye on W3C's technical reports page.

6. XML is new, but not that new

Development of XML started in 1996 and it has been a W3C Recommendation since February 1998. Before XML there was SGML, developed in the early '80s, an ISO standard since 1986, and widely used for large documentation projects. The development of HTML started in 1990. The designers of XML simply took the best parts of SGML, guided by the experience with HTML, and produced something that is no less powerful than SGML, and vastly more regular and simple to use. Some evolutions, however, are hard to distinguish from revolutions.... And it must be said that while SGML is mostly used for technical documentation and much less for other kinds of data, with XML it is exactly the opposite.

7. XML leads HTML to XHTML

There is an important XML application that is a document format: W3C's XHTML, the successor to HTML. XHTML has many of the same elements as HTML. The syntax has been changed slightly to conform to the rules of XML. A format that is "XML-based" inherits the syntax from XML and restricts it in certain ways (e.g, XHTML allows "<p>", but not "<r>"); it also adds meaning to that syntax (XHTML says that "<p>" stands for "paragraph," and not for "price," "person," or anything else).

8. XML is modular

XML allows you to define a new document format by combining and reusing other formats. Since two formats developed independently may have elements or attributes with the same name, care must be taken when combining those formats (does "<p>" mean "paragraph" from this format or "person" from that one?). To eliminate name confusion when combining formats, XML provides a *namespace* mechanism. XSL and RDF are good examples of XML-based formats that use namespaces. *XML Schema* is designed to mirror this support for modularity at the level of defining XML document structures, by making it easy to combine two schemas to produce a third which covers a merged document structure.

9. XML is the basis for RDF and the Semantic Web

W3C's Resource Description Framework (RDF) is an XML text format that supports resource description and metadata applications, such as music playlists, photo collections, and bibliographies. For example, RDF might let you identify people in a Web photo album using information from a personal contact list; then your mail client could automatically start a message to those people stating that their photos are on the Web. Just as HTML integrated documents, images, menu systems, and forms applications to launch the original Web, RDF provides tools to integrate even more, to make the Web a little bit more into a Semantic Web. Just like people need to have agreement on the meanings of the words they employ in their communication, computers need mechanisms for agreeing on the meanings of terms in order to communicate effectively. Formal descriptions of terms in a certain area (shopping or manufacturing, for example) are called ontologies and are a necessary part of the Semantic Web. RDF, ontologies, and the representation of meaning so that computers can help people do work are all topics of the Semantic Web Activity.

10. XML is license-free, platform-independent, and well-supported

By choosing XML as the basis for a project, you gain access to a large and growing community of tools (one of which may already do what you need!) and engineers experienced in the technology. Opting for XML is a bit like choosing SQL for databases: You still have to build your own database and your own programs and procedures that manipulate it, but there are many tools available and many people who can help you. And since XML is license-free, you can build your own software around it without paying anybody anything. The large and growing support means that you are also not tied to a single vendor. *XML isn't always the best solution, but it is always worth considering.*

XML AND CSS

We now turn to how XML and CSS can be used together. There are basically two ways: CSS can be used with Web languages that are written in XML or CSS can be used to display documents that are written only in XML. The best example of a Web language that is written in XML is XHTML, which is a cousin of HTML. XHTML imposes a few restrictions on how tags and attributes are written, but otherwise looks the same as traditional HTML documents.

The other way to use XML and CSS together is to combine a CSS style sheet with a document that's written only in XML. For example, the following document is an XML document written in a (hypothetical) format for aircraft maintenance manuals:

```
<manual>
  <aircraft>
    <brand>Boeing</brand>
    <type>747</type>
  </aircraft>
  <date>8 June 1998</date>
  <chapter type="main">
    <par>  Wipe the aircraft regularly
    with a soft cloth.      </par>
  </chapter>
</manual>
```

It has none of the familiar HTML elements, but other than that, it doesn't look too strange. A simple style sheet for this document may be as follows:

```
manual {display: block; margin-left: 10%}
aircraft {display: block: margin: 2em;
   font-size: xx-large}
chapter {display: block; margin-top: 1em}
date, par {display: block}
```

Inheritance works like in HTML. So, in the example, the *brand* element will be xx-large because it inherits the font size from the *aircraft* element.

In most of the examples in this book, we have written the selectors of style rules in capitals because in HTML, lowercase and uppercase letters are interchangeable. XML is different in that respect. A style sheet for an XML-based document must use selectors with exactly the same letters as the elements in the document. Spelling "manual" as "MANUAL" does not work.

EXPERIMENTING WITH XML

Recent versions of Internet Explorer, Opera, and FireFox support XML combined with CSS. The basic rules are as follows:

1. If you use an element *<abc>*, you must end it with *</abc>*. Unlike HTML, no tags may be omitted.
2. If the element is empty (has no end tag), you must end it with a slash: *<xyz/>*.
3. If you use an attribute *att*="*value*", make sure you put quotes around the value. Unlike in HTML, all attributes, even simple ones, must be quoted.
4. Style sheets cannot be in the same file as the XML document. Instead, put a line like this at the top of the XML document (note the two question marks):

```
<?xml-stylesheet href="my-style.css"?>
```

- This works the same as <link rel="stylesheet" href= "my-style.css"> in HTML. In fact, as in HTML, you can add "title" and "type" attributes, and you can have multiple alternative styles. But unlike in HTML, you cannot use capital (for example, "HREF" is not correct).

- The browser doesn't have a built-in style for any XML-based documents, so all elements will be displayed inline. You'll have to use the **display** property.

But most of all, don't forget that these experiments are not documents that you can share with the world, like HTML. It may seem that you have a meaningful format, with names like "manual," "aircraft," "date," or "chapter," but without proper documentation, nobody can be sure what you mean by them. "Manual" could mean "by hand," and "chapter" might be a sub-group of a club or society. The larger the group of people you want to share this format with, the better the documentation must be.

SOME EXAMPLES

Here are some examples of (hypothetical) XML-based formats and their possible style sheets.

The first example could be an electronic program guide. The structure is simple. The guide consists of number of "day" elements, each containing "program" elements, which in turn contain start and end times, the program's name, a short description, a code for programming a video recorder, and some elements that indicate whether the program is in stereo and in wide screen. Consider this code:

```
<?xml-stylesheet href="guide.css"?>
<guide>
  <day>
    <date>1 Jan 2000</date>
    <program>
      <start>06.00</start><end>09.30</end>
      <name>Good morning, world!</name>
      <description>News, weather, and interviews
      </description>
      <code>tv://channel2000/20000101T0600-0930</code>
      <stereo/>
    </program>
    <program>
      <start>23.40</start><end>01.15</end>
      <name>Late(st) news</name>
      <description></description>
      <code>tv://channel2000/20000101T2340-0115</code>
```

```
        <stereo/>
        <wide/>
      </program>
    </day>
  </guide>
```

The XML starts with a link to a style sheet "guide.css." A simple style sheet to make this readable could be as follows (see Figure 16.1):

```
day {display: block}
program {display: block}
description {display: block}
code {display: none /* Don't show the code */}

guide {background: black; color: white; padding: 1em}
day {font-size: large; margin: 1em 0}
program {margin: 1em 2em; text-indent: -2em}
start, end {font-weight: bolder}
end:before {content: "-"}
end:after {content: ". "}
name {color: red}
stereo:before {content: "stereo "}
wide:before {content: "16:9 "}
stereo, wide {font-size: small}
```

Figure 16.1 The "guide" document with the first style sheet.

1 Jan 2000

06.00–09.30. Good morning, world! News, weather, and interviews stereo

23.40–01.15. Late(st) news stereo 16:9

The information could also be displayed in tabular format: every program is one row and each field is a column (see Figure 16.2).

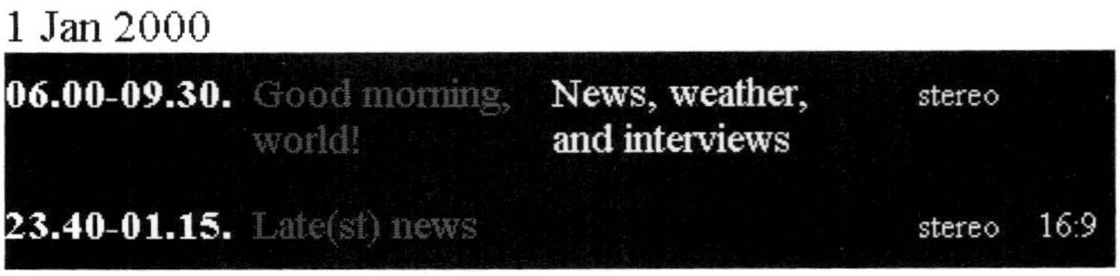

Figure 16.2 The "guide" document with the second style sheet.

1 Jan 2000

| **06.00-09.30.** | Good morning, world! | News, weather, and interviews | stereo | |
| **23.40-01.15.** | Late(st) news | | stereo | 16:9 |

```
guide {display: table}
day {display: table-body}
date {display: caption}
program {display: table-row}
start, end, name, description, stereo, wide {
  display: table-cell}
code {display: none} /* Don't show the code */
date {font-size: larger; text-align: left}
guide {background: black; color: white}
program {vertical-align: baseline}
name, description, stereo, wide {padding: 0.5em}
start, end {font-weight: bolder}
start:after {content: "-"}
end:after {content: ". "}
name {color: red}
stereo:before {content: "stereo "}
wide:before {content: "16:9 "}
stereo, .wide {font-size: smaller }
```

For more information on the style properties for tables, see Chapter 17, "Tables."

The next example could be part of a dictionary. The document consists of **GLOSS** elements, containing **HEAD** and **SENSE** elements, the latter in turn containing **DEF** and **EX** elements:

```
<?xml-stylesheet href="dict.css"?>
<dictionary>
  <gloss><head>pen</head>
    <sense type="n" num="1">
      <def>Goose feather used for writing.</def>
    </sense>
    <sense type="n" num="2">
      <def>Fenced area for keeping sheep.</def>
      <ex>At night, the sheep are in the pen.</ex>
    </sense>
  </gloss>
  <gloss><head>pen-knife</head>
    <sense type="n">
      <def>Knife for sharpening pens (1).</def>
    </sense>
  </gloss>
</dictionary>
```

The style sheet is contained in a file called dict.css. We want every **GLOSS** to be a block, with the **HEAD** outdented. The **HEAD** term will be bold, the definition will be italic. The type of the word ("n" for nouns) will be taken from the attribute and inserted before the definition. If multiple senses exist for a word, there will be a **NUM** attribute with a number and the style sheet will insert that number before the definition.

```
gloss {
  display: block;
  margin-left: 1em;
  text-indent: -1em;
}
head {
  font-weight: bold
}
sense:before {
  content: attr(type) ". ">;
}
sense[num]:before {
  content: attr(num) ". " attr(type) ". ";
}
def {
  font-style: italic
}
```

Figure 16.3 shows how this might be rendered. See Chapter 6, "The fundamental objects," for information about the :before pseudo-element and the use of the **content** property to display the value of an attribute.

Figure 16.3 Possible rendering of a dictionary.

pen 1. n. *Goose feather used for writing.* 2. n. *Fenced area for keeping sheep.* At night, the sheep are in the pen.
pen-knife *Knife for sharpening pens (1).*

There are two set of rules for the **SENSE** element. The second one is only used if there is a **NUM** attribute and, in that case, the value of the **content** property is taken from this rule instead of the earlier one. The effect is to display both the **NUM** and **TYPE** attributes. See Chapter 4 for more information on constructing selectors and on how they determine the precedence of rules.

Chapter 17

Tables

Tables visually show relations between pieces of data. Lists do the same, but tables allow you to show multiple relations at the same time. Each cell in a table holds a number or some short text that has some relation to other data in the same column or the same row.

To make it easier to see the structure of the table, rules (i.e., lines) are often added between the rows or columns (or both), sometimes only between certain groups of rows or columns. Colors and changes in font can, of course, also be used. Cells don't have margins (although there is a **cell-spacing** property that works in a somewhat similar way), but padding is available.

CSS2 offers two ways of setting borders on cells. In one model, called *collapsing borders,* there is only one border between two cells; in the other, called *separate borders,* there are two. Depending on what "look" you are trying to achieve, and on personal preference, you may find one or the other easier to use.

THE PARTS OF A TABLE

Tables are made up of rows and columns, which in turn contain cells. That is the general idea, but in practice, tables can be more complex. For example, some cells can be in two or more columns at the same time. Here is an HTML table with a style sheet that makes the boundaries of the cells visible by means of a simple border (see Figure 17.1).

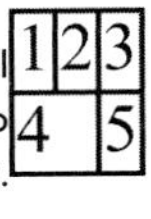

Figure 17.1 A small table. Cell 4 spans two columns.

```
<TABLE>
   <TR><TD>1   <TD>2   <TD>3
   <TR><TD COLSPAN=2>4   <TD>5
</TABLE>
```

with style:

```
TABLE {border-collapse: collapse}
TD {border: solid}
```

We'll explain why we need collapse in the next section.

The HTML table model, which is the basis for CSS's table model, is actually quite complex, if all parts are considered. But luckily, most tables are simple and need only a small part of the full model.

The essential parts of any table, the parts that cannot be omitted in HTML, are the table itself (the box that contains all the rows and cells), the rows, and the cells. The rows are boxes inside the table, and the cells are boxes inside the rows. The complication that cells can span several rows is handled by saying that a cell box can actually extend outside the row box.

Here is a table in which the row boxes are made visible by giving them each a different background. The cells are shown the same way as before, with a border (see Figure 17.2):

Figure 17.2 A table with differently colored rows.

```
<TABLE>
   <TR CLASS=r1><TD> 1 <TD> 2 <TD ROWSPAN=2> 3
   <TR CLASS=r2><TD COLSPAN=2> 4
   <TR CLASS=r3><TD> 5 <TD> 6 <TD> 7
</TABLE>
```

and the style:

```
TABLE {border-collapse: collapse}
TD {border: solid}
TR.r1 {background: #F99}
TR.r2 {background: #9F9}
TR.r3 {background: #99F}
```

There are a number of optional parts in a table, which are needed for more complex tables. The caption is one. It is typically one or a few lines of text above or below the table.

Rows can also be grouped into row groups, which puts all of them into a box and allows them to be visually distinguished as a group. There are three kinds of row groups: the ordinary group, of which there can be as many as desired; the table head, of which there can be at most one; and the table foot, which can also only be used once per table. The latter two behave in a special way: A table head group, if present, is always shown above any other rows, and a foot is always shown after any other rows. Furthermore, if a table is so large that it is broken among several pages, the head and foot are repeated on each page.

Figure 17.3 shows an example of a table with three row groups, visually delimited by a thick line between them. The style sheet is

```
TBODY {border-bottom: thick; border-top: thick}
```

and the HTML source

```
<TABLE>
  <TBODY CLASS=nov>
    <TR><TH>1-10 <TD> 45 <TD> 67 <TD> 34
    <TR><TH>11-20 <TD> 54 <TD> 76 <TD> 43
    <TR><TH>21-30 <TD> 57 <TD> 78 <TD> 23
  <TBODY CLASS=dec>
    <TR><TH>1-10 <TD> 57 <TD> 67 <TD>84
    <TR><TH>11-20 <TD> 75 <TD> 56 <TD>85
    <TR><TH>21-31 <TD> 75 <TD> 91 <TD>48
  <TBODY CLASS=jan>
    <TR><TH>1-10 <TD> 72 <TD> 64 <TD>85
    <TR><TH>11-20 <TD> 35 <TD> 63 <TD>87
    <TR><TH>21-31 <TD> 71 <TD> 19 <TD>38
<TABLE>
```

1-10	45 67 34
11-20	54 76 43
21-30	57 78 23
1-10	57 67 84
11-20	75 56 85
21-30	75 91 48
1-10	72 64 85
11-20	35 63 87
21-30	71 19 38

Figure 17.3 A table with three row groups.

Tables can also have column and column group elements, which the style sheet can use to visually distinguish columns. The next section shows an example of a table with all the optional parts. We'll use it to explain the collapsing borders model.

COLLAPSING BORDERS MODEL

The first of the two methods for setting borders on tables allows you to set borders on all parts of a table: the outer edge of the table itself, each of the rows, columns, groups of rows and columns, and, of course, the cells themselves. However, no matter how many style rules you write, in the end, there will only be one border between every pair of cells or on the outside of the table.

For example, if you specify a border style for the rows, for the cells and for the row groups, there will be places in the table where all three of these declarations apply. The border that is drawn there is the one that is the "strongest," in the sense of the most visible. For example, if these are the style rules

```
TBODY { border: thick double }
TR { border: medium solid }
TD { border: medium dotted }
```

the strongest is the `thick double`, next is the `medium solid`, and the weakest is the `medium dotted`. The result is that there will be a dotted line between all cells, and a solid line between all rows, except at the edge of a row group (**TBODY**), where the border will be a thick double line.

Thicker lines are stronger than thinner lines, and double lines are stronger than single ones, which are in turn stronger than dashed lines and dotted lines. The "3D" styles (ridge, outset, groove, and inset) are the weakest of all, but that is because they are more commonly used with the separated borders model, which is explained later. If the specified styles for the cells, rows, columns, etc., differ *only* in color, a different rule is applied: The cell's border style wins over the row, row over row group, and so on in the following order: cell, row, row group, column, column group, and table.

Here is an example of a complex table. We use it in several examples in the following sections. First, here's the HTML code:

```
<TABLE SUMMARY="The count of things each person saw,
   organized by thing, time of day and person">
<CAPTION>What we saw on our trip
   to the beach</CAPTION>
<COLGROUP>
   <COL CLASS=when><COL CLASS=who>
<COLGROUP>
   <COL CLASS=dog><COL CLASS=cat><COL CLASS=croco>
<COLGROUP>
   <COL CLASS=bak><COL CLASS=ant><COL CLASS=book>
<COLGROUP>
   <COL CLASS=yel><COL CLASS=pur><COL CLASS=blk>
<THEAD>
   <TR><TH> <TH> <TH COLSPAN=3>Animals
      <TH COLSPAN=3>Shops <TH COLSPAN=3>Cars
   <TR><TH>When? <TH>Who?
      <TH>Dogs <TH>Cats <TH>Crocodiles
      <TH>Bakeries <TH>Antiques <TH>Book
      <TH>Yellow <TH>Purple <TH>Black
</THEAD>
<TBODY>
```

```
<TR><TH ROWSPAN=3>Morning
   <TH>Judy
   <TD>4 <TD>0 <TD>0
   <TD>4 <TD>6 <TD>2
   <TD>0 <TD>0 <TD>5
  <TR><TH>Alan
   <TD>3 <TD>1 <TD>0
   <TD>3 <TD>2 <TD>1
   <TD>1 <TD>0 <TD>2
  <TR><TH>Tim
   <TD>2 <TD>0 <TD>2
   <TD>2 <TD>1 <TD>7
   <TD>0 <TD>0 <TD>1
 </TBODY>
 <TBODY>
  <TR><TH ROWSPAN=3>Afternoon
   <TH>Judy
   <TD>2 <TD>1 <TD>0
   <TD>4 <TD>2 <TD>2
   <TD>0 <TD>1 <TD>1
  <TR><TH>Alan
   <TD>2 <TD>1 <TD>0
   <TD>1 <TD>2 <TD>3
   <TD>0 <TD>0 <TD>1
  <TR><TH>Tim
   <TD>4 <TD>4 <TD>1
   <TD>3 <TD>3 <TD>6
   <TD>1 <TD>1 <TD>5
 </TBODY>
</TABLE>
```

We'll first show a style that uses only borders to indicate the way the information is grouped: A thick double border below the headings, a thick border underneath the groups of rows, and a thin border between the groups of columns (see Figure 17.4).

What we saw on our trip to the beach

When	Who	Animals			Shops			Cars		
		Dogs	Cats	Crocodiles	Bakeries	Antiques	Books	Yellow	Purple	Black
Morning	Judy	4	0	0	4	6	2	0	0	5
	Alan	3	1	0	3	2	1	1	0	2
	Tim	2	0	2	2	1	7	0	0	1
Afternoon	Judy	2	1	0	4	2	2	0	1	1
	Alan	2	1	0	1	2	3	0	0	1
	Tim	4	4	1	3	3	6	1	1	5

Figure 17.4 Table borders example.

The style sheet that draws these borders is rather simple:

```
TABLE { border-collapse: collapse }
COLGROUP { border-left: thin solid }
THEAD { border-bottom: thick double }
TBODY { border-bottom: thick solid }
TABLE { border: hidden }
TH { text-align: left }
```

We've thrown in a text-align: left because it looks better than the default style for HTML, which centers all **TH** elements. But, the real trick is in the fifth line. The border style hidden is a "style" that is peculiar to tables, and in fact to the collapsing borders method of creating borders.

If you look at the first line, you see that a thin rule is specified for the left side of all column groups. But, we don't want a rule on the left side of the first column group. The hidden style gets rid of that extra border. Because this border is shared with the table itself, we can set a style on the table that overrides the border. The same happens with the third rule: Setting a thick rule below the row groups produces one rule too many, but the hidden style on the table takes it away.

Setting the style to none wouldn't have helped because none is the weakest style of all. In fact, all cells implicitly have a border: none, but any other border style overrides it.

SEPARATED BORDERS MODEL

In the separated borders model, you can only set borders on cells, and on the table itself, not on rows, columns, or groups of rows or columns. Every cell has its own borders, so there are never any conflicts. This method is not so easy if you want to visually delimit row or column groups with borders, but it works well for the "3D" border styles, especially inset and outset. Here is an example (see Figure 17.5):

```
TABLE { border-collapse: separate;
  border: 0.2em outset; cell-spacing: 0.2em }
TD, TH { border: 0.1em inset }
```

This makes use of the **cell-spacing** property, which works only for the separated borders model. separate is the initial value for the **border-collapse** property, so we could have omitted it, but we set it here explicitly for clarity.

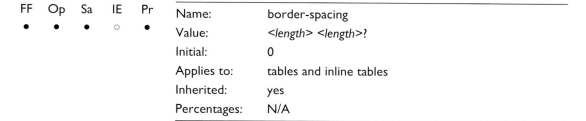

What we saw on our trip to the beach										
When?	Who?	Animals			Shops			Cars		
When?	Who?	Dogs	Cats	Crocodiles	Bakeries	Antiques	Book	Yellow	Purple	Black
Morning	Judy	4	0	0	4	6	2	0	0	5
Morning	Alan	3	1	0	3	2	1	1	0	2
Morning	Tim	2	0	2	2	1	7	0	0	1
Afternoon	Judy	2	1	0	4	2	2	0	1	1
Afternoon	Alan	2	1	0	1	2	3	0	0	1
Afternoon	Tim	4	4	1	3	3	6	1	1	5

Figure 17.5 Table borders example.

FF   Op   Sa   IE   Pr
•   •   •   •   •

Name:	border-collapse
Value:	collapse | separate
Initial:	separate
Applies to:	tables and inline tables
Inherited:	yes
Percentages:	N/A

The **border-collapse** property determines what border model a table uses. If all tables in a document use the same model (which they usually do), you can set the property most easily on the **BODY** element, and all tables will inherit it.

FF   Op   Sa   IE   Pr
•   •   •   ○   •

Name:	border-spacing
Value:	*<length> <length>?*
Initial:	0
Applies to:	tables and inline tables
Inherited:	yes
Percentages:	N/A

border-spacing is only used by tables with the separated borders model. It determines the space between every pair of borders. You cannot set it on individual cells. Whatever the value of **border-spacing** is for the table element, it is used throughout the table. You can, however, set different values for the space between vertical borders and between horizontal borders. If the property has only one value, it will be used for both horizontal and vertical spacing. If it has two, the first gives the horizontal space (between columns) and the second the vertical space (between rows).

Borders for empty cells

FF	Op	Sa	IE	Pr
●	●	●	○	○

Name:	empty-cells
Value:	show | hide
Initial:	show
Applies to:	table cells
Inherited:	yes
Percentages:	N/A

The separated borders model distinguishes between empty cells and non-empty cells. Normally, borders are drawn around all cells, but the **empty-cells** property makes it possible to suppress borders if the cell has no content. This property can be set for each cell individually, but usually, you would set it on the table, or even on the **BODY** element, to apply to the entire document. Figure 17.6 shows the effect.

empty-cells: show

empty-cells: hide

Figure 17.6 The effect of the **empty-cells** property.

ALIGNMENT

In normal paragraphs, text can be aligned on the left, right, or center, or can be justified, by setting the **text-align** property. Text in table cells can be aligned in the same way. See Chapter 7, "Space inside boxes," for the full definition of **text-align**.

The content of cells can also be aligned vertically across rows because the contents of cells are not necessarily the same height, but the cells are. The **vertical-align** property, which otherwise determines the vertical position of words in a line, can also be applied to table cells to align the contents of cells in a row.

Of the **vertical-align** property, only the values `baseline`, `top`, `bottom`, and `middle` apply to table cells. The initial value, `baseline`, ensures that the baseline of the first text line in a cell lines up with the first baseline of all other cells in the row that have their **vertical-align** property set to `baseline`. Figure 17.7 shows the four different alignments.

Some text over two lines	Some text over three lines	Large text	Small text	baseline
Some text over two lines	Some text over three lines	Large text	Small text	top
Some text over two lines	Some text over three lines	Large text	Small text	middle
Some text over two lines	Some text over three lines	Large text	Small text	bottom

Figure 17.7 The four vertical alignments applicable to table cells. From top to bottom: `baseline`, `top`, `middle`, and `bottom`.

SIZES

Browsers normally determine the width and height of each cell automatically, finding a balance between the available width for the entire table and the widths of the individual columns. Most browsers follow a recipe similar to the following:

1. Try to format each cell without introducing line breaks. If the resulting table fits between the margins of the table's parent, this will be the final layout.

2. If the table won't fit without adding line breaks in the cells' content, try first to make the table exactly as wide as the parent's margins allow. If the cells' content can be broken into lines so that the table fits, this will be the chosen layout.

3. If there is no possibility to make the table narrow enough to fit in the parent, make each column as narrow as possible, and let the table stick out on the right.

This usually results in a reasonable table, but seldom a beautiful one. If you want a certain column to take more space at the cost of another, or if you want several columns to be the same width, you have to set the **width** property of some cells or columns.

Setting the **width** property on a cell or column has a slightly different effect than on other elements. On normal elements, it sets the exact width; on table cells and columns, it sets the minimum width. If the content of a normal element is too wide for the specified value of **width**, the content sticks out and overlaps the border (see the **overflow** property in Chapter 8). But, if the content of a table cell is too wide for the given **width**, the width itself is increased, and that of all other cells in the column as well.

If different cells in the same column have different **width**s, the maximum width is used. The width of a cell that spans several columns imposes a minimum on the sum of the widths of the columns it spans.

If you set the **width** property on the **TABLE** element itself, that, also, acts as a minimum width: If the columns together require more than the specified width of the table, the table's width will be increased. On the other hand, if the specified width is larger than what the columns require, the columns are made wider. This is often used to make a table as wide as its parent (or wider):

```
<STYLE>
  TABLE {width: 100%; border-collapse: collapse}
  TD {border: thin solid}
</STYLE>
...

<TABLE>
  <TR><TD>This <TD>table <TD>needs
  <TR><TD>only <TD>little <TD>space
</TABLE>
```

This is rendered as a full-width table:

This	table	needs
only	little	space

You can use percentages for the widths of cells or columns, and the browser tries to make that column as wide as specified. But because it is possible to create circular dependencies (the width of the columns is a percentage of the table's width, but the table's width depends on the columns), browsers may choose to handle only the most simple cases (for example, when the table's width is given explicitly and is larger than the minimum required width).

Be careful when using percentages because it is easy to forget the borders and padding. Setting the column widths of a four-column table to 25 percent only makes sense if the borders and padding are zero; otherwise, the sum of the widths will be more than 100 percent, which is obviously impossible. Here is an example with percentages:

```
TABLE {border-collapse: separate; cell-spacing: 4%}
TD {width: 20%}
```

This works for a four-column table. The four columns and the five spacing areas add up to 100 percent. However, if you want your columns to be all the same width, the easier way is to use the fast size algorithm.

Fast size

FF	Op	Sa	IE	Pr
●	●	●	●	●

Name:	table-layout
Value:	auto | fixed
Initial:	auto
Applies to:	tables and inline tables
Inherited:	no
Percentages:	N/A

If the table is simple and sufficiently regular that you can set the size of each column explicitly and be sure that the sizes are wide enough, you can tell the browser to use your sizes directly without checking each cell's minimum requirements. The advantage is that the browser gains time. It can start formatting and displaying the first row, using the column widths that you gave in the style sheet, without waiting for the rest of the table.

Of course, any failures are the designer's responsibility. If a cell can't be made narrow enough to fit the preset width, results are undefined. Usually, some text ends up overlapping the text in the next cell.

The property that controls whether the browser uses the fast mode is **table-layout**. Not all browsers look at this property; some use the normal mode anyway, deeming it fast enough. Here is an example of a style sheet using the fast table algorithm. It creates a table with a preset width and all columns the same width:

```
TABLE {table-layout: fixed: width: 100%}
```

Two conditions must be met before the fast algorithm can be used: **table-layout** must be fixed, and **width** must *not* be auto, both on the table element. If these two properties are set as required on the table element, the widths of the columns are computed after the first row without waiting for the other rows. First, all the column elements are inspected (elements **COL** in HTML). If there are any with a **width** property other than auto, their columns are the indicated width. For the other columns, the **width** property of the cells in the first row is checked. If any **width** properties are not auto, their value will be used for the columns. If no columns are left without a width, the **width** of the table element is not used, and the width of the table is instead computed from the column widths, plus any paddings and borders. Otherwise, the columns that don't have a width yet will divide the remaining space.

That leads to three possible situations:

1. All columns have an explicit width, for example:

```
TABLE {table-layout: fixed; width: 100%}
COL {width: 4.5em}
```

If we apply this to our large "trip to the beach" table (shown previously), which has 11 columns, we get a table of 49.5em plus any borders and paddings. The **width** property of the **TABLE** is ignored (although it has to be set to something; if you set it to auto, the fast algorithm will not be used).

2. Only some columns have an explicit width, for example:

```
TABLE {table-layout: fixed; width: 50em}
COL.when, COL.who {width: 4em}
```

Applied to the same table, this makes the first two columns 4em wide, and the remaining columns equally divide the remaining space. Assuming three borders of 0.1em and padding for all cells of 0.3em, that leaves 42em − 3 × 0.1em − 22 × 0.3em = 35.1em for the remaining nine columns, or 3.9em for each column.

3. No columns have an explicit width, for example:

```
TABLE {table-layout: fixed; width: 55em}
```

This makes all columns equally wide. You may not be interested in the exact width of the columns, but if you wish, it can be computed: Using the same example, the columns will be (55em − 3 × 0.1em − 22 × 0.3em)/11 = 48.1em/11 ≈ 4.4em.

SETTING BACKGROUND COLORS

All parts of a table have a background. The initial value of **background** is transparent, but all elements − cells, rows, row groups, columns, column groups, and of course the table itself − can be given a color and a background image. Here is an example in which a row, a column, and a cell have been given a background color:

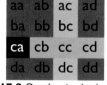

Figure 17.8 Overlapping backgrounds.

```
<TABLE>
  <COL CLASS="a"><COL CLASS="b">
    <COL CLASS="c"><COL CLASS="d">
  <TR CLASS="a"><TD>aa <TD>ab <TD>ac <TD>ad
  <TR CLASS="b"><TD>ba <TD>bb <TD>bc <TD>bd
  <TR CLASS="c"><TD ID="c1">ca <TD>cb <TD>cc <TD>cd
  <TR CLASS="d"><TD>da <TD>db <TD>dc <TD>dd
</TABLE>
```

with the style sheet:

```
TABLE {background: green; border-collapse: collapse}
COL.c {background: rgb(191,191,191)}
TR.c {background: rgb(255,170,0)}
#c1 {background: black; color: white}
TD {padding: 0.25em}
```

As Figure 17.8 shows, the background of the table is hidden by the column background, which in turn is hidden by the row. The cell is on top of everything.

Column groups (**COLGROUP**) and row groups (**THEAD**, **TFOOT**, and **TBODY**) can also be given backgrounds. Column groups are in front of the table background, but behind the columns, row groups are in front of columns and behind rows.

POSITIONING THE CAPTION

The default position for the caption of a table is above the table, but with the **caption-side** property, you can cause it to be displayed below the table instead.

FF	Op	S	IE	Pr
●	●	●	○	○

Name:	caption-side
Value:	top | bottom
Initial:	top
Applies to:	table-caption elements
Inherited:	yes
Percentages:	N/A

The rule to use is

```
CAPTION { caption-side: bottom }
```

INLINE TABLES

By default, tables in HTML are displayed as blocks: They end the previous paragraph, and any text after it will be in a new paragraph. However, CSS also supports inline tables, that will not break the line, but are displayed in the sentence in which they occur. Here is how that looks:

Magic squares are formed by placing the numbers 1, 2, 3, etc. in a square grid in such a way that the sum of the numbers in each row and each column is the same. A magic square with 9 cells, such as this

3	5	7
4	9	2
8	1	6

has a sum of 15 for every row and every column. Try it with squares of 16 and 25 cells.

Tables are put inline with the **display** property:

```
TABLE { display: inline-table }
```

XML AND TABLES

At the start of this chapter, we showed the various parts of a table in HTML. The same parts can occur in an XML-based format, but in that case, the browser probably has no built-in knowledge about which XML element corresponds to which part of the table. To help with that, the **display** property has keywords for each of the parts. The keywords are as follows:

- table (corresponding to **TABLE** in HTML) – Specifies that an element defines a block-level table.
- inline-table (doesn't exist in HTML) – Like table, but the table doesn't start on a new line. Instead, it is placed inline.
- table-row (in HTML: **TR**) – Specifies that an element is a row of cells.
- table-row-group (in HTML: **TBODY**) – Specifies that an element groups one or more rows.
- table-header-group (in HTML: **THEAD**) – Like table-row-group, but wherever it occurs in the table, it is always displayed before all other rows and rowgroups (but after any captions). On printed pages, the header group is often repeated on each page, in case the table is too long for one page.
- table-footer-group (in HTML: **TFOOT**) – Like table-row-group, but it is always displayed after all other rows and rowgroups (but before captions). Like table-header-group, this element is often repeated at the bottom of all pages if a long table is printed.
- table-column (in HTML: **COL**) – Specifies that an element describes a column of cells. Column elements cannot have content, but they may be useful for setting column widths, borders, and backgrounds.
- table-column-group (in HTML: **COLGROUP**) – Specifies that an element groups one or more columns.
- table-cell (in HTML: **TD**, **TH**) – Specifies that an element represents a table cell.

- table-caption (in HTML: **CAPTION**) – Specifies a caption for the table.

For example, if some document contained markup similar to this:

```
<timetable>
  <title>
    Airport bus time table
    <from>Black Lake Hotel</from>
    <to>Pine International Airport</to>
  </title>
  <fields>
    <bus>Bus no.</bus>
    <dep>Departure time</dep>
    <tim>Journey time</tim>
    <ar2>Arrival terminal 2</ar2>
    <ar1>Arrival terminal 1</ar1>
  </fields>
  <rec>
    <bus>501</bus>
    <dep>06:25</dep>
    <tim>85 min.</tim>
    <ar2>07:50</ar2>
    <ar1>08:00</ar1>
  </rec>
  <rec>
    <bus>301</bus>
    <dep>06:50</dep>
    <tim>140 min.</tim>
    <ar2>09:10</ar2>
    <ar1>09:20</ar1>
  </rec>
  ...
  <rec>
    <bus>515</bus>
    <dep>17:55</dep>
    <tim>115 min.</tim>
    <ar2>19:50</ar2>
    <ar1>20:00</ar1>
  </rec>
</timetable>
```

A good way to present this information is in tabular form. The `<timetable>` element becomes a table, `<field>` is a heading row, `<rec>` is a normal row, and so on. A skeleton of a style sheet could be as follows:

```
timetable {display: table}
fields {display: table-header-group}
rec {display: table-row}
bus, dep, tim, ar2, ar1 {display: table-cell}
title {display: table-caption}
```

This is enough to display the data in tabular form. We flesh out the skeleton next with some padding and other style properties to make it look better, but let's first take a look at why this works. If you look closely, you can see that not all the parts of a table are present. For example, `<fields>` has been made a `table-header-group` (corresponding to the **THEAD** in HTML), and its children are `table-cell` (like **TH/TD** in HTML), but there is no row element to contain those cells.

The table model of CSS allows many elements to be omitted. Where necessary, they are automatically inserted. In the previous style sheet, the `table-row` that must enclose the children of `<fields>` is automatically inserted between the `<fields>` element and its children. It is created as a so-called *anonymous box,* which means it has no corresponding element in the source document and no name; hence, you cannot set properties on it. You can tell its presence indirectly because the cells are correctly lined up in a row, but you cannot make the row box itself visible.

Let's add a few more properties to make the table easier to read: some horizontal rules, padding, and so on. Figure 17.9 shows the result.

Airport bus time table Black Lake Hotel - Pine International Airport

Bus no.	Departure time	Journey time	Arrival terminal 2	Arrival terminal 1
501	06:25	85 min.	07:50	08:00
301	06:50	140 min.	09:10	09:20
515	17:55	115 min.	19:50	20:00

Figure 17.9 XML table example.

```
title {font-style: italic}
fields {font-weight: bold;
  border-bottom: medium solid}
rec {border-bottom: thin solid black}
bus, dep, tim, ar2, ar1 {padding: 0.5em}
to:before {content: " - "}
```

Because CSS automatically inserts missing elements in a table, it is sometimes possible to use the table layout for something that, at first sight, doesn't look like a table at all. For example, the following (hypothetical) markup could be rendered as a table (see Figure 17.10):

```
<scene-list>
  <scene><name>Opening scene</name>
    <item>Camera 1 left</item>
    <item>Camera 2 on rails</item>
    <item>Camera 3 close-up</item>
  </scene>
  <scene><name>Balcony scene</name>
    <item>Camera 1 left</item>
    <item>Camera 2 close-up</item>
  </scene>
</scene-list>
```

Opening scene	Camera 1 left	Camera 2 on rails	Camera 3 close-up
Balcony scene	Camera 1 left	Camera 2 close-up	

Figure 17.10 A table created from a list.

We can align the cameras in columns:

```
scene-list {display: table; border-collapse: collapse}
scene {display: table-row}
name, item {display: table-cell;
  border: thin solid; padding: 0.5em}
name {font-weight: bolder}
```

Chapter 18

The CSS saga

The saga of CSS starts in 1994. One of the authors of this book works at CERN – the cradle of the Web – and the Web is starting to be used as a platform for electronic publishing. One crucial part of a publishing platform is missing, however: There is no way to style documents. For example, there is no way to describe a newspaper-like layout in a Web page. Having worked on personalized newspaper presentations at the MIT Media Laboratory, Håkon saw the need for a style sheet language for the Web.

Style sheets in browsers were not an entirely new idea. The separation of document structure from the document's layout had been a goal of HTML from its inception in 1990. Tim Berners-Lee wrote his NeXT browser/editor in such a way that he could determine the style with a simple style sheet. However, he didn't publish the syntax for the style sheets, considering it a matter for each browser to decide how to best display pages to its users. In 1992, Pei Wei developed a browser called "Viola," which had its own style sheet language.

However, the browsers that followed offered their users fewer and fewer options to influence the style. In 1993, NCSA Mosaic, the browser that made the Web popular, came out. Stylewise, however, it was a backward step because it only allowed its users to change certain colors and fonts.

Meanwhile, writers of Web pages complained that they didn't have enough influence over how their pages looked. One of the first questions from an author new to the Web was how to change fonts and colors of elements. At that time, HTML did not provide this functionality – and rightfully so. This excerpt from a message sent to the *www-talk* mailing list early in 1994 gives a sense of the tensions between authors and implementors:

> In fact, it has been a constant source of delight for me over the past year to get to continually tell hordes (literally) of people who want to -- strap yourselves in, here it comes -- control what their documents look like in ways that would be trivial in TeX, Microsoft Word, and every other common text processing environment: "Sorry, you're screwed."

The message is available from the archives at http://www.webhistory.org/ www.lists/www-talk.1994q1/ 0648.html

The author of the message was Marc Andreessen, one of the programmers behind NCSA Mosaic. He later became a co-founder of Netscape, a company eager to fulfill the request of authors. On October 13, 1994, Marc Andreessen announced to *www-talk* that the first beta release of Mozilla (which later turned into Netscape Navigator) was available for testing. Among the new tags the new browser supported was **CENTER**, and more tags were to follow shortly.

The original is online at http://www.w3.org/People/ howcome/p/cascade.html

Three days before Netscape announced the availability of its new browser, Håkon published the first draft of the *Cascading HTML Style Sheets* proposal. Behind the scenes, Dave Raggett (the main architect of HTML 3.0) had encouraged the release of the draft to go out before the upcoming "Mosaic and the Web" conference in Chicago. Dave had realized that HTML would and should never turn into a page-description language and that a more purpose-built mechanism was needed to satisfy requirements from authors. Although the first version of the document was immature, it provided a useful basis for discussion.

Among the people who responded to the first draft of CSS was Bert Bos, the co-author of this book. At that time, he was building Argo, a highly customizable browser with style sheets, and he decided to join forces with Håkon. Both of the two proposals look different from present-day CSS, but it is not hard to recognize the original concepts.

The Argo browser was part of a project to make the Internet accessible to scholars in the Humanities. It featured plug-ins (which it called "applets") before Netscape added them. See http://odur.let.rug.nl/~bert/ stylesheets.html and http://www.let.rug.nl/~bert/ argo.html.

One of the features of the Argo style language was that it was general enough to apply to other markup languages in addition to HTML. This also became a design goal in CSS and "HTML" was soon removed from the title of the specification. Argo also had other advanced features that didn't make it into CSS1, in particular, attribute selectors and generated text. Both features had to wait for CSS2.

Robert Raisch's message to www-talk is at http://www.webhistory.org/ www.lists/www-talk.1993q2/ 0445.html

"Cascading Style Sheets" wasn't the only proposed style language at the time. There was Pei Wei's language from the Viola browser, and around 10 other proposals for style sheet languages were sent to the *www-talk* and *www-html* mailing lists. Then, there was DSSSL, a complex style and transformation language under development at ISO for printing SGML documents. DSSSL could conceivably be applied to HTML as well. But, CSS had one feature that distinguished it from all the others: It took into account that on the Web, the style of a document couldn't be designed by either the author or the reader on their own, but that their wishes had to be combined, or "cascaded," in some way; and, in fact, not just the reader's and the author's wishes, but also the capabilities of the display device and the browser.

As planned, the initial CSS proposal was presented at the Web conference in Chicago in November 1994. The presentation at Developer's Day caused much discussion. First, the concept of a balance between author and user preferences was novel. A fictitious screen shot showed a slider with the label "user" on one side and "author" on the other. By adjusting the slider, the user could change the mix of his own preferences and those of the author. Second, CSS was perceived by some as being too simple for the task it was designed for. They argued that to style documents, the power of a full programming language was needed. CSS went in the exact opposite direction by making a point out of being a simple, declarative format.

WWW3, the third conference in the WWW series, was held on April 10–14, 1995, in Darmstadt, Germany

At the next WWW conference in April 1995, CSS was presented again. Both Bert and Håkon were there (in fact, this was the first time we met in person) and this time, we could also show implementations. Bert presented the support for style sheets in Argo, and Håkon showed a version of the Arena browser that had been modified to support CSS. Arena had been written by Dave Raggett as a testbed for new ideas, and one of them was style sheets. What started out as technical presentations ended up in political discussions about the author-reader balance. Representatives from the "author" side argued that the author ultimately had to be in charge of deciding how documents were presented. For example, it was argued that there may be legal requirements on how warning labels had to be printed and the user should not be able to reduce the font size for such warnings. The other side, where the authors of this book belong, argued that the user, whose eyes and ears ultimately have to decode the presentation, should be given the last word when conflicts arise.

Cascading Style Sheets

To subscribe to the mailing list or search the archives, see http://lists.w3.org/Archives/Public/www-style

Outside of the political battles, the technical work continued. The *www-style* mailing list was created in May 1995, and the discussions there have often influenced the development of the CSS specifications. Now, almost 10 years later, more than 16,000 messages exist in the archives of the mailing list.

In 1995, the World Wide Web Consortium (W3C) also became operational. Companies were joining the Consortium at a high rate and the organization became established. Workshops on various topics were found to be a successful way for W3C members and staff to meet and discuss future technical development. It was therefore decided that another workshop should be organized, this time with style sheets as the topic. The W3C technical staff working on style sheets (namely the two authors of this book) were now located in Sophia-Antipolis in Southern France where W3C had set up its European site. Southern France is not the worst place to lure workshop participants to, but because many of the potential participants were in the U.S., it was decided to hold the workshop in Paris, which is better served by international flights. The workshop was also an experiment to see if it was possible for W3C to organize events outside the U.S. Indeed, this turned out to be possible, and the workshop was a milestone in ensuring style sheets their rightful place on the Web. Among the participants was Thomas Reardon of Microsoft, who pledged support for CSS in upcoming versions of Internet Explorer.

At the end of 1995, W3C set up the HTML Editorial Review Board (HTML ERB) to ratify future HTML specifications. Because style sheets were within the sphere of interest of the members of the new group, the CSS specification was taken up as a work item with the goal of making it into a W3C Recommendation. Among the members of the HTML ERB was Lou Montulli of Netscape. After Microsoft signalled that it was adding CSS support in its browser, it was also important to get Netscape on board. Otherwise, we could see the Web diverge in different directions with browsers supporting different specifications. The battles within the HTML ERB were long and hard, but CSS level 1 finally emerged as a W3C Recommendation in December 1996.

In February 1997, CSS got its own working group inside W3C and the new group set out to work on the features which CSS1 didn't address. The group was chaired by Chris Lilley, a Scotsman recruited to W3C from the University of Manchester. CSS level 2 became a Recommendation in May 1998. Since then, the group has worked in parallel on

CSS3 (which is still to come) and CSS 2.1 (which is described in this book).

The W3C working group, whose official name is "Cascading Style Sheets and Formatting Properties Working Group," because they do more than just CSS, has about 15 members, delegated by the companies and organizations that are members of W3C. They come from all over the world, so the "meetings" are usually over the phone, and last about an hour every week. About four times each year, they meet somewhere in the world. Recent venues have been Provo, Redmond, San Francisco, and Paris. In Paris, the meeting was held at the offices of EDF-GDF, the French electricity and gas company. At that meeting, the group was offered a superb dinner: French cuisine overlooking Paris and the Seine – one of the few glamourous moments in the history of a hard-working technical working group.

BROWSERS

The CSS saga is not complete without a section on browsers. Had it not been for the browsers, CSS would have remained a lofty proposal of only academic interest. The first commercial browser to support CSS was Microsoft's Internet Explorer 3, which was released in August 1996. At that point, the CSS1 specification had not yet become a W3C Recommendation and discussions within the HTML ERB were to result in changes that Microsoft developers, led by Chris Wilson, could not foresee. IE3 reliably supports most of the color, background, font, and text properties, but it does not implement much of the box model.

The next browser to announce support for CSS was Netscape Navigator, version 4.0. Since its inception, Netscape had been sceptical toward style sheets, and the company's first implementation turned out to be a half-hearted attempt to stop Microsoft from claiming to be more standards-compliant than Netscape. The Netscape implementation supports a broad range of features – for example, floating elements – but the Netscape developers did not have time to fully test all the features that are supposedly supported. The result is that many CSS properties cannot be used in Navigator 4.

Netscape implemented CSS internally by translating CSS rules into snippets of JavaScript, which were then run along with other scripts. The company also decided to let developers write JSSS, thereby bypassing CSS entirely. If JSSS had been successful, the Web would have had one more style sheet than necessary. This, fortunately for CSS, turned out not to be the case.

Meanwhile, Microsoft continued its efforts to replace Netscape from the throne of reigning browsers. In Internet Explorer 4, the browser display engine, which among other things is responsible for rendering CSS, was replaced by a module code-named "Trident." Trident removed many of the limitations in IE3, but also came with its own set of limitations and bugs. Microsoft was put under pressure by the Web Standards Project (WaSP), which published "IE's Top 10 CSS Problems" in November 1998 (see Figure 18.1).

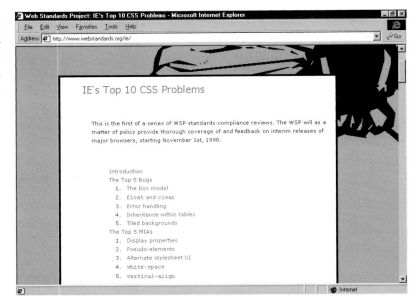

Figure 18.1 The WaSP project tracks browser conformance to W3C Recommendations. One of their first reviews was the CSS support in Microsoft Internet Explorer.

Subsequent versions of Internet Explorer have improved the support for CSS, but important functionality is still missing (for example, "fixed" positioning, generated text, and user-selectable style sheets). In this book, we review Version 6 of Internet Explorer.

Figure 18.2 Opera's "small-screen rendering" transforms pages into columns.

The third browser that ventured into CSS was Opera. The browser from the small Norwegian company made headlines in 1998 by being tiny (it fit on a floppy!) and customizable while supporting most features found in the larger offerings from Microsoft and Netscape. Opera 3.5 was released in November 1998, and supported most of CSS1. The Opera developers (namely Geir Ivarsøy) also found time to test the CSS implementation before shipping, which is a novelty in this business. One of the authors of this book, Håkon, was so impressed with Opera's technology that he joined the company as CTO in 1999. Since then, Opera Software has grown and now has about 200 employees. One important market for Opera's browser is mobile phones. By reformatting pages to fit on a small screen (@media handheld is handy here), the Web has been freed from the desktop (see Figure 18.2).

The people at Netscape responded to the increasing competition with a move that was novel at the time: They released the source code for the browser. With the source code public, anyone could inspect the internals of their product, improve it, and make competing browsers based on in. Much of the code, including the CSS implementation, was terminated shortly after the release, and the "Mozilla" project was formed to build a new generation browser. CSS was in important specification to handle and countless hours have been spent by volunteers to make sure pages are displayed according to the specification. Several browsers have been based on the Mozilla code, including Galeon and Firefox.

Apple is often seen as a technology pioneer, but for a long time, it did not spend much resources on Web browsers. Apple left it to Microsoft to build a browser for its machines, and Internet Explorer for Mac actually had better support for CSS than the Windows version of the browser. In 2003, Microsoft discontinued support for the Mac and Apple announced a new browser called "Safari." Safari isn't entirely new – it is based on the open source Konqueror browser, which was developed for the KDE system running on Linux.

Cascading Style Sheets

Tantek Çelik is an editor of the CSS 2.1 specification and for a long time he was a Microsoft employee. His efforts within the company resulted in very good support for CSS in Internet Explorer for the MacIntosh. Unfortunately, the code has not been ported to the Windows platform.

For Web designers, it is good news to have several competing products based on Web standards. Although some efforts to test that your pages display well in all browsers are necessary, the fact that Web pages can be displayed on a wide range of machines is a huge improvement from the past:

Anyone who slaps a "this page is best viewed with Browser X" label on a Web page appears to be yearning for the bad old days, before the Web, when you had very little chance of reading a document written on another computer, another word processor, or another network.
—Tim Berners-Lee in Technology Review, July 1996

BEYOND BROWSERS

The CSS saga isn't only about Web browsers. Many people outside of the few that program Web browsers have made important contributions to CSS over the past years. Some of them are mentioned in the Preface and we use the few remaining paragraphs of this book to expand on some of them.

The CSS1 test suite was an landmark development for CSS and W3C. When the first two CSS implementations came out and could be compared, we realized there was a problem. You could not expect the style sheet tested only in one browser to work in the other browser. To rectify the situation, Eric Meyer – with help from countless other volunteers – developed a test suite that implementors would test against while there still was time to fix the problems. Todd Fahrner created the "acid" test which became the ultimate challenge. See Figure 18.3.

Brian's "index dot CSS" is available from http://www.blooberry.com/indexdot/css/index.html

When a test suite is available, someone must do the testing. Brian Wilson has done a remarkable job of testing CSS implementations and making the results available on the Web.

Without compelling content, CSS hasn't served its purpose. Dave Shea created the CSS Zen garden to show fellow graphics artists why CSS should be taken seriously. He, along with the many people who created submissions, showed people how to use CSS creatively.

The Web site for the Prince formatter is http://www.yeslogic.com

The Web has been trapped on the desktop for too long. Making it available on mobile phones is one important escape. Michael Day and Xuehong Liu have shown us another way out: The Prince formatter

Figure 18.3 The acid test.

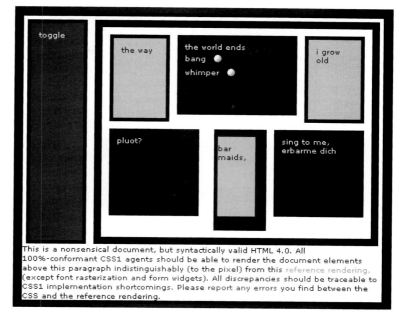

converts HTML and XML documents to PDF and is entirely based on CSS. This product enabled the authors of this book to abandon traditional word processors and use the same standards we preach. This book has been written entirely in HTML and CSS.

Appendix A

HTML 4.0 quick reference

This appendix gives a brief overview of HTML 4.0. This version of HTML is the first to contain the elements and attributes necessary for effective use of style sheets, in particular **STYLE** and **CLASS.** There are, in fact, two versions of HTML 4.0: HTML 4.0 and HTML 4.0 "Transitional." The latter contains a number of tags (the so-called "extensions") that existed in HTML 3.2, but are now deprecated in favor of style sheets. We describe only HTML 4.0 here, which doesn't contain the extensions.

The following text focuses on the elements that are most useful in combination with a style sheet. Other elements are also mentioned, but with less explanation. For the same reason, not all the possible attributes are described. The rules for how elements can be nested have been stratified by leaving out some cases that are allowed in HTML 4.0. The result is simpler to explain than the full rules, but a little more restrictive.

The text is not a tutorial on HTML. It assumes you've read at least Chapter 1, "The Web and HTML." This appendix focuses on the list of HTML elements and the rules for combining them.

DOCUMENT STRUCTURE

An HTML 4.0 document consists of elements nested inside other elements. Each element starts with a *start tag* <...> and ends with an *end tag* </...>.

In some cases, one or both of the tags may be omitted. In general, it is safest to always include both of them. When a document is created with the help of a dedicated HTML editor, the tags are inserted automatically by the editor.

At the highest level, a document consists of one element, called **HTML**. Inside that are two elements, **HEAD** and **BODY**:

```
<HTML>
  <HEAD>...</HEAD>
  <BODY>...</BODY>
</HTML>
```

Elements can have attributes, which have a name and a value, separated by an equals sign (=). The value is enclosed in quotes ("..." or '...'). Attributes are listed only in the start tag, never in the end tag:

```
<EM CLASS="surname">
<A REL='copyright' HREF='copy.html'>
```

Element names and attribute names can be spelled with capital or small letters, or even mixtures of the two. The previous example can also be written as follows:

```
<em class="surname">
<a rel='copyright' href='copy.html'>
```

THE HEAD ELEMENT

The head contains information about the document. It is normally not displayed. The elements that can occur in the **HEAD** are **BASE**, **ISINDEX**, **MAP**, **META**, **LINK**, **STYLE**, and **SCRIPT**.

TITLE

There must be exactly one **TITLE** element. It can contain only text, no other elements. The title is often displayed in the title bar of a window.

STYLE

The **STYLE** element can contain a style sheet, as described in Chapter 2, "CSS." An attribute **TYPE** must be added that declares the type of style language (for example, <STYLE TYPE="text/css">).

LINK

LINK specifies a relationship between the document and some other document. The relationship is a keyword that is put in the **REL** attribute. The URL of the other document is put in the **HREF** attribute. There may be zero or more **LINK** elements. The element has no content and the end tag must be omitted. The relation "stylesheet" is used to associate a style sheet with a document:

```
<LINK REL="stylesheet"
  HREF="http://example.com/sty/rf.css">
```

META

The **META** element attaches various kinds of meta-information about the document. The element has no content and the end tag must be omitted.

BASE

BASE can contain the URL of the document itself or the URL that serves as the base for relative URLs in the document. The URL is included as the value of the **HREF** attribute. The element has no content and the end tag must be omitted.

Here is an example of a typical **HEAD**:

```
<HEAD>
  <TITLE>The oak tree</TITLE>
  <LINK REL="author" HREF="../people/Jones">
  <STYLE TYPE="text/css">
    H1 {font-family: Helvetica, sans-serif}
    BODY {font-family: Bodoni, serif}
  <STYLE>
</HEAD>
```

THE BODY ELEMENT

BODY can contain three types of elements: container elements, bridge elements, and special elements. *Container elements* can contain exactly the same elements as the **BODY**. These elements create divisions, interactive forms, long quotations, and other high-level structures. *Bridge elements* contain text and text-level elements. Paragraphs and headings are examples of bridge elements. *Special elements* include lists, tables, and certain elements for interactive forms.

All the elements that can appear in the **BODY** can appear any number of times. All of them accept these five attributes: **CLASS**, **STYLE**, **ID**, **LANG** (to indicate the language in which the element is written), and **DIR** (to indicate the writing direction: ltr is left-to-right, rtl is right-to-left for Hebrew and Arabic).

Container elements

The container elements are **DIV**, **BLOCKQUOTE**, **ADDRESS**, **FORM**, and **FIELDSET**.

DIV is a general division, such as a chapter, section, abstract, or note. It is customary to indicate the type of division in the **CLASS** attribute (for example, <DIV CLASS="verse">).

BLOCKQUOTE is a quotation consisting of one or more paragraphs.

ADDRESS is a name and/or address, usually after a heading or a blockquote, or at the end of the document, to indicate the author of the document or the quotation.

FORM is a container for an interactive form. The **ACTION** attribute contains the URL of the server that will process the form. The **METHOD** attribute contains the method used to send the form data to the server, either get, post, or put.

The **FIELDSET** element groups a part of a form. In addition to all other elements that can occur in **BODY**, it can also have one **LEGEND** element in its content, which, if present, must be the first element in the **FIELDSET**. Browsers can use the **FIELDSET** to activate a set of form elements together. The **LEGEND** is a bridge element.

Bridge elements

The bridge elements are **P**, **H1**, **H2**, **H3**, **H4**, **H5**, **H6**, and **PRE**. The **P** is a normal paragraph. **H1** to **H6** are headings of different levels. **H1** is the most important. **PRE** means "preformatted." Typically, the **white-space** property for this element is set to pre (see Chapter 6, "The fundamental objects").

Special elements

The special elements are **OL**, **UL**, **DL**, **HR**, and **TABLE**. **OL** and **UL** are simple lists. They contain only **LI** (list item) elements (one or more). The **LI** element itself acts like a container element: It accepts the same content as the **BODY** element. **UL** is typically shown with a bullet as a label and **OL** typically uses numbered labels. For example (compare Figure A.1):

* First item
* Second item

1. First item
2. Second item

Figure A.1 Unordered and ordered lists.

```
<UL>
   <LI><P>First item</P></LI>
   <LI><P>Second item</P></L>
</UL>
<OL>
   <LI><P>First item</P></LI>
   <LI><P>Second item</P></LI>
</OL>
```

DL is a definition list. It contains one or more definitions, where each definition consists of one or more **DT** (term) elements, followed by one or more **DD** (definition) elements. The **DT** element is like a bridge element: It contains text and text-level elements. The **DD** is a container: It contains the same elements as **BODY**. Figure A.2 shows how the following **DL** example might look.

term A
    Definition of term A

term B1
term B2
    Definition for terms B1 and B2

Figure A.2 Definition list.

```
<DL>
   <DT>term A</DT>
   <DD><P>Definition of term A</P></DD>
   <DT>term B1</DT>
   <DT>term B2</DT>
   <DD><P>Definition for terms B1 and B2</P></DD>
</DL>
```

HR is an element without content and without an end tag. Its purpose is to separate paragraphs without grouping them. It is usually rendered as a horizontal rule (hence its name) or simply as white space.

The **TABLE** element creates a table. A table has a complex structure (see Chapter 17, "Tables"), but the main part consists of rows of cells. The content of the table starts with three optional parts: a **CAPTION**, a **THEAD**, and a **TFOOT** (in that order); after that are one or more **TBODY**, which contain the actual table.

The **CAPTION** is a bridge element: It may contain only text and text-level elements. It defines a caption that can be displayed above or below the table.

The **THEAD** contains the first few rows of the table, those that contain the column headings. Putting those headings in the **THEAD** allows certain browsers to treat them specially, but they can also be put in the table's body. **TFOOT** also contains column headings, possibly the same, but they're meant to be at the bottom of the columns. For small tables, it is okay to omit the **TFOOT** and put any headings directly in the table's body.

The table's body is contained in one or more **TBODY** elements. In large tables, rows can be grouped together into multiple **TBODY**s. For small tables, a single **TBODY** suffices.

THEAD, **TFOOT**, and **TBODY** all have the same structure. They contain one or more **TR** (Table Row) elements. Each **TR** contains zero or more table cells.

There are two types of table cells: **TH** and **TD**. The former is for table headings, and the latter for table data. **TH** and **TD** act like containers: They can contain the same elements as the **BODY** element. **TH** and **TD** can have two attributes: **COLSPAN** and **ROWSPAN**. They indicate, respectively, how many columns and how many rows the cell spans. The default is 1.

Here is an example of a simple table. (To make it easier to read, all end tags are omitted; according to HTML 4.0, this is allowed.) Figure A.3 shows the result.

	Year 1996			
	Q1	**Q2**	**Q3**	**Q4**
cars	365	320	258	191
bicycles	165	208	358	391
trains	35	45	53	72

Figure A.3 A simple table.

```
<TABLE>
  <TBODY>
    <TR>
      <TH ROWSPAN=2>
      <TH COLSPAN=4><P>Year 1996
    <TR>
      <TH><P>Q1
      <TH><P>Q2
      <TH><P>Q3
      <TH><P>Q4
    <TR>
      <TH><P>cars
      <TD><P>365
      <TD><P>320
      <TD><P>258
      <TD><P>191
    <TR>
      <TH><P>bicycles
      <TD><P>165
      <TD><P>208
      <TD><P>358
```

```
    <TD><P>391
  <TR>
    <TH>trains
    <TD><P>35
    <TD><P>45
    <TD><P>53
    <TD><P>72
</TABLE>
```

TEXT-LEVEL ELEMENTS

Text-level elements are mixed with text inside the bridge elements and inside the element **DT**. Text-level elements indicate the function of a certain word or a phrase. Here is an example of a paragraph with text and several text-level elements. Note that text-level elements can be nested inside each other. Figure A.4 shows the result of the example.

A *square* is a rectangle of which all sides are of equal length. *Squares should **not** be used for solving problem A.*

```
<P>A <DFN>square</DFN> is a rectangle
of which all sides are of equal
length. <EM CLASS="instruction">Squares
should <STRONG>not</STRONG> be used for
solving problem A.</EM></P>
```

Figure A.4 **DFN**, **EM**, and **STRONG** elements.

All text-level elements accept the attributes **CLASS**, **LANG**, **DIR**, and **STYLE**.

Most text-level elements can be nested inside each other arbitrarily, but a few have restrictions. The unrestricted ones are **ACRONYM**, **ABBREV**, **B**, **BDO**, **CITE**, **CODE**, **DFN**, **EM**, **I**, **KBD**, **LABEL**, **Q**, **SPAN**, **STRONG**, **SUB**, **SUP**, **VAR**, and **LEGEND**. The ones with restrictions are **A**, **BR**, **IMG**, **INPUT**, **SELECT**, and **TEXTAREA**.

Normal text-level elements **EM** and **STRONG** mark words or phrases that need emphasis or strong emphasis. **DFN** contains a word or term that is being defined. The first occurrence of a new term in a technical document is often marked this way. **CODE** and **KBD** are mostly used when talking about computer-related topics. They indicate literal code (such as a word from a program or a command) and literal text to type on the keyboard. **VAR** indicates a variable, either in a computer program or in a formula. **SUB** and **SUP** are for subscripts (like the 2 in H_2O) and superscripts (like the 2 in $E=mc^2$). Although HTML doesn't have support for mathematical formulas, these elements can help create the most simple one.

ACRONYM and **ABBREV** mark acronyms (abbreviations that are pronounced as a single word, such as NATO, NASA, UNICEF, and Benelux) and abbreviations (such as USA, viz., i.e., W3C, and CSS). Marking them might allow a smart browser to expand them, but it is especially useful for a speech synthesizer.

B and **I** indicate that words were bold or italic in the text from which the current words are derived. They are useful when the text is converted from a document format that doesn't allow the role of the words to be encoded. For text entered directly in HTML, **EM** and **STRONG** are usually better choices.

CITE encloses a bibliographic reference (a type of link that is not a hyperlink), such as *(Raggett 1996)*. **Q** encloses a short quotation or a word that is used metaphorically. The appropriate quote marks are inserted by the browser; for example, the sentence: He said: <q>Hello!</q>.

A **LABEL** is used in conjunction with a form element (**SELECT**, **TEXTAREA**, **INPUT**, **FIELDSET**) or with an **OBJECT** element to provide a description for it. Usually, it occurs near that other element. It has an extra attribute, **FOR**, which is required and that contains the ID of the element that it is associated with. Typically, in a browser, clicking a label activates the element to which it is joined and puts the cursor on it.

LEGEND can occur only inside a fieldset and provides a caption for the group of form controls enclosed by the fieldset.

The **BDO** element is needed for certain rare cases that can occur in documents that contain both left-to-right text (such as English) and right-to-left text (such as Hebrew). It stands for Bi-Directional Override. It has a required attribute, **DIR**, that is either ltr or rtl. Depending on this attribute, it tells the HTML program that the content is left-to-right or right-to-left, even if the characters inside the element would normally be used in the opposite direction. (This is different from the **DIR** attribute that all elements have, and that indicates only the default direction, for those characters that don't have a definite direction. For more information, see the CSS2 specification.)

SPAN is a general-purpose element that can be used when none of the other text-level elements is suitable. It must have either a **CLASS** attribute to indicate the role of the element or a **STYLE** attribute to set a style directly; for example, to mark people's names, you could do the following:

```
<SPAN CLASS="person">Berners-Lee</SPAN>.
```

Restricted text-level elements

Restricted text-level elements differ from normal text-level elements in what can be nested inside them. Apart from **A**, they don't allow other text-level elements in their content.

A is perhaps HTML's most important element: It is the source anchor of a hyperlink. Besides the normal attributes (**CLASS**, **ID**, **STYLE**, **LANG**, and **DIR**), it has a required attribute **HREF** that contains the URL of the target anchor. It accepts all text-level elements in its content except other **A** elements.

The **BR** indicates a forced line break, without starting a new paragraph. It has no content and no end tag.

The **IMG** element inserts images and other simple objects. It has a required attribute, **SRC**, which holds the URL of the image, and another required attribute, **ALT**, which can hold short text that is displayed when the image itself can't be displayed (for example, <IMG SRC="w3c_48x48" ALT="W3C logo">). The element has no content and no end tag.

INPUT is an element used in interactive forms. It creates a button or a short text field, depending on the value of the (required) **TYPE** attribute: text, password, checkbox, radio, submit, reset, file, hidden, or image. It has a required **NAME** attribute and a **VALUE** attribute that is required for some values of the **TYPE** attribute. **INPUT** has no content and no end tag. Here are some examples of input elements (Figure A.5 shows how they typically look):

Figure A.5 Examples of **INPUT** elements.

```
<FORM ACTION="xx">
  <P><INPUT TYPE="text" NAME="fld9" VALUE="initial">
    Name
  <P><INPUT TYPE="radio" NAME="r7" VALUE="a" CHECKED>
    Option 1
  <P><INPUT TYPE="radio" NAME="r7" VALUE="b">
    Option 2
  <P><INPUT TYPE="radio" NAME="r7" VALUE="c">
    Option 3
  <P><INPUT TYPE="checkbox" NAME="pu8">
    Check if you are sure
  <P><INPUT TYPE="submit" VALUE="Send!" NAME="sub-a">
    <INPUT TYPE="reset" VALUE="Reset">
<FORM>
```

SELECT is a list or menu for use in an interactive form. It can contain only one or more **OPTION** elements or **OPTGROUP** elements that, in turn, contain **OPTION** elements. An **OPTION** element contains only text, no other elements. The **SELECT** element has a required **NAME** attribute with an arbitrary text as its value. For other attributes, refer to a full HTML specification. Figure A.6 shows the result of this code:

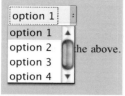

Figure A.6 Example of a
SELECT.

```
<FORM ACTION="xx">
  <P><SELECT NAME="hh44">
    <OPTION SELECTED>option 1</OPTION>
    <OPTION>option 2</OPTION>
    <OPTION>option 3</OPTION>
    <OPTION>option 4</OPTION>
  </SELECT>
  <P>Select one of the above.
</FORM>
```

TEXTAREA is another element for interactive forms. It represents a fill-in field of more than one line. It can contain text but no other elements. It has three required attributes: **NAME**, **ROWS**, and **COLS**. **NAME** contains an arbitrary text. **ROWS** contains a number indicating the height of the field. **COLS** contains the width of the field. Other attributes are optional:

```
<FORM ACTION="xx">
<TEXTAREA NAME="kk12" ROWS=3 COLS=15>
Edit this text.
</TEXTAREA>
</FORM>
```

OBJECT is a sophisticated element. It can insert images into text, include applets (small programs that run inside a document), and in general put arbitrary multimedia objects inside the text, including other HTML documents. In principle, it makes **IMG** obsolete, but **IMG** is retained for simple cases. The most important attribute of **OBJECT** is **DATA**, which contains a URL that points to an external object. It has several other attributes, which are used for some types of objects. Because this is only a quick reference, we can't list all the different multimedia objects and their attributes here.

Although **OBJECT** is itself a text-level element, its content is the same as that of **BODY**. However, in the ideal case, that content is not displayed. The intention is that the content is only displayed when the object itself could not be displayed, for whatever reason. The content constitutes an alternative, in the same way that the **ALT** attribute of **IMG** is an alternative. But, the alternative of **OBJECT** is much richer; it can be almost a complete HTML document. Here is a simple example:

```
<P>Look at yourself:
  <OBJECT DATA="nonexistent.ngf">
    <P>Your browser failed to load the
    NGF image. If it had worked, you
    would have seen a gold edged
    mirror that reflected your face.<P>
  </OBJECT>
</P>
```

BUTTON: a text-level container element

A **BUTTON** element is a bit like a 1-cell inline table (see the section "Inline tables" in Chapter 17). It can occur only in bridge elements and text-level elements, but it is itself a container. It is normally used as a submit or reset button in a form, with the difference that the label is not restricted to one line of text without markup, but can be any HTML text. Usually, it is rendered with an outset border, but different browsers may show it slightly differently. Here is an example (see Figure A.7):

Figure A.7 Examples of **BUTTON** elements.

```
<P>Press
  <BUTTON STYLE="width: 8em">
    <H2>Red</H2>
    <P>to select red</P>
  </BUTTON>
or
  <BUTTON STYLE="width: 8em">
    <H2>Green</H2>
    <P>to select green</P>
  </BUTTON>
...</P>
```

SPECIAL CHARACTERS

A few characters can be entered by name. This may be useful when the HTML file is to be sent over old mail systems or when your keyboard doesn't allow you to enter those characters in an easier way. For example, instead of "é," you can enter "é" (including the & and the ;). Here is a complete list:

Letter	Code	Letter	Code	Letter	Code
á	&aacute;	é	&eacute;	í	&iacute;
Á	&Aacute;	É	&Eacute;	Í	&Iacute;
â	&acirc;	ê	&ecirc;	î	&icirc;
Â	&Acirc;	Ê	&Ecirc;	Î	&Icirc;
à	&agrave;	è	&egrave;	ì	&igrave;
À	&Agrave;	È	&Egrave;	Ì	&Igrave;
ä	&auml;	ë	&euml;	ï	&iuml;
Ä	&Auml;	Ë	&Euml;	Ï	&Iuml;
å	&aring;	ó	&oacute;	ú	&uacute;
Å	&Aring;	Ó	&Oacute;	Ú	&Uacute;
æ	&aelig;	ô	&ocirc;	û	&ucirc;
Æ	&AElig;	Ô	&Ocirc;	Û	&Ucirc;
ç	&ccedil;	ò	&ograve;	ù	&ugrave;
Ç	&Ccedil;	Ò	&Ograve;	Ù	&Ugrave;
ð	&eth;	ö	&ouml;	ü	&uuml;
Ð	&ETH;	Ö	&Ouml;	Ü	&Uuml;
ñ	&ntilde;	ø	&oslash;	ý	&yacute;
Ñ	&Ntilde;	Ø	&Oslash;	Ý	&Yacute;
ß	&szlig;	õ	&otilde;	ÿ	&yuml;
þ	&thorn;	Õ	&Otilde;	©	&copy;
Þ	&THORN;	™	&trade;	®	&reg;
&	&amp;	<	&lt;	>	&gt;
"	&quot;		&shy;		
—	&mdash;	–	&ndash;		
	&zwj;		&zwnj;		

A non-breaking space ( ) is exactly like a normal space except that it will never be broken at the end of a line. A soft hyphen (­) is an invisible mark in the text that indicates that a line may be broken at that point if needed, in which case it will expand to the appropriate type of hyphen to indicate that the word continues on the next line. A thin space ( ) is a space that is about half as wide as a normal space.

An em space ( ) is a space that is as wide as the em of the current font. An en space ( ) is half the width of an em space.

A zero-width non-joiner (‌) is an invisible mark between two letters to indicate that the two letters should not be combined visually. It can be used to avoid a ligature. In Western languages, it is almost never necessary. In some Oriental languages, it is more common. A zero-width joiner (‍) is the opposite. It combines two letters into a ligature that would otherwise not be combined.

XHTML 1

Since 2000, HTML 4 has a successor, called XHTML 1. It has exactly the same elements as HTML 4, but it is written using XML syntax. The XML syntax will make it easier in the future to combine XHTML with other XML-based languages, such as MathML (for mathematical expressions), SVG (for diagrams, maps, and other graphics) and SMIL (for multimedia) into a single format for many different types of documents.

In this book, we used HTML 4 for the examples, but all browsers also accept XHTML 1. The syntax differences are small:

- All element names must be written in lowercase in XHTML:

HTML	XHTML
<P>	<p>
<H1>	<h1>
<OL>	<ol>
<DIV>	<div>
etc.	

- All elements that don't have an end tag in HTML need a slash (/) just before the > in XHTML:

HTML	XHTML
<img>	<img />
<hr>	<hr />
<link>	<link />

```
<meta>       <meta />
<base>       <base />
<isindex>    <isindex />
<input>      <input />
```

- All elements whose end tag may be omitted in HTML have a required end tag in XHTML:

HTML   **XHTML**
```
<html>...    <html>...</html>
<body>...    <body>...</body>
<p>...       <p>...</p>
<li>...      <li>...</li>
<dt>...      <dt>...</dt>
<dd>...      <dd>...</dd>
```

- In HTML, attributes that consist of only letters or digits, without any spaces or other symbols, don't need quote marks. In XHTML, all attributes, without exception, need to be quoted:

HTML   **XHTML**
```
rowspan=2        rowspan="2"
class=property   class="property"
width=45         width="45"
id=fig17         id="fig17"
etc.
```

- In HTML, some attributes don't have a value; their presence is enough. In XHTML, they require a value that is the same as their name:

HTML   **XHTML**
```
checked    checked="checked"
selected   selected="selected"
```

- XHTML files must have a DOCTYPE just before the <html>. Currently, that looks like this:

```
<!DOCTYPE html PUBLIC "-//W3C//DTD XHTML 1.1//EN"
  "http://www.w3.org/TR/xhtml11/DTD/xhtml11.dtd">
<html>
...
```

This indicates the first element of the format (html), the unique name for the format, including the version number (-//W3C//DTD XHTML 1.1//EN), and finally, the place on the Web where one can find a formal grammar for this format.

Appendix B

Reading property value definitions

The box on page 95 describes how to read CSS property definitions. One of the fields, however, was omitted because explaining it requires a few pages. The *Value* field is written in a formal syntax to ensure preciseness, but the end result isn't always readable to humans. This appendix describes how to read the Value field.

Here is an example of a property defininition.

FF	Op	Sa	IE	Pr
●	●	●	●	●

Name:	font-style
Value:	normal │ italic │ oblique
Initial:	normal
Applies to:	all elements
Inherited:	yes
Percentages:	N/A

The Web sites of the vendors are http://www.microsoft.com http://www.mozilla.org http://www.opera.com http://www.apple.com http://www.yeslogic.com

The "button bar" on the left side indicates how major browsers support each property. The browser categories are IE6 (Microsoft Internet Explorer for Windows, version 6), FF (Firefox version 1.0), Op7 (Opera version 7.2), Sa1 (Safari version 1.0), and Pr4 (Prince version 4). The first four products are browsers, and Prince is a CSS formatter that prints HTML and XML documents.

The buttons have the following meaning:
- ○ The property is not supported by the browser.
- ◑ The property is partially supported by the browser.
- ● The property is, for most practical purposes, fully supported by the browser.

"Index dot CSS" is available from http://www.blooberry.com/ indexdot/css/index.html

For more detailed information about browser support, Brian Wilson's "Index Dot CSS" is the best source. For example, it tells you how the Mac version of IE4 differs from the Windows version. The buttons on the left indicates to what extent major browsers support the property. See the separate box on what the abbreviations and buttons mean.

The *Name* field is the first field in the formal definition. It simply lists the name of the property.

The *Value* field gives the possible values of the property. The previous example says that this particular property accepts one of three keywords as value: `normal`, `italic`, or `oblique`.

If a property offers many possible values or many possible complex combinations of values, you may find square brackets, vertical bars, and other symbols in this area. The syntax is defined in a shorthand notation using certain symbols:

- Angle brackets: < and >
- Vertical bars: | and ||
- Regular brackets: [ ]
- Question mark: ?
- Asterisk: *

Keywords are also used. A *keyword* is a word that appears in a value. Keywords must appear literally, without quotes, angle brackets, or other marks. Examples are `italic`, `oblique`, `thick`, `thin`, and `medium`. The slash and comma also must appear literally when used in a value.

When these symbols are used in this shorthand, they have special meanings. All other characters that appear in a value stand for themselves. Note that spaces may be inserted between all values; they can also often be omitted, as long as the result is unambiguous. Here is an explanation of what each symbol means:

Angle brackets < > The words between the angle brackets < and > specify a type of value. The most common types of values are `length` (*<length>*), `percentage`, `color`, `number`, and `url`. We discuss most of these in this chapter. We talked about `url` in Chapter 1, "The Web and HTML," and we dealt with `color` in Chapter 10, "Colors."

More specialized types include some you've already seen: `font-weight`, `text-align`, `font-style`, `text-decoration`, and `background`. We describe these under the properties to which they apply in Chapters 4–8. For example, if the definition of a property (let's take the **color** property as an example) includes this line:

Name:	font-style
Value:	*<color>*

It means that the property accepts values of type color, for example red. As a result, in the style sheet, you might find

```
H2 { color: red }
```

The url value is handled a little differently from the others. Instead of simply typing a URL, you type url followed by the actual URL in parentheses, with no space between the two: url(images/tree.png) or url(http://www.w3.org/pub/WWW). Here is an example of its usage:

```
BODY { background: url(bg/marble.png) }
```

MULTIPLE VALUES

If multiple values must occur in a certain order, they are given as a list. The following example could be used in the definition of a property that always required a color and a number (there is no such property in CSS1; this is just an example):

Value:	*<color>* *<number>*
Example:	red 7.5
Example:	#CECECE 25

Vertical Bars | and ||: A single vertical bar | separates alternative values. For example, in A|B, the | separates A and B; either A or B will be used. You may have any number of alternatives. *One and only one of the alternatives must occur.* In the following examples, exactly one of the listed values must occur:

Example:	normal
Example:	{ font-style: normal }
Example:	left	right	center	justify
Example:	right
Example usage:	H1 { text-align: right }

A double vertical bar ‖ also separates alternative values; for example, A ‖ B. However, the ‖ means that either A or B or both must occur. Further, they may occur in any order. In the following example, there may be a color or a url or both, and their order is not important:

Example:	red url(logos/logo.png)
Example:	url(logos/logo.png) black
Example:	#00FF00
Example:	url(logos/logo.png)

Another example, slightly more complicated, is taken from the definition of the border property, which has a value defined as follows. The types `border-width` and `border-style` are defined in Chapter 8, "Space around boxes."

Example:	*1pt dotted blue*
Example:	*dotted*
Example:	black 0.5pt
Example:	P.note { border: red double 2px }

Curly brackets { }: Curly brackets { } indicate that the preceding value may occur at least A and, at most, B times. This is written as {A, B}. For example, in the following example, a `length` value may occur one, two, three, or four times:

Example:	2em
Example:	2em 3em
Example:	2em 3em 4em
Example:	2em 3em 4em 5em
Example usage:	P { margin: 2em 3em 4em 5em }

In this example, we use the **margin** property to set a different margin for each of the four sides of a **P** element. See Chapter 8 for a complete definition of **margin**.

Question marks (?), asterisks (*), and plus (+): Any type or keyword may be followed by one of the modifiers +, *, or ?. A plus

Appendix B: Reading property value definitions

(+) indicates that the preceding item may be repeated. The item must occur *one or more times*.

Value:	<percentage>+
Example:	0% 50% 50% 11% 0.1%
Example:	37.5%

An asterisk (*) indicates that the preceding item may be repeated, but it may also be omitted. It may occur zero or more times.

Value:	<length>*
Example:	12pt 12ex 3.5mm 12pt 12pc 3.6mm
Example:	1.1in.

Note that the last example has no value at all.

A question mark (?) indicates that the preceding type or keyword is *optional*.

Value:	<url>? <color>
Example:	url(http://www.w3.org/pub/WWW) black
Example:	white

In this example, the available values are a url and a color. <url> is followed by a ?, while <color> is not. Hence, the URL may be omitted, but the color may not. The background property has a value similar to that and, in that property, the presence of both values means that the color is displayed with the image on top of it. If the image pointed to by the url is unavailable, just the color is displayed.

Regular brackets [ ]: Regular ("square") brackets group parts of the definition together. A question mark, asterisk, or other special symbol that follows the closing bracket applies to the entire group. The following example shows a group with a vertical bar inside and curly braces on the outside to indicate that the entire group may be repeated between one and four times.

Value:	[<length> | <percentage>]{1,4}
Example:	12pt 10pt 12pt 5pt
Example:	10%
Example:	10% 10% 1px
Example usage:	ADDRESS { padding: 5% 1em }

In each case, there are between one and four values, and each of the values is either a length or a percentage.

Here is another, more complex example. It is a simplification of the definition of **font-family**.

Value:	[<family-name> ,]* <generic-family>
Example:	helvetica, arial, sans-serif
Example:	serif
Example usage:	EM { font-family: Helvetica, Arial, sans-serif }

The group has an asterisk to indicate that it can occur zero or more times. The group itself consists of a family-name and a comma. In the first example, the group occurs twice – there are two families and two commas – while in the second example, the group is completely absent; just generic-family appears.

TYING IT ALL TOGETHER

The following are examples of how to read the syntax shorthand. The first example is of the **line-height** property.

Name:	line-height
Value:	normal | <number> | <length> | <percentage>

In this case, there is only one value, but it can be either the keyword normal or a number, length, or percentage. Here are some example style rules that use the property:

```
P.intro { line-height: 14pt }
DIV.warning { line-height: normal }
H1, H2, H3 { line-height: 1.0 }
H4 { line-height: 120% }
```

Appendix B: Reading property value definitions

The second example comes from the **text-decoration** property, which we discussed in Chapter 5. This example uses the single vertical bar, double vertical bar, and regular brackets.

Name:	text-decoration
Value:	none	[underline || overline || line-through || blink]

This is interpreted as follows:

1. The value is either the keyword, none, or one or more of the keywords in the group within the regular brackets.
2. If you choose none, you're done. If you choose the bracketed group, you have other choices. The group has four keywords. The double vertical bars indicate that one or more of these must occur. If you choose more than one, the order in which they are used doesn't matter.

Thus, there is a large number of possible values. Here are some of them:

- underline overline
- overline underline
- none
- underline blink line-through
- blink

Because the order of the keywords doesn't matter for the **text-decoration** property, there are really only 15 different decorations you can set with it, but you can write some of them in more than one way.

Appendix C

System colors

In addition to being able to assign predefined color values to text, backgrounds, and so on, CSS2.1 allows authors to specify colors in a manner that integrates them into the user's graphic environment. Style rules that take into account user preferences thus offer the following advantages:

- They produce pages that fit the user's defined look and feel.
- They produce pages that may be more accessible as the current user settings may be related to a disability.

The set of values defined for system colors is intended to be exhaustive. For systems that do not have a corresponding value, the specified value should be mapped to the nearest system attribute or to a default color.

Table C.1 lists additional values for color-related CSS attributes and their general meaning. Any color property (e.g., **color** or **background-color**) can take one of the following names. Although these are case-insensitive, it is recommended that the mixed capitalization shown below be used to make the names more legible.

System color name	Description
ActiveBorder	Active window border.
ActiveCaption	Active window caption.
AppWorkspace	Background color of multiple document interface.
Background	Desktop background.
ButtonFace	Face color for three-dimensional display elements.

System color name	Description
ButtonHighlight	Dark shadow for three-dimensional display elements (for edges facing away from the light source).
ButtonShadow	Shadow color for three-dimensional display elements.
ButtonText	Text on push buttons.
CaptionText	Text in caption, size box, and scrollbar arrow box.
GrayText	Grayed (disabled) text. This color is set to #000 if the current display driver does not support a solid gray color.
Highlight	Item(s) selected in a control.
HighlightText	Text of item(s) selected in a control.
InactiveBorder	Inactive window border.
InactiveCaption	Inactive window caption.
InactiveCaptionText	Color of text in an inactive caption.
InfoBackground	Background color for tooltip controls.
InfoText	Text color for tooltip controls.
Menu	Menu background.
MenuText	Text in menus.
Scrollbar	Scroll bar gray area.
ThreeDDarkShadow	Dark shadow for three-dimensional display elements.
ThreeDFace	Face color for three-dimensional display elements.
ThreeDHighlight	Highlight color for three-dimensional display elements.
ThreeDLightShadow	Light color for three-dimensional display elements (for edges facing the light source).
ThreeDShadow	Dark shadow for three-dimensional display elements.
Window	Window background.
WindowFrame	Window frame.
WindowText	Text in windows.

Table 18.1 System colors in CSS 2.1.

Index

CSS QUICK REFERENCE (continued from inside front cover)

Name	Values	Initial value	Applies to	Inherited?	Percentages	Page
display	inline | block | list-item | run-in | inline-block | table | inline-table | table-row-group | table-header-group | table-footer-group | table-row | table-column-group | table-column | table-cell | table-caption | none | inherit	inline	all elements	no	N/A	125
empty-cells	show | hide | inherit	show	'table-cell' elements	yes	N/A	334
float	left | right | none | inherit	none	all elements	no	N/A	193
font-family	[[<family-name> | <generic-family>] [, <family-name> | <generic-family>]*] | inherit	depends on user agent	all elements	yes	N/A	94
font-size	<absolute-size> | <relative-size> | <length> | <percentage> | inherit	medium	all elements	yes	refer to parent element's font size	104
font-style	normal | italic | oblique | inherit	normal	all elements	yes	N/A	107
font-variant	normal | small-caps | inherit	normal	all elements	yes	N/A	109
font-weight	normal | bold | bolder | lighter | 100 | 200 | 300 | 400 | 500 | 600 | 700 | 800 | 900 | inherit	normal	all elements	yes	N/A	110
font	[['font-style' || 'font-variant' || 'font-weight']? 'font-size' [/ 'line-height']? 'font-family'] | caption | icon | menu | message-box | small-caption | status-bar | inherit	see individual properties	all elements	yes	see individual properties	113
height	<length> | <percentage> | auto | inherit	auto	(1)	no	see prose	193
left	<length> | <percentage> | auto | inherit	auto	positioned elements	no	refer to width of containing block	207
letter-spacing	normal | <length> | inherit	normal	all elements	yes	N/A	162
line-height	normal | <number> | <length> | <percentage> | inherit	normal	all elements	yes	refer to the font size of the element itself	157
list-style-image	<uri> | none | inherit	none	elements with 'display: list-item'	yes	N/A	131
list-style-position	inside | outside | inherit	outside	elements with 'display: list-item'	yes	N/A	132
list-style-type	disc | circle | square | decimal | decimal-leading-zero | lower-roman | upper-roman | lower-greek | lower-latin | upper-latin | armenian | georgian | none | inherit	disc	elements with 'display: list-item'	yes	N/A	130
list-style	['list-style-type' || 'list-style-position' || 'list-style-image'] | inherit	see individual properties	elements with 'display: list-item'	yes	N/A	132
margin-right margin-left margin-top margin-bottom	<margin-width> | inherit	0	(3)	no	refer to width of containing block	171
margin	<margin-width>{1,4} | inherit	see individual properties	(3)	no	refer to width of containing block	171
max-height	<length> | <percentage> | none | inherit	none	(4)	no	see prose	198
max-width	<length> | <percentage> | none | inherit	none	(4)	no	refer to width of containing block	198
min-height	<length> | <percentage> | inherit	0	(4)	no	see prose	198
min-width	<length> | <percentage> | inherit	0	(4)	no	refer to width of containing block	197
orphans	<integer> | inherit	2	block-level elements	yes	N/A	270
outline-color	<color> | invert | inherit	invert	all elements	no	N/A	188
outline-style	<border-style> | inherit	none	all elements	no	N/A	189
outline-width	<border-width> | inherit	medium	all elements	no	N/A	189
outline	['outline-color' || 'outline-style' || 'outline-width'] | inherit	see individual properties	all elements	no	N/A	188
overflow	visible | hidden | scroll | auto | inherit	visible	(6)	no	N/A	204
padding-top padding-right padding-bottom padding-left	<padding-width> | inherit	0	(5)	no	refer to width of containing block	176
padding	<padding-width>{1,4} | inherit	see individual properties	(5)	no	refer to width of containing block	176
page-break-after	auto | always | avoid | left | right | inherit	auto	block-level elements	no	N/A	269
page-break-before	auto | always | avoid | left | right | inherit	auto	block-level elements	no	N/A	268